Invitatio
POLITICS

Invitation to POLITICS

Michael Laver

MARTIN ROBERTSON · OXFORD

© Michael Laver, 1983

First published in 1983 by
Martin Robertson & Company Ltd.,
108 Cowley Road, Oxford OX4 1JF

All rights reserved. No part of this publication
may be reproduced, stored in a retrieval system,
or transmitted, in any form or by any means,
electronic, mechanical, photocopying, recording
or otherwise, without the prior written permission
of the copyright holder.

Except in the United States of America,
this book is sold subject to the condition
that it shall not, by way of trade or otherwise
be lent, re-sold, hired out, or otherwise circulated
without the publisher's prior consent in any form of
binding or cover other than that in which it is
published and without a similar condition including
this condition being imposed on the subsequent
purchaser.

British Library Cataloguing in Publication Data

Laver, Michael
  Invitation to politics.
  1. Political science
  I. Title
  320   JA66

  ISBN 0-85520-573-3
  ISBN 0-85520-574-1 Pbk

Typeset by Katerprint Co Ltd, Cowley, Oxford
Printed and bound in Great Britain
by T. J. Press Ltd, Padstow

Contents

1	Introduction	1
2	Why We Need Governments	17
3	When We Don't Need Governments	47
4	Who is Governed?	67
5	What Governments Do	88
6	Making Collective Decisions	144
7	Where Decisions are Made	159
8	How Governments Decide	192
9	Politics between Governments	216
10	Conclusion: the Politics of the Future	240
	Notes on Further Reading	254
	References	260
	Index	263

1

Introduction

WHAT IS POLITICS ABOUT?

Politics is about groups of people. It is about the interplay of hopes and fears, aims and aspirations, that can be found in any human group. The result may be bitter conflict or fruitful co-operation. Conflict arises when people want things that are in short supply, or when they want things that are incompatible. Co-operation arises because nobody can go it alone. Even the most miserable misanthrope that ever there was needs other people if she is going to get what she wants. Even Robinson Crusoe (who was no misanthrope) survived mainly by putting into practice the lessons learned from his social past (not to mention half a shipload of artefacts conveniently salvaged from it).

Most typically of all, however, politics is about the characteristic blend of conflict and co-operation that can be found so often in human interactions. Pure conflict is war. Pure co-operation is true love. Politics is a mixture of both. I will go further, and claim that *any* mixture of conflict and co-operation is politics.

Take a crude example from everyday motoring life. You, a motorist in something of a hurry, approach a pedestrian crossing complete with pedestrian, crossing. She is crossing slowly and you are driving fast. Unless someone takes evasive action, you are on a collision course. Yet each of you would prefer the other to back down. You are loath to lose precious seconds by hitting the brake. She is unwilling to scuttle off the crossing in an undignified hurry. Whatever happens next is the result of a little bit of motoring politics. This is because, while there may be a winner and a loser, both can lose, and lose big, if the collision course is not altered.

Politics is also about institutions and ideologies, elections and parties, power, authority and all of those other things that people write books about. These things, however, are interesting because they are aspects of politics, not because they are subjects in their own right. Indeed, treating them as subjects in their own right creates a considerable risk of missing the point.

Consider voting, for example. It is no use taking voting and elections out of their political context. Elections offer choices, but any election offers only a limited range of choices. The actual choices on offer depend upon ideology of those in power and upon the institutions that these people operate. Thus, in a system in which killing people is considered to be a bad thing, mass genocide is rarely offered as an expedient for population control. In a system in which our public representatives are free to make money by acting as private consultants, we should not be too surprised that we have never been asked to pass judgement on this matter. The electorate might well disapprove, but it is not they who set the political agenda.

There is a particular danger in studying institutions out of context. This is an especially seductive course of action, since institutions are often so visible. It might seem natural, for example, to concentrate our attention for a while upon the Cabinet. Cabinet meetings can be observed to take place, and you can even kick a Cabinet Minister. In moments of self-doubt, when abstract concepts such as power, social welfare or democracy seem to run like sand through our fingers, there is something reassuring about an institution. Yet the same institutions look very different in different countries and at different times. In theory, this point seems obvious. In practice, of course, people tend to concentrate their resources upon a single subject, such as the British Cabinet, 1964–70.

Introduction

This effectively takes the matter out of context, however much lip service may be paid to the need to make imaginative comparisons across culture and time.

The same danger presents itself when people study countries. Nobody can deny that foreign travel broadens the mind. We clearly need a few area specialists to tell us what goes on inside the White House, where Argentina is, or whatever. As far as politics in general is concerned, however, countries are not necessarily very useful as objects of study in their own right. Knowing all that there is to be known about France means knowing an awful lot. It might make you an ideal contestant in a TV quiz show, but it will not necessarily make you any the wiser about the ways of politics.

Many of the headings under which politics is discussed, therefore, beg most of the questions that need to be answered. An obvious rejoinder to this point is that the world is a difficult and complicated place, and that it is not possible to talk about everything at once. It certainly is not possible to talk about everything at once, but this does not automatically imply that we need talk about only one thing at a time. Any sensitive author, of course, tries hard to set specific discussions in general context. How ever hard anyone tries, however, it is almost impossible to write something under a heading such as 'elections', 'Cabinets', 'legislatures' or even 'ideologies' without starting to think of such matters as subjects in their own right.

In this book therefore, I have deliberately forsaken such headings. My basic intention is to describe the blend of conflict and co-operation that is politics, and to look at practical manifestations of politics in a range of contexts.

The most important of these contexts, of course, is government. This is hardly controversial. However, I precede my discussion of the politics of government with a discussion of why we have governments at all, and of what happens when we do not. It might on the face of it seem rather peculiar to discuss what governments do while questioning the need for government in the first place. After all, governments have been with us for thousands of years, and they are hardly going to disappear all of a sudden. However, one of the main subjects of political debate in the West concerns the circumstances in which governments *should* regulate our lives. Extensions and contractions, at the margins, of the scope of government activity are crucial to the politics of every Western system. Thus, the subject matter of my argument is politics. While many of my illustrations come from government, this is merely because government is such an important aspect of politics in most modern societies.

The focus of this book, therefore, is political activity and political processes rather than political institutions and political systems. The analogies that run through the argument concern the recurrence of the same types of process or behaviour in a variety of different contexts. The need for communities to regulate social behaviour, for example, is the same whether we are dealing with a family, a village, a nation, a group of national governments or even the criminal underworld. While the institutions may differ radically, the functions that they serve can be remarkably similar. Striking analogies can be made between underground crime syndicates and overground governments, or between heavy-handed patriarchs and dictators. Usually, such analogies are plausible because the politics of the two situations turns out to be pretty much the same.

The reason for such similarities is generally that the particular interplay of conflict and co-operation that is involved produces the same broad patterns of human interaction. Whether we are talking about keeping the family kitchen in a state of reasonable tidiness, about preserving a beautiful stretch of countryside from litter and pollution or about protecting the crops of a continent from acid rain, we are talking about producing public benefits by restraining individual action. Whether the institution involved is a nuclear family or an international organization, the problem it addresses is the same.

The argument that follows deals with 'wants' rather than 'needs'. In choosing to do this, I have already chosen one fork at a major ideological junction. Many would have chosen to

Introduction

do quite the reverse. Nobody can deny that needs and wants are often quite different. Even we who are called adults regularly want things that we don't need and need things that we don't want. In concentrating upon wants, I have deliberately chosen the easy path. Wants, after all, tend to be felt consciously. Needs, on the other hand, may well be obscure even when they are important. I may want a colour television, a home computer and a video recorder. You may wisely deduce that such wants illustrate a deep-seated unconscious need for self-fulfilment. You may well be right, but it is difficult to be certain about such things. At the very least I am quite sure that I want a home computer. However snooty you might be about my cravings for consumer hardware, you will find it difficult to deny that.

By concentrating upon conscious desires rather than upon real needs, I have resigned myself to a somewhat passive political stance. This is concerned more with how things *are* than with how they *should be*. Since I view politics as conflict and co-operation over the satisfaction of private desires, my concerns will tend to be of a more practical, 'how-to-do-it' variety. If I had chosen to focus upon need, my discussion of politics would inevitably have involved a much more radical prescription for action.

Another important constraint on the scope of this book is its overwhelming preoccupation with the politics of broadly Western political systems. Many of the notions that we shall discuss can be applied much more universally. I have deliberately restricted my range of examples, however, precisely because I portray politics as a process for resolving the problem of conflicting human desires. In order to do this in even a slightly persuasive manner, I am convinced that you must be able to think yourself into the minds of the participants. We may feel at least generally capable of doing this when people are broadly 'like us'. Since I do not believe that there is any such thing as a universal 'human nature', however, I feel much less confident about my ability to think myself into the minds of people brought up in radically different cultures.

This is a major limitation of my approach. While we can sit

back in the comfort of our armchairs and write about parliamentary procedure in Nepal, for example, we can be much less certain about what Nepalese workers might look for in a trade union. I do not, however, regard this limitation as a shortcoming. To my mind it is simply further evidence of the futility of taking institutions out of context. If it is possible to say sensible things about Nepalese institutions while knowing nothing of the people of Nepal, we should begin to wonder whether it is sensible to talk about Nepalese institutions in the first place.

This book, therefore, is about the political interplay of conflict and co-operation in Western societies. Before rolling up my sleeves and getting on with things, however, I want to take a little time to emphasize two matters that will set my general argument in context. Much of this book, as I have already indicated, is concerned with the interaction between government and community. An important aspect of politics involves precisely this relationship, while many of my examples concern government as a part of the process of politics. In the following section, I will discuss the distinction between politics and government, since so much of what we read tends to present these two quite different processes as if they were simply alternative ways of describing the same thing. After this, I will discuss the relationship between practical politics and social science. The study of politics has these days been turned into an academic discipline. There is even a subject, political science, that purports to treat politics in an objective scientific manner. Other academic disciplines, such as sociology, psychology and economics, are also concerned with social and economic relationships. Academic social science, therefore, has quite a lot to say about the subject matter of this book, and I need to take at least a page or two to discuss this relationship. The following two sections, therefore, will tell you what this book is not about. It is neither an *Invitation to Government* nor an *Invitation to Political Science*. As an *Invitation to Politics* it discusses both of these important matters, but as means to an end rather than as the end itself.

Introduction

POLITICS AND GOVERNMENT

The process of politics transforms the hopes and fears of us all into some sort of end product. This process can take place at many levels. One level, quite possibly the most important level in developed nations today, is the level of the state. This explains why many people see 'politics' and 'government' as almost interchangeable terms. In universities, which are meant to be well up on such matters, it usually seems to be a rather arbitrary decision which results in one 'Department of Politics' and another 'Department of Government'. There is a real concentration, both in the academic and in the popular mind, upon the politics of states.

The fact that politics goes on between *states* is, of course, recognized in the existence of a quite separate subject, interestingly entitled inter*national relations.* You will not find much in the international relations literature about how the Scots get along with the English but, such jibes aside, inter-state politics is generally recognized as an important subject in its own right.

Below state level, local politics is obviously a matter of academic and popular concern. It is rarely considered to be as lively and as interesting a topic as the politics of the state, a factor reflected both by the relatively small number of academics who work in this area and by the relatively low turn-out at local elections. This is despite the fact that a change of local government can often have a much more immediate and significant effect on a voter's day-to-day life than a change at state level. Local taxes are often quite heavy; whole local services such as education, public transport and housing touch us all and *are* affected by local election results. In practice, however, local politics is usually seen as a part of the administration of the state.

I have included discussions of inter-state politics as well of the politics of everyday life to illustrate the point that many of the more interesting features of politics do not emerge from the study of government. The politics of small group decision-making, for example, are unique. There is simply nothing quite like going into a meeting with a few others, whose hopes and fears you know well, and trying to come out with a result. In a similar way, inter-state politics are overwhelmingly influenced by their inevitably anarchic character. It seems reasonable to assume that there never will be a world government, so that international relations will always be a matter of politics without government. With these vital qualifications in mind, most of the examples that follow concern the politics of government. Before going any further, therefore, it is worth taking a little time to spell out just what government is. The answer is simple, though it is not obvious.

Governments take decisions, but the process of government is much more than the politics of decision-making. The committee of your local tennis club, after all, takes decisions from time to time. The crucial difference between a government and your local tennis club is that decisions taken by governments can be *enforced*. The politics of enforcement are far from straightforward, although they do have a relatively simple bottom line. This is force. If you insist on playing tennis in stiletto heels, your local tennis club can ask you to desist. If you refuse, it can expel you. If you refuse to be expelled, it can attempt to prevent you from gaining access to its facilities. If you are determined to gain access, a point will come at which it will either call the police or take legal action against you. It then hands its problem over to the state. If you continue to defy the state, a point will come at which you will, quite simply, be forcibly restrained. In this sense, government is the ultimate source of coercion in social affairs. Government, however, involves much more than coercion. After all, I could twist your arm behind your back until you were in so much pain that you gave me all of your money. That ability does not make me a government. Another crucial component of what we mean by a government is the notion of legitimacy. Legitimacy is a much less tangible notion than that of force. It basically comprises an acceptance by people (though which people is a matter of continuous debate) that it is meet and right for someone to behave in the way that he or she does. The government is the agency that controls a monopoly of *legitimate force*.

The role of legitimacy in the definition of government has two main functions, one practical, the other moral. Social life

Introduction

would in practice be intolerable if governments had to use actual physical force all of the time to maintain order. This would be a tremendously costly and disruptive process. While driving along and minding your own business, for example, you come across a policeman directing traffic. He signals you to stop, but you refuse. You drive on, narrowly missing him and proceding on your way in a north-westerly direction. He takes your number and radios it to central control. Soon a number of police cars are in hot pursuit and signalling you to stop. You refuse. Eventually one of the police cars forces you to stop, and the policeman asks you to get out of the car. You refuse. Eventually, you are dragged kicking and screaming down to the police station and thrown into a locked cell.

Once in a while, I suppose, this little drama may actually take place, but traffic control would be a chaotic and intolerable business if every driver responded in this way to instructions issued by agents of the state. Most people pragmatically accept that they should take orders from policemen, even when they disagree with them. Such pragmatism may be very narrow and may concern only the trade-off between obeying policemen on point duty or being hauled off to a locked cell. Or it may be rather broader, involving a recognition that if nobody obeyed policemen on point duty, driving life would descend into chaos. Either way, however, this justification for the ceding of authority to agents the state is pragmatic. This ceding of authority, however grudging, is part of the process of giving legitimacy.

Morally, legitimacy flows to governments constituted in a manner that has previously been agreed, tacitly or explicitly, by the population. This enables people to distinguish between *liking* what governments actually do and *accepting* them as legitimate. Once more, however, the matter is not clear-cut.

Many British governments in recent times have been very unpopular. Few British people, however, have regarded them as illegitimate in the sense that these governments did not have the right to do what they did. Most people in practice went along with what was done, even when they bitterly disagreed with it.

The situation is complicated by the fact that Britain does not have a written constitution. Since formal legitimacy in Britain is not spelt out in black and white, it is sometimes a matter of debate. Thus, when central government suspends an elected local council because it does not conform with government policy, there are (disputed) grounds for calling this action illegitimate, for claiming that central government is acting beyond its legitimate authority. (Such instances have, in the past, resulted in local councillors, such as those at Clay Cross, being physically coerced and sent to jail). In the same way, some people objected to Britain's entry into the EEC on the grounds that no single British government had the legitimate authority to cede certain state powers to an international organization.

By and large, however, people are well able to separate the notions of legitimacy and popularity. This begs one important question: for whom is a government legitimate? It is unlikely that any government will be unanimously accepted as legitimate by the entire population that is subject to its powers of coercion. This problem is nowhere more evident than in Northern Ireland, where some not only dislike the government in power, but refuse to accept its authority to govern. Those who feel most strongly about this show their feelings by refusing to recognize the legitimacy of courts of law, of the police force and of other coercive agents of the British state. The British government is not regarded as legitimate by a minority of those it claims as its subjects in Northern Ireland. The result is violence.

Violence must inevitably be used by a government that is determined to pursue its right to govern in the face of opposition from those who do not accord it legitimacy. It is not inevitable, but it is likely, that disloyal 'subjects' will resist with violence of their own. The key question raised by Northern Ireland concerns just how many people may refuse to give a government legitimacy before it ceases to be a legitimate government at all and becomes an agent of oppression. A related question concerns what is to be done when a population is so divided that significant minorities are never likely to accord legitimacy to the same government.

Introduction

There are no obvious answers to these questions, but two things are clear. An administration can continue to rule in the absence of popular legitimacy, though this will tend to be a bloody and costly process. A ruler can, however, mobilize sufficient force to keep a population at bay, at least for a time. In the second place, a government needs much more than mere agreement with its policies if it is to be regarded as legitimate. It is not enough for a government to have legitimacy only among those who agree with it. This in turn means that legitimacy simply among the majority is not enough. Government legitimacy is in question if it is withheld by a substantial minority.

I will return to the matter of constitutional change in a later chapter. For the moment, however, it is sufficient to note that those states that do have written constitutions usually require a qualified majority of two-thirds or three-quarters of the population before their constitutions may be amended. This thereby defines a defiant minority of a third or a quarter of the population as tolerable for the purposes of constitutional legitimacy. This is a relatively generous assumption. Even a 10 per cent minority with intense feelings can generate a violent crisis of legitimacy.

Thus, while we can quite easily define a government as an agency that monopolizes the forces of legitimate coercion, the notion of legitimacy can be difficult to pin down. Very little that is truly convincing has been written on this subject, though it is one that tends to worry academics more than politicians. In practice, the presence or absence of government legitimacy is easy to spot. While we might find it difficult to write down what we mean by a legitimate government, we can usually recognize a crisis of legitimacy when we see one.

It is the coercive nature of government action, of course, that makes the role of government a subject of such intense political controversy. We all, except the most avid libertarians, accept a need for *some* government. A large part of public debate, however, concerns just how broadly the scope of legitimate coercion should range. Those who believe ardently in the principle of *laissez-faire* see the government's only role as the ultimate guarantor of the contracts necessary to conduct 'free' trade. Others are inclined to cast their net more widely, seeing every private action as having a public consequence, and seeing the regulation of these 'spillovers' (see chapter 2) as a necessary function of government. In addition there are those, including both conservatives and radicals, who see government coercion as being necessary to enforce and implement moral values, although they obviously disagree over which values are important. This book will not tell you which of these groups are right about the role of government. Rather, it attempts to set their arguments in the same general context, so that they can argue *with* each other rather than *past* each other, as is so often the case.

POLITICS AND SOCIAL SCIENCE

Once upon a time, I was both a student of politics and a hitchhiker. Many motorists, having generously offered me a ride, would ask me what I did for a living. I learned very quickly that being a student of politics is even worse than being a student of medicine. Not everyone, after all, has a bad back. Very nearly everyone has some view or another about the state of the nation, and is keen to get it off his or her chest. Few people can imagine that there is more to political science than sitting back in a comfortable armchair, taking a pull on a beaker of sherry, and getting down to a good old political discussion. I have since taught politics for several years at various universities. And I am coming around to the view that those motorists were right. Many of the people who come to study political science are interested in politics, and many of them quickly become bored or frustrated with the seeming inability of most political science ever to get to the point.

There are good reasons for this, and there are bad ones. Any attempt to be scientific, or even merely systematic, about anything involves doing things carefully and deliberately. It is no use arguing for the sake of arguing with all and sundry about the first political sort of a thing that comes into your head. It is rarely much good downing even a whole bottle of sherry and retiring to a quiet corner to await inspiration (although this technique has, on occasion, produced spectacular results). The whole point about the academic approach is that it is methodical, and that methodical analysis can produce interesting, non-obvious and worthwhile results.

The danger, of course, is that there can be a very fine line between being methodical about a task and plodding through it. Much of political science, as of everything else, is merely plodding rather than systematically inspired. Having sampled a few pieces of the turgid, uninspired and indigestible stodge that is sometimes served up, many people write off the whole enterprise as a useless waste of time. They become indiscriminately hostile, unable to sort good from bad and willing to switch off at the first sight of a long sentence or a piece of jargon. By and large they are right, of course, but good science has long sentences and jargon too, for perfectly justifiable reasons.

I begin, therefore, by defending social science with a plea that you give it a chance, however unappetizing it may sometimes look. You will discover, of course, that most things that look unappetizing indeed turn out to taste unappetizing, but you will also discover that you can't always tell.

This is not to excuse the unfortunate fact that the social sciences are particularly prone to the obfuscation of the obvious. The reasons for this are bad but understandable. Social scientists lack self-confidence. In particular, they lack self-confidence when they compare themselves with their colleagues in the physical sciences. Not only are nuclear physicists or biochemists able with ease to spend mind-boggling sums of money on entire buildings full of impressive-looking hardware, but there is also absolutely no chance that an innocent bystander looking at one of their publications would understand even the title, much less the content. The self-doubting social scientist looks with a mixture of envy and awe at a position of such apparent power. Many of them begin to wish that their own outpourings were a little less easily comprehended by all and sundry. Maybe fewer people would then be able to hurt their pride by accusing them of talking nonsense.

Some social scientists have attempted to redress this seeming injustice by 'professionalizing' the discipline. One obvious way of doing this is to fill the literature with weird concepts and incomprehensible formulae, the very technique that seems to work so well for the nuclear physicist. The intention is to ensure that nobody will be able to accuse social scientists of talking nonsense, since nobody will be able to understand what social scientists are saying. This response stems, as I have suggested, from insecurity, since it is based upon a sneaking suspicion on the part of some social scientists that those who would otherwise accuse them of talking nonsense might indeed be right. This insecurity is, of course, unnecessary, since an awful lot of monumental nonsense has been talked in the natural sciences, and nobody has thought any the less of natural scientists for it. The insecurity, however, is real, and its unfortunate consequence is the obfuscation of the obvious.

All of this means that the academic study of revolution, of violence, of sexual behaviour, even of party politics is rarely as exciting as many people expect, if what they are expecting is argument or action. Nevertheless, some aspects of the academic approach (rarely the long sentences or the jargon, but certainly the methodical style) are invaluable aids to our understanding. Social scientists are in the business of making careful generalizations about the world; if you refuse to make careful generalizations, you will be knocked down and killed the first time that you try to cross a busy road.

All of the social sciences are relevant to the study of politics. This is one of the many reasons why I have not attempted to write an *Invitation to Political Science*, since this would obscure an important point. I make no distinction at all between political science and sociology. It is impossible to know where one begins and the other ends and senseless to even try to decide. Each, when it deals with institutions, tends to pick different institutions to deal with, such as the 'legislature' on one hand or the 'family' on the other. I hope

Introduction

that I have already shown, and I shall certainly show in what follows, that such distinctions are redundant when they are not misleading.

There is also a vast area of overlap between sociology/political science and the study of economics. Differences here, however, are a matter more of theoretical style than of substance. Economists tend to deal with well-defined models of the world, based upon very restrictive assumptions about the ways in which people behave. They tend to be more willing, therefore, to sacrifice realism to theoretical elegance. There is a lot to be said for this way of going about things. It forces people to be methodical, and it (sometimes) forces people to be explicit about the assumptions they make. Since the main subject matter of economics is human behaviour in the market and since, in capitalist societies, the behaviour of the market is crucial to us all, it is difficult for anyone who is interested in politics to know too much about economics. However, because economists in practice impose such rigid constraints and assumptions upon their models, it is vital to know about *more* than economics. Some of the greatest political sillinesses that I have ever heard uttered have come from the mouths of very clever professional economists. This problem arises, I think, because it is obvious to most people who are interested in politics that they need a sound grasp of economics. Many people who are interested in economics, however, regard it as a subject in its own right.

Of the other social sciences, history, philosophy and psychology are obviously important. With the exception, perhaps, of physiological aspects of psychology, most of these so-called distinctive disciplines have remained separate either by accident, or because of their history or for administrative convenience. As a consequence, of course, different styles and traditions can and do emerge, and superficial differences can be huge.

In a discussion such as this, it is all too easy to end up concluding that everything is jolly interesting, useful and relevant to politics and worth a quick browse. I will, therefore, nail my colours to the mast. Anyone who is interested in studying politics must have some understanding of economics or at least of what economists are saying. Excursions into other academic disciplines are always good for the soul. When they are necessary, however, the need will be obvious to all concerned.

PLAN OF CAMPAIGN

For all of the reasons that I have just given, this book is *not* a Cook's Tour of political science. I have tried, instead, to organize it in a logical fashion. I begin with the need for government at all (chapter 2), and discuss those circumstances in which government will not, indeed, be necessary (chapter 3). Most of these circumstances depend upon the existence of some form of coherent community to take over necessary tasks of social control. Thus, I move on in chapter 4 to discuss some of the factors that might tend to draw communities together. From this I move to discuss in chapter 5 the types of things that governments do when they *are* needed, looking at the production of goods and services, the planning and co-ordination of social activity and the redistribution of welfare. In chapter 6, I look at the problems facing any social group when it must decide what, *in particular*, it wants to do. Governments tend to solve these problems in various ways, depending upon how they are organized. Chapters 7 and 8, therefore, look at decision-making by governments. While governments tend to regulate interaction between individuals, there are few institutions to regulate interactions between governments. Politics between governments (chapter 9) is inevitably more anarchic. Finally, and by way of a review of the main themes that I have discussed, I look in chapter 10 at the politics of the future. We are told by many that we are entering another industrial revolution. If this is true, many aspects of what now makes up a community may change, as they did during and after the last industrial revolution. As a consequence politics may be transformed in ways that we can hardly imagine. Obviously I cannot write about things that I cannot imagine. I have done my best, however, to imagine as much as I can.

2

Why We Need Governments

DO WE NEED *THIS* GOVERNMENT?
DO WE NEED *ANY* GOVERNMENT?

I have already said that quite a lot of politics is about government. Immediately we face a paradox. How can politics be about government if, when we in the West change the government in power, we often seem to change very little? In very broad terms, such change-overs have remarkably little effect upon whole countries. The general growth and decline of nations seems to take place more or less regardless of the personnel in power. We could take many of the members of most Western governments and load them into a giant spaceship. We could fire them off to the uttermost end of the universe. Life on Earth would hardly be any different.

This does not mean that the particular government with its finger on the trigger is irrelevant. Major details of national life are clearly affected by changes of administration. Some governments spend enormous sums of money on nuclear missile systems; others do not. Some make people pay for personal health care as they use it; others make us all pay, even when we are healthy. Some put their faith in the market; others feel that the market works only if it is highly co-ordinated and regulated. Nevertheless, when it really comes down to actually *doing* something, governments are usually more remarkable for their similarities than for their differences. If Britain were to switch from the most left-wing to

Invitation to Politics

the most right-wing of likely governments, you or I would notice far less difference than if we were to move from Britain under the Conservatives to the United States under the Republicans or (setting aside the language difference) to Italy under the Christian Democrats.

The differences, of course, seem important because it is these that are emphasized when we are offered a choice of government. To many individuals, they are clearly crucial. Someone who would be working for a living under one government might be unemployed under another. This means that we can all think of answers to the question 'Do we need *this* government?' And those reasons are perfectly valid. Given the broad similarities between all governments, however, we find it much harder to answer the question 'Do we need *any* government?'

Most of us have taken a trip on an iron ship. Many of us would be hard-pressed to explain why iron ships float. We prefer to take the buoyancy of iron ships for granted, particularly when we are riding around in one. In the same way, we tend to take the need for governments for granted, especially when we are choosing one. If we wish to go systematically into the matter of floating ships, we proceed by looking at the conditions under which such floating takes place. We discover that they float better when they are hollow, when they have no holes below the waterline, when they are not too heavily laden and when they do not fall over. In the same way, we must look at the conditions under which governments are needed. These usually boil down to people in general wanting governments in general because they fear that social life without them would be intolerable. The main purpose of this chapter is to look in more detail at why people imagine that life without government would be worse than life with it.

Life without government is anarchy. The very word 'anarchy' scares many people, who equate it, quite simply, with chaos. Many facets of human life, however, are conducted without government, yet in a perfectly orderly manner. Both everyday life and international relations (two matters to which I shall be returning) proceed usually

Why We Need Governments

without, and sometimes even despite, government action. Anarchy is not chaos. It is the orderly self-regulation of social affairs. In this sense, anarchy is all around us.

It is much easier for a group to regulate itself in an orderly manner if it is relatively small. This should be obvious to all from everyday experience. It is why nearly all theories of anarchy see human interaction as fundamentally a matter for small groups. Quite how small is small depends upon the context. If a group of people are sharing a flat, ten may find it much more difficult to organize the cooking and the cleaning than five. Twenty sharers in a giant flat may even begin to create something that looks a little like a government in order to discipline the slob who leaves tea leaves in the sink, or the insomniac who practises the trombone at four in the morning. On the other hand, a much bigger group may have no trouble at all in getting its members to pitch into a battle against marauding foreigners. Whatever the context, however, an effective anarchistic group is never going to be anything like the size of a nation or a country, as we think of these things today.

Anarchists agree that social interaction on a national scale would be impossible without government. They simply think that it is also unnecessary. On the other side of the fence, almost everyone else believes that large-scale social interaction is inevitable in the modern world. This may be because they believe that national feeling is a potent force. It may be because people now want high-technology hardware, like nuclear power stations or supersonic airliners, that can be produced only by huge social units. It may be because they favour social policies that can be put into effect only by planning on a really large scale. Those on opposite sides of the debate do not deny that small communities can regulate themselves or that large groups need to be organized along more coercive and more institutional lines. Both sides see the alternatives as regulation by government or by community. They simply disagree over when and where each alternative is either viable or desirable.

Your belief in the ability of groups to regulate themselves is influenced by your view of human nature. Since there are as

Invitation to Politics

many views of human nature as there are members of the human race, it is difficult to generalize. We will need, however, to make some assumptions about human nature in order to get the show on the road. We can, of course, make any assumptions which amuse us, filling our world with the most wild and woolly characters we can think of, even filling it with saints. In order to construct a useful model of society, however, the assumptions we make should be at least a little realistic. I will review three basic possibilities, starting with the most optimistic.

NICE PEOPLE GET ALONG WITHOUT GOVERNMENT

The inhabitants of a small but densely populated island somewhere off the coast of Europe had never bothered to invent government. They were a modest, generous and sociable race of people who had no great ambitions beyond a warm hearth, a full belly and a few rags on their backs to keep out the cold winds of winter. Since their desires were modest, there was enough of everything to go around. Since people were generous when their neighbours fell off cliffs, banged their heads on the overhanging branches of massive oak trees or otherwise incapacitated themselves, the injured were well provided with basic necessities. Since people were sociable, they responded to major disasters by getting together and working something out.

The inhabitants of this small but densely populated island were by no means hermits. They worked together when necessary, building lighthouses, draining land and repelling foreign invaders. Once in a while, of course, some would take the view that a particular project was misguided. The construction of a large and potentially dangerous pressurized water reactor, needed to warm the hearths of Albion more cheaply, did raise one or two eyebrows. However, the doubters were sociable beings and went along with the consensus. When it came to paying for the pressurized water reactor, all worked a little harder to make their contributions. Each felt that an obligation to the community was more

Why We Need Governments

important than a personal misgiving about the project. The reactor blew up, killing thousands and maiming many more. Children were born with horrible deformities; others began to die in extreme but mysterious pain. Folks got together to decide what to do.

They were all agreed upon the benefits of a warm hearth. They mostly agreed that the pressurized water reactor had seemed like a good idea at the time. Some thought that it was still a good idea. The first reactor had been missing a few nuts and bolts; the new one would be indestructible. After all, everyone can learn from mistakes. Others were less convinced, and thought that building another reactor would be an act of suicidal folly. No one believed that those in favour of the reactor were bad, just stupid. Many felt that they must stand up and oppose the reactor in the interests of all. Facing them were many who sincerely believed that the pressurized water reactors were the very best things that had ever been invented (provided that all of the nuts and bolts were in place). They believed that it was their civic duty to build another one, having given the victims of the first a decent burial.

Both sides were in total agreement over what life was all about. Both had a highly developed social conscience. Neither was at all greedy or nasty in any way. Each thought that the other was totally and dangerously misguided. Neither could accept the policy proposed by the other. Unfortunately, it was not as if one faction lived in one part of the country, while the other lived elsewhere. If this had been the case, they could have agreed to go their separate ways. They lived side by side. The anti-nuclear group just could not allow the others to go on with their project. The nuclear lobby could not allow the project to be stopped. In the best of all possible worlds, there was a civil war. Would a government have stopped it?

The inhabitants of Albion might have anticipated such a problem. They might have realized that the fact that they agreed upon *ends* was no guarantee that they would agree over the best *means* to achieve them. (The fact that they agreed upon the need for energy was no guarantee that they would agree upon the need for pressurized water reactors.) Recognizing that controversial collective decisions would have to be taken, they might have set up some mechanism for making this easier. They could all have agreed to abide by the results of such a process, however much they privately disagreed with those results.

The issue is now clear. Would people abide by collective decisions with which they fundamentally disagreed, or would there be a need for those decisions to be imposed, ultimately by the use of force, on dissenters? If decisions must be enforced, there is an argument for some form of collective agency with a monopoly over the use of 'legitimate' force. This agency is a government.

In terms of most of the routine collective decisions arising in an island inhabited by such pleasant and well-meaning individuals, there seems to be little to be said for government. If people agree to abide by collective decisions, and if they are then confronted with a decision with which they disagree, they will go along with the decision anyway. They will do so in the hope and understanding that – win a little, lose a little – there will be future occasions on which they will get their way in the face of opposition from others. For most matters which may arise, it will never seem worth undermining the principle of voluntary individual acquiescence to the collective will.

Such acquiescence will be put to a severe test when a major issue emerges. When the decision in question is very important, it may seem to many that undermining the principle of give and take is regrettable, but necessary. The long-term benefits gained by a community in which everyone gets along with everyone else are huge, but they are not infinite. At the very least, certain decisions may destroy the very community that does the deciding, leaving it no time to enjoy any long-term benefits. The Albion Anti-Nuclear Lobby (ANNUL) sees no point in going along with what it regards as an auto-destructive collective decision to build another pressurized water reactor. This is despite the fact that ANNUL is a firm believer in the need to accept the give and take of normal political interaction. It is, in this case, prepared to fight it out.

Why We Need Governments

If a group such as this is divided over a major issue, there are really only two possibilities. The group can split into two. This would produce groups once more united on major matters. This is the traditional solution, adopted by the groups in which people existed for the millennia before modern states emerged. Indeed, it is still the solution adopted in many of the informal social groups to which we all belong. You prefer to say the Mass in Latin? You think that Boy Scouts ought still to wear shorts? You can't change the way in which your group does these things? You form a breakaway group of kindred spirits and get your own way without conflict or interference. Provided that the group can sustain itself, that enough of the faithful prefer a Latin Mass and enough Boy Scouts are prepared to get their knees cold, then this is the obvious solution. In this case major internal disputes do not generate a need for government. Subdivision of the group restores a situation in which the members can get along without formal enforcement.

If the group cannot subdivide, its problems are obviously more serious. Subdivision may be impossible because one or both subgroups would not be large enough to be self-sustaining. Or there may just not be enough space left for the breakaway faction to inhabit. In some cases subdivision would not solve the problem anyway. (In matters such as nuclear disarmament, for example, dissidents would need to go to another planet before they could have things their own way without interfering with others.) Forced to coexist, the two factions must either fight it out or work it out. If they are unable to work it out, civil war looks probable. But a government is unlikely to resolve this problem.

Remember that we are dealing with altruists. Concerned with the well-being of others, an altruist may be prepared to bear private punishments in order to further social objectives. Thus altruists may resist government imposition of important collective decisions for the same reason that they would refuse to participate in the principle of voluntary acquiescence. As governments down the ages have discovered, an altruist can make a formidable opponent. She is impervious, when roused, to most of the conventional mechanisms of social control. Governments cannot solve such problems, which therefore provide no justification for government in the first place.

This world inhabited by sociable altruists with modest material desires seems to have no need for a government to monopolize the legitimate forces of coercion. The fact that there is no government, however, does not mean that there will be no political institutions. A large group may well require some formal mechanism for making collective decisions. If it is too large to assemble conveniently in a single place, agreement will have to be reached about when decisions have to be taken, about which decisions have to be taken, and so on. Mechanisms for solving these problems are many and varied, though most involve some method of delegating decision-making to a representative group. It is not hard to see why a legislature and a bureaucracy might emerge, even in a rather small society. Legislatures and bureaucracies, however, should not be confused with governments. The process of *making* decisions is quite separate from the problem of *enforcing* them. Enforcement is necessary only in the absence of consent. It is thus possible to imagine a society which had a legislature (to make collective decisions) without a government (to enforce them). In practice the two usually appear inseparable, and the distaste for government felt by most anarchists is usually matched by their distaste for legislatures and bureaucracies. The practical solutions they advocate usually involve the organization of collective decision-making around small groups, for which formal institutions will not be necessary.

SELFISH PEOPLE FIND IT HARDER TO GET ALONG WITHOUT GOVERNMENT

There are many ways to be less than nice. We will not, however, be too pessimistic at this stage. Imagine that people are rather greedy and self-centred, but are also essentially sociable. They are positively not spiteful, jealous or vain. The arguments in favour of government now become stronger,

Why We Need Governments

and take two basic forms. In the first place, people who are less than nice need government for their own good. In the second place, government may be needed for the good of others.

When people are nice, they can trust one another. Recognizing the need to get together in order to produce a few home comforts, they enter into dealings with one another, free from suspicion. No one has any particular incentive to double-cross a partner. When people are greedier and more self-centred, the incentives to double-cross are much greater. Yet they still need to make mutually beneficial agreements, even in the absence of trust. This provides one potential role for government.

When people are nice, they are concerned about the effects of their actions upon others. A nice person who enjoys listening to loud music late at night worries about keeping the neighbours awake. An altruist even turns the sound down, reducing her own pleasure in order to increase the pleasure of others. A selfish person sees no private benefit at all in so doing. Yet when everyone behaves like this, all may be worse off. It may become impossible to snatch forty winks at any time. The incessant cacophony produced by a society of selfish music lovers might reach such a level that all wished everyone else would stop, yet none would see any benefit in restraining her own noise pollution. This is a problem of collective action. All, collectively, want something. None, individually, is prepared to contribute towards it. Solving collective-action problems presents another role for government.

The need to make contracts and to solve collective-action problems may cause greedy people to want government for their own good. Each may have desires which cannot be fulfilled without some agency which monopolizes the forces of legitimate coercion. A further problem arises, however, if collective decisions are taken that involve attempts to increase overall social welfare. In order to make the group *as a whole* (as opposed to each individual member) better off, it may be necessary to help some at the expense of others. The most extreme example arises when one member of the group controls all of the wealth and the rest are dying of starvation. It is most improbable that the single wealthy person will be so happy that this cancels out the misery of the starving masses. Some redistribution from rich to poor clearly increases overall social well-being.

It is unlikely that a selfish individual would favour a decision that increased social welfare at her own expense. However, sociable people, even greedy ones, may well not object to decisions which leave them untouched while increasing the welfare of others. It is likely, therefore, that some of the collective decisions on the social agenda will include attempts to increase overall welfare. Such policies may well involve redistribution. Some form of legitimate coercion will be necessary to effect this, since the starving masses will need to do rather more than decide that the millionaire *should* redistribute some of her wealth. They will need to take it from her.

Thus contracts, collective action and a desire to maximize social well-being all generate possible roles for government in a group that does not consist entirely of altruists.

Making contracts

We must all deal with others, yet even a deal that promises great things for everyone can go sour. It may well turn out that one party to the deal wishes that she had never got herself involved. She has to decide whether she will honour the deal at great cost, or back out and cut her losses. If *all* parties feel like this, there's no problem. The deal can be dissolved by mutual consent. If one or more parties want to go through with the deal while others want to back out of it, they then face the problem of enforcement.

Now, very few deals can be constructed that depend upon neither trust nor enforcement. When I go to the market and buy a pound of apples, I hand over the cash with one hand and take the apples with the other. No trust is required. However, if only this type of 'instantaneous' transaction were possible, many valuable deals could not be made. I could never borrow money, bet, invest, insure, or buy and sell

Why We Need Governments

anything that was so expensive that I could not carry the cash around with me. (By cash I mean gold sovereigns, silver dollars, or something else that has intrinsic value. After all, what is a dollar bill or a pound note, but a promise? And what is a promise without trust?) People clearly will want to make deals that cannot be consummated instantaneously. They must either trust each other or rely upon 'outside' enforcement. This need for enforcement in the absence of trust means that contract enforcement is one of the few powers allowed to government by extreme proponents of capitalist *laissez-faire*. All but the most rabid 'anarcho-capitalists' like to see contracts enforced, even if they see no other justification for government intervention in social life.

To get a feel for contract enforcement without government, think about what happens when you buy or sell a second-hand car through the small ad columns of your local newspaper. Even a clapped-out second-hand car these days costs more money than you feel like giving a total stranger for her birthday. You put an ad in the paper and a total stranger shows up on your doorstep. She likes the car and wants to buy it. Now things get embarrassing. She is obviously not carrying a sack full of cash just in case she likes your car, so she can't pay you in cash here and now. Maybe you could let her have the car, and she could come back tomorrow with the money? Maybe you could let her write you a cheque? Maybe you could, but I will tell you one thing: you wouldn't get me to part with my car on those terms. I'd want the cash before I gave her the keys. That tall, dark stranger could be anybody; why should I trust her?

If she didn't have enough cash, I'd even want a deposit before I promised not to sell it to anyone else. Why else would I make such a promise? Now she has to trust me and has no more incentive to do so than I have to trust her. Who knows how many deposits I might collect from innocent people that evening before disappearing with the car and the proceeds? The only foolproof way is to carry all of the cash around with you, and to close the deal on the spot.

The private used-car market is a good example of the type of problem that confronts people who are less than nice if they don't have a government. In this case, the difficulty of identifying and tracing the total stranger who appears on your doorstep means that the legitimate enforcement supposedly on offer from government is not much use. You are more or less on your own and have to devise some way of making sure the deal sticks.

Things are completely different when you are dealing not with a stranger but with someone you will see over and over again. In this case, deals may not need to be enforced, but may tend to enforce themselves. The incentive to double-cross someone is greatly reduced by the knowledge that you may need to deal with her again. If you keep your word today, you will be believed tomorrow. You break a verbal contract only if the incentives are so great that they outweigh all of the future benefits of honesty. Now, if you were a colleague of mine, I might even let you try out my rusty old banger for a few days before I pressed you for the cash.

'Outside' contract enforcement is less necessary when people expect to deal with each other again. It is thus less needed by a *community*, since one of the defining characteristics of a community is the long-term interaction of its members. Within a community contracts may be honoured, even at short-term cost, because people need to make contracts again. You or I often keep our word, even when we would quite like to break it, because we want people to go on believing us. We know that our word is a valuable thing, and we may well depend on it the next time we want to borrow a fiver or hear a few juicy secrets. In a long-standing community, therefore, contracts may simply enforce themselves.

In contrast, when we are dealing simply with a collection of individuals who expect no continuing interaction, we have no incentive to make short-term sacrifices in the hope of long-term benefits. We thus have no incentive to be honest when this is inconvenient. If we break our word, the injured party may refuse to deal with us in the future. But we will never need to deal with her in the future, so who cares? In this context, contracts do need to be enforced, and a role for government emerges. Once more (and this is a point we shall see over and over again) it is a role for government which is much more important when community is weak than when it is strong. Put crudely, contract enforcement is a task that government takes over when community fails.

Collective-action problems

Almost every action I take has public consequences. I am writing these words for all sorts of private reasons, yet they will one day be published. I am no Karl Marx, but these words of mine will still have some effect on the lives of others. They may bore a potentially great concert pianist to death, while the paper they are printed on may help keep a lumberjack in employment. The most superficial comparison of the writings of Karl Marx and Michael J. Laver will, however, demonstrate quite conclusively that some actions have more significant public consequences than others. These range in scale from the slight smell of garlic that wafts on to the street when I make spaghetti sauce to the destruction of half the planet by a megalomaniac US President who was trying to impress her new boyfriend. They may be good, bad or a matter of opinion (like my frying garlic). They need a name, and I shall call them 'spillovers'. This is not a particularly attractive name, but it is more attractive and self-explanatory than some of the alternatives that may be found lurking among shelves of technical books and articles. The word 'spillover', when I use it in this book, will mean the public consequences of an individual action. Controlling bad spillovers and stimulating good ones are matters that cause problems of collective action.

When people talk of collective-action problems, the conversation usually turns to lighthouses. In many ways a lighthouse is a private sort of thing. It may be home for a lighthouse keeper. It can be sold, fenced off, demolished and generally 'owned'. Some people may like the idea of living in tall, thin buildings perched on dangerous rocks and may be prepared to build things that look very like lighthouses for their purely personal pleasure. Even so, they would be unlikely to put a powerful light on the top, a light that flashed at regular intervals so that their house could serve as a useful navigational aid for passing sailors. It is this light that makes the lighthouse something more than a tall, thin building, and this aspect of a lighthouse is a spillover. Spillovers such as this can be greatly prized by large numbers of people, yet can be very difficult to produce.

Sometimes, however, spillovers just happen. I have just cut the hedge in my front garden. I hate cutting this malevolent green privet monster, but I cut it anyway. When I have finished cutting it, the whole street looks a little nicer. When I don't cut it, my neighbours wish I would. My neat hedge provides a positive spillover for my neighbours, but I certainly do not cut it in order to produce this. The hedge finds itself cut because I enjoy the view from my front windows, a view that is obscured when the privet gets out of control. Once I am cutting anyway, I cut neatly. I'd rather have a neat hedge than a ragged one, and the extra effort is rather small. Selfish person that I am, I nonetheless produce the beneficial spillover of a neat hedge for my neighbours. I produce it because my costs are worth the benefits *to me,* and I give the spillovers to the neighbours for nothing.

Social life, however, is not always as neat as my front hedge. Two factors can make the public consequences of private actions cause serious political problems. As in the case of building a lighthouse, *social benefits* may arise from actions which have *private costs*. As in the case of the noxious gases pouring from the exhaust pipe of my car, individuals may get the *private benefits* while *society* pays the *costs*.

Lighthouses are expensive. They must be very tall, very thin, and strong enough to survive on dangerous rocks. If people cannot be found who regard living in such buildings as just what they want to do, lighthouse keepers must be paid. It is extremely unlikely that the benefits to a single sailor are so great that she will decide to build a lighthouse entirely at her own expense, and provide navigational assistance to all and sundry as a free gift. If sailors want lighthouses, therefore, they cannot rely on free gifts but must share the cost if the benefits are to seem worthwhile. The more that a valuable spillover generates private costs, the less likely it is to be

Why We Need Governments

produced by a single individual and offered to others as a free gift.

My car generates the reverse problem, pollution. This is the classic unwanted spillover. I like driving in my car. It gets me from A to B, and B is where I want to be. My car costs me money, of course. I have to feed it petrol and fix its broken motor from time to time. But getting from A to B is so valuable to me that I am prepared to pay those costs, and still feel that I have come out ahead. I get a good deal because I don't pay all of my costs, but hive some of them off on society. My car pumps poison into the atmosphere. It *must* do so. If the exhaust pipe is blocked up, the car will stall. If the exhaust pipe is diverted into the car, the gases will kill me. Exhaust gases generate many social costs. They cause brain damage in children, erode the façades of buildings that are part of our cultural heritage, cause smog and so on. Unless I am some kind of altruist, however, you can't really expect me to stop driving around just for the good of society. Yet all of those exhaust gases pose quite a problem. The more an unwanted spillover is the result of private benefits, the more likely it is to be produced anyway and forced upon everyone else.

A final example gives perhaps the most tangible expression to the collective action of problems caused by spillovers. It concerns canine excrement. Most people who own dogs like to own dogs. Most also 'take them for a walk' at least once a day. Dogs do, of course, need lots of exercise, but the real point of this exercise is to allow them to poop on the pavement. One of the costs of owning a dog is that they can rarely be trained to use lavatories and tend to leave their droppings around and about. Dog owners fob these costs off on society, on the children and adults who step in the turds and on the road sweepers who have to clean them up. A disease that can cause blindness in children is transmitted in little puppies' poopies. Dog owners choose to do this. They could just as easily let their pets relieve themselves at home, and pay the full cost of dog ownership, but they rarely do. Once more, the result is a collective action problem. Once more this could be resolved by community. Interestingly, however, dogs' walks often tend to be taken a little away from the owner's immediate environment, or in public parks with an ever-changing clientele.

The main problem with spillovers is that they tend to be indiscriminate. Good spillovers can be enjoyed by everyone if they are enjoyed by anyone. Bad spillovers are foisted on all if they are foisted at all. Selected people can usually be prevented from enjoying or suffering only when everyone is so prevented. This is quite different from the traditional private goods that are taken to market. If I've got a sackful of apples, I can give them to whoever I want, and I will probably want to give them to whoever gives me the most money. When I cut my front hedge, everyone can look at it. Even my worst enemies get the benefit, whether or not I want them to do so.

This important social property makes spillovers impossible to market in the normal way. Since you can't exclude people from them, you can't expect people to pay for things that they can enjoy anyway. If you build a lighthouse, for example, you will find it difficult to sell its services. What could you do? You could lay a huge minefield around the lighthouse. This could serve to exclude all, save those whom you issue with a chart, from the area of sea within which your light was an aid to navigation. But the cost of laying the mines and printing the charts would exceed any likely revenue.

Once you build that lighthouse, it will be there for all to see and to use. There's nothing that you can really do about it. If you wish to make a living in the navigation industry, train as a river pilot. You can market your services very easily, assisting only when paid, and letting all who refuse to pay simply run aground.

Since most spillovers are indiscriminate, they tend to cause problems of collective action. Because people can enjoy whether or not they contribute, selfish people will not contribute. They will take free rides, which is why they are called free riders. How would selfish sailors build a lighthouse? Each would reckon that if the lighthouse was going to be built anyway, her contribution would not be missed. If it was not going to be produced anyway, the contribution would be wasted. All sailors want a lighthouse, with its valuable spillovers, but no lighthouse is built.

One of the best examples of a very valuable spillover which presents collective-action problems is research into, and implementation of, policies which control infectious diseases. Everyone benefits from public health, and they benefit whether or not they have contributed towards the cost. The enforcement of public hygiene standards, for example, helps everyone, yet is very expensive. Selfish people allow everyone else to contribute to the high cost and take a free ride on the benefits. As yet, no means exists to educate germs or viruses to attack only free riders, and thus to enable a pay-as-you-use system to operate. Yet if everyone takes free rides, hygiene standards collapse and everyone is worse off. Although free riders would contribute if their contribution made a difference, each individual contribution makes a difference only in the smallest of groups.

The basic elements of the collective action are thus:

(1) Some actions with private benefits have social costs. Other actions with private costs have social benefits.
(2) Social costs and benefits are more or less universally distributed over all.
(3) Except in small groups, individuals will not voluntarily incur private costs for social benefits or forgo private benefits to reduce social costs.
(4) Social costs will therefore be high, and social benefits low. All will be worse off than they would if successful collective action could be organized.

While government can solve collective-action problems, enabling the construction of lighthouses where none would otherwise be built, there are two important circumstances in which the collective-action problem disappears. The first arises when the group is small. The second arises when one individual finds it worthwhile to generate social benefits single-handedly.

When the group is small, two factors save the day. In the first place, it is possible that the contribution of each individual is critical. Imagine that three or four of us are sitting in a railway compartment at the beginning of a long voyage. We may all want to smoke. We recognize, however, that if all smoke, the air will quickly become unbreathable. In a small group such as this the logic of the situation is quite clear. Each of us makes a noticeable and worthwhile contribution to clean air by not smoking. In the second place it is possible in a small group for this tacit agreement to emerge: no one smokes if none smoke; if someone smokes, however, none should feel bound to restrain herself. Each then knows that she, and she alone, can break the tacit smokers' truce. The conditional nature of the deal means that each individual's behaviour makes a critical difference to air quality. Each can destroy the deal single-handedly.

This type of deal, of course requires an element of continuity in the group. My restraint today is in the interest of longer-term objectives. Others will do the same thing for the same reason. If no one expects to be around to reap the benefits, no one will bother to contribute. Continuity, as well as small size, are needed if a group is to solve its collective-action problems. Continuity and small size, of course, are two of the central properties of community. Thus one of the solutions to collective-action problems that avoids centralized coercion depends, once more, upon community.

This, for example, is the key to the dramatic decline in the quality of life that is often experienced by those who are rehoused from small terraced streets to large, modern housing projects. It is by now well known that the level of litter and vandalism is much higher in modern high-rise blocks. The terraced street tends to be a small community, in which a few people tend to see each other regularly. The size of the group is such that each member makes a significant contribution to the protection of the public environment. As a community, the give and take of long-term interaction also allows for a tacit 'litterers' truce' to emerge. Everyone can do her bit on condition that everyone else goes on doing his bit. The tower block houses a much larger group. Crucially, the inhabitants face outwards rather than in on each other. It is hard to see what the others are doing, even if you know who they are, which is less likely anyway. The conditions for community are undermined. Litter, vandalism and other problems of collective action increase.

When social benefits are produced by someone as an unintended side-effect of a private activity that she is enjoying anyway, the collective-action problem may disappear once more. (Someone who is spiteful or jealous may refuse to give others free gifts, but we all come on to this problem later.) Positive spillovers that can be produced by single individuals tend to be a rather neglected subject, although some are vital. Art and innovation are prime examples.

A great inventor has just come up with a cure for hangovers that works every time. This discovery clearly has huge positive spillovers. The knowledge that she could not stop others from reaping the fruits of her labours, however, did not weaken the inventor's determination to perfect the cure, despite the need for an intensive series of costly and painful practical experiments. As with most artists, the personal benefits to this inventor are sufficient in themselves. The fact that the world at large benefits is icing on the cake. Free riders may have a field day, but the good is worth enough to the producers of art or innovation for them to produce regardless.

Many valuable spillovers, however, have few private benefits. Many have private costs. They require co-operation if they are to be produced at all. When the group is large, free-riding is likely. Anarchistic solutions based on conditional co-operation ('I'll help if all help') may work for small communities. In larger groups free riders may need to be forced, *for their own good*, to pull their weight in the productive process. Forcing people to contribute towards the cost of producing social benefits is an important potential role for government. Thus selfish sailors may thank a government for building them a lighthouse and forcing them to pay for it. Others may well be relieved when a government eradicates bubonic rats by enforcing public health regulations. In these cases, government steps in when community fails. When slum dwellers move to a large and impersonal housing project, community is undermined, as we have seen. This generates a greater need for government. If people won't pick up their own litter, government employees may be needed to do the job. If people can't control their own vandals, they will want a police force to take over.

To sum up, private actions have public consequences. These spillovers may cause problems of collective action. Problems may not arise if the group is small and stable (a community) or if private interest and public interest co-incide. For larger and less stable groups, all may be made better off by a government that forces people to co-operate (for example, over public health and hygiene) for their own good.

Thus, as was the case with contracts, solutions to the collective-action problem tend to depend either upon community self-help or upon government. These arguments in favour of government depend upon the failure of community. Their relevance is determined largely by the size and stability of the group concerned. Small and stable groups may be able to dispense quite easily with government. Large size and high turnover force a group to rely upon government if its members are to engage in any collective endeavour.

Increasing social welfare

People who are selfish but sociable, and definitely not spiteful, may well favour policies that help others. They may want to increase overall social well-being for a number of reasons.

In the first place, there may be all sorts of rather intangible benefits. Policies that hold out a vague promise of making all better off may still be favoured by the selfish, even if they produce no direct benefit to the individual. The healthy may be in favour of increased public provision of personal health care if they are comforted by the thought that *should* they happen to be struck down in their prime, they will be looked after. Selfish able-bodied people may not begrudge provision for the sick or the aged, on the grounds that there is a chance that they may reap the benefits of this in the future. At the very least, such policies provide peace of mind, and every insurance executive knows that people are prepared to pay for peace of mind.

Why We Need Governments

In the second place, people may hope for indirect, selfish benefits from helping others. Most of us are now aware that the good fortune of one can lead to the good fortune of others. Local shopkeepers lose out when local unemployment rises. They may thus favour policies that help others by reducing local unemployment, even when these are of no *direct* benefit to them. Increasing the welfare of some can have a knock-on effect upon the welfare of others.

In the third place, we are, after all, dealing with sociable people. It is quite possible to want as much as you can get for yourself, yet not to begrudge the good fortune of others. If I do not gamble, and if you make a fortune as a result of a spectacular betting coup, there is no reason for me to feel bad. I may even relish your good fortune. After all it has cost me not one penny.

Thus, either because of a selfish belief in the notion that what's good for the group is good for the individual, or because of a more sociable concern for the welfare of others when this does not conflict with their own well-being, selfish people may be concerned to increase social welfare. Achieving such increases presents any group with huge problems. Not least of these is the little matter of deciding what actually constitutes an increase in social welfare and what does not.

Such decisions are easy in extreme cases. If whole populations can be saved from starvation, we face no problem in deciding that all are better off. In general, when a policy makes everyone happier, we can assume that social well-being is increased. The problems arise when some are made better off at the expense of others, or if we are looking for the policy that is the best possible in the circumstances. In each of these cases, we are faced with the fundamental problem of comparing the value attached by different people to the same thing. If we cannot make such comparisons, then we cannot add these evaluations together. If we cannot add them together, then we cannot arrive at any estimate of the total value of a policy.

Pretend, for the moment, that I am a university professor with a commitment to the overall welfare of my students. One of the things that is just a little bit within my control is whether they leave university with a good degree or a mediocre one. Not only can I teach as well as I am able, but also I can use some of my very restricted influence at examiners' meetings. This influence, however, is limited to my ability to help at most one student in any year. (If I make impassioned speeches in favour of the entire group, my special pleading is disregarded.) I decide to use my influence on behalf of the student who most wants a good degree, in order to maximize the welfare of the group. I am left with the problem of deciding who this person is.

I could put the problem to the group, asking each to tell me how much she wants a good degree. One may tell me, 'I really want a good degree' while another may say, 'I really, really, really, really, want a first.' A third may get down on her knees and plead, 'I want that first more than anything else in the whole world.' I am still faced with two problems. In the first place, why should I believe what anyone says? If all students are altruists, I have some hope that their answers will be sincere. If they are not, then I must be aware of the likelihood that once a student wants a good degree, even a little bit, she has every incentive to exaggerate the strength of her desire. In the second place, even if I decide to believe my students, I must still compare one expressed desire with another. The person who wants a first more than anything else in the entire world may not want anything much. She may be a listless and poorly motivated sort of person with little ambition. The person who 'just' wants a first may want many other things even more badly. But she may still get a lot more value out of a good degree than the poorly motivated pudding. I have no yardstick for comparing the value that each student places on the favour I may do her.

Such yardsticks exist in practice, but they are all imperfect. One student might announce that she would murder her maiden aunt for a first. This could give me the idea of making my speech on behalf of the person prepared to commit the most spectacular murder. I would, however, be assuming that the cost of murdering a maiden aunt was the same for all students, clearly a suspect proposition. I might look for another yardstick, and consider money. I could give the first to the student prepared to donate the largest sum of money to a charity of my choosing. But this would simply favour the richest students. Such yardsticks are known as *numéraires* and are used as aids to comparison. They reduce everything to the same commonly valued denominator. In theory, no *numéraire* is perfect. In practice, some are better than others. At the end of the day, we have to do something.

Setting aside for a moment the technical difficulty of deciding which actions increase social welfare, we can attempt to solve the practical problem of taking necessary decisions in two basic ways. In the first place, social welfare may obviously be increased by greater *efficiency*. We may all be better off if more is produced. In the second place, social welfare may be increased by *redistribution*. Redistribution may work because each individual does not value every single gobbet of wealth to the same degree. Obviously, you greatly prize the gobbet of wealth that stands between you and death by starvation. The gobbet of wealth that enables you to build a heater for your second indoor swimming pool is less critical. Life will go on without it. Crudely, if we take the second swimming pool heater away from one person, and in the process save another from starvation, we have increased social welfare. In the terms used by economists, this arises from the fact that most people receive a *diminishing marginal utility* from added wealth. Another thousand means less to a millionaire than to a pauper. Taking it from the millionaire and giving it to the pauper increases social well-being.

Almost nobody would deny that it is a good thing to increase social welfare. Few would disagree with the general idea that it is desirable to increase the efficiency of production in order to do this. As we have seen, if we make everyone better off, we do not even need to tackle the problem of comparing the views of different people in order to know that we have increased social welfare. Problems arise when we want to redistribute wealth. Redistribution forces us to compare the evaluations of different individuals. Worse, there is a real possibility that redistribution and productive efficiency may sometimes be incompatible, though this argument works both ways.

Invitation to Politics

Many increases in efficiency involve redistribution. The classic case arises during industrial revolutions which, by definition, increase productive efficiency. Almost inevitably they also redistribute wealth. Some parts of the productive process disappear, at considerable cost to those previously involved. New classes are created. No one doubts that the revolution in information technology that will be brought about by micro-chip electronics will increase our ability to produce. This will be of little comfort to the thousands who will lose their jobs, and who will not be redeployed because the need for workers will be reduced. It may well be the case that redistribution (quite possibly from poor to rich) results in a loss of overall social welfare. This loss may more than cancel out the gains arising from increased efficiency.

The other side of this argument is that certain inequalities in the distribution of wealth may promote efficiency. This is an argument put forward by supporters of free-enterprise capitalism, who claim that inequalities produce incentives, and incentives produce efficiency. Such people may admit that inequalities of wealth, taken on their own, result in a society with a lower level of overall welfare than could be achieved by redistribution. They add, however, that the efficiency gains that arise from incentives more than compensate for this. The traditional theorists of free enterprise argued that *everyone* even the poorest, might well be better off in a situation of efficient inequality than they would in a situation of equal inefficiency. This is as much a practical question as a philosophical one. Most people answer it in their own way, from their own observations of the effects of incentives on efficiency. It is not enough, however, to convince yourself that incentives increase the overall efficiency of the system. Incentives must enhance efficiency by enough to compensate for the loss of welfare arising from the inevitable inequalities that must be involved.

Increasing social welfare thus provides several roles for government. These relate to the redistribution of wealth, to the efficiency of production and to the interaction between redistribution and efficiency.

Unless altruists are involved, redistribution will rarely be

Why We Need Governments

voluntary. In the absence of government, any involuntary redistribution that takes place will tend to consist of the strong taking things that belong to the weak. If wealth and strength go together, this will result in redistribution from poor to rich. As we have seen, this will tend to reduce overall social welfare. Redistribution that increases social welfare will tend, therefore, to depend upon coercion imposed from the outside, usually by governments.

Government coercion can also promote productive efficiency. Advertising, for example, is usually defended by advertisers because it expands the size of the market and allows more efficient large-scale production. In certain circumstances advertising may generate efficiency gains that exceed its costs. However, most free market competition will force producers to advertise *whether or not this is the case*. Even in a shrinking market rival advertisers may slug it out at great cost, in a desperate attempt to retain their market shares. A government that banned advertising in certain market sectors might well increase social welfare. After all, the inhabitants of Albion can only eat so much food. At the very least, once people are eating as much as they possibly can without bursting, further advertising cannot increase efficiency by expanding the food market. Banning food advertising would, quite simply, result in fewer wasted resources.

There are, of course, many other sources of inefficiency in the market. For example, the process of competition may lead to the emergence of a single, monopolistic producer. Once a monopoly has achieved, production can become very inefficient as competitive forces cease to operate. A government may therefore promote social welfare by controlling monopolies and by increasing competition between private producers.

Even in a market with neither advertising nor monopolies, the process of unregulated competition can be inefficient. A standard example is the 'hog cycle'. One year producers breed too many hogs. When they try to sell these, the price plummets. Next year, given this year's low prices, they hardly produce any hogs at all, since hogs are unprofitable. The price rockets. The year after, they over-produce again.

And so it goes on. The best level of production is never achieved, and inefficiency reigns. A government that intervened and effectively regulated hog prices or production would increase social welfare.

Opponents of government intervention in private production usually claim that such intervention is bad because it promotes inefficiency. I will reserve consideration of this point until my discussion of what governments do (chapter 5), although it is worth pointing out that such criticisms are usually based upon alleged deficiencies of bureaucratic decision-making rather than upon the notion of government itself. For the moment, we should simply note that government intervention can conceivably increase efficiency in those areas of private production where unregulated competition is manifestly inefficient.

The final role for government in this context arises when redistributing wealth and increasing the efficiency of production are incompatible. Some form of outside intervention then seems imperative. Just as redistribution is unlikely without either altruism or force, the sacrifice of efficiency to gain greater social welfare seems unlikely to arise from unregulated human interaction. Some redistributions of wealth (including redistributions which create more, as well as less, equality) may increase social productivity. Unless we are prepared to take the Darwinian view that only the most productive social systems will survive, outside intervention may well be imperative.

WHEN PEOPLE ARE SPITEFUL AND JEALOUS AND VAIN

Greed is not the most edifying motivation, but it is certainly not the worst that we can imagine. Greedy people may hurt others in pursuit of their private objectives, but at least they do so only as a means to an end. Spiteful people hurt others for fun. A greedy person might happen to want the possessions of others, but a covetous person will do this simply because the others have them. A greedy person may want more than everyone else because she wants as much as possible. A vain person wants more than the others because she just likes having more than the others.

It might seem that this is splitting hairs. After all, when someone bangs you over the head with a cosh and rifles your pockets, you don't much care whether she is covetous, vain, or just plain greedy. Your pockets are rifled and your head aches either way. True as this undoubtedly is, the social implications of simple greed are rather less dismal than those of covetousness, spite and vanity, which depend on the relative rather than the absolute well-being of individuals. Spiteful, covetous and vain people really are about the worst that we can imagine. After all, if two people are motivated by greed, there are many deals that they can concoct to make them both better off. They will still, therefore, want and need to get together, even to trust one another. Many of these deals will be of little use to the vain or covetous, who can hardly deal with each other at all. Almost any deal imaginable is going to make one side better off than the other, even when both come out way ahead.

Imagine that we are both covetous, and that you want to buy my rusty car. I am leaving the country and need to sell it quickly, while you need a cheap car. I could sell it to a dealer for £250, and the dealer would resell to you for £400. If I offer the car directly to you at £350, we both stand to gain, although you gain £50 to my £100. If you were covetous or spiteful, you would rather force me to sell to the dealer. You would do this, at some cost to yourself, because the deal would involve a greater cost for me. You gain an advantage even though you lose money. The tables would be turned if you came to me first with a firm offer of £300. In that case if I were covetous or spiteful, I might sell to the dealer at a loss of £50, in order to force you to pay the extra £100 that he would charge you. If we were both simply greedy, we would regard such spiteful gestures as ridiculous. We would try hard to work out a deal, since simply greedy people do not see a relative advantage as something worth paying for.

The problem of enforcing contracts is faced anyway by greedy men. It will be greatly exacerbated for the spiteful, the covetous and the vain. In the first place, far fewer mutually acceptable contracts will be available to them. (For the greedy, any deal that makes both better off may be acceptable. The spiteful accept only deals that leave relative advantage undisturbed.) The notion of mutual benefit that lies at the root of most voluntary deals simply evaporates when such dismal creatures are involved. In the second place, those deals that are eventually struck will be much more unstable. Any unforeseen development is likely to distort the fragile equilibrium that balances the relative advantage of two people. There are many changes of circumstance in which two greedy people can see themselves as still benefiting from a deal. Two covetous people are going to want to welsh on a deal as soon as circumstances change. The equilibrium between two covetous wills is unstable. For them, a deal can be balanced only in the sense that you can, in theory, balance a pencil on its point. Try it.

The same dismal logic applies to the production of public benefits and spillovers. These will be valued by the covetous only if they involve no redistribution at all. As we shall see, few public benefits can satisfy this criterion. Any form of redistribution is clearly impossible without outside coercion, since redistribution, by definition, disturbs relative advantage. The very notion of increasing social welfare has no meaning for the covetous and spiteful. Since one man's relative gain is always another's relative loss, they find themselves locked in a confrontation with no scope for mutual gain.

There is little more to say. We have painted a picture of people that is so pessimistic that the only possible consequence will be a state of perpetual disorder. The only possible solution is the imposition of a powerful government. With such dismal assumptions about human nature, little else is plausible.

THE CASE FOR GOVERNMENT

The case for government depends upon how you feel about human nature. In two circumstances the position is straightforward, and I have treated these rather briefly.

Why We Need Governments

If we make optimistic assumptions, and regard people as modest, altruistic and sociable, then government is not absolutely necessary, though some form of decision-making structure may be needed in all but the smallest of groups. This structure may need to be quite complex and bureaucratic if the group is large and concerned with specialized issues. Superficially it may look like government, but there will be no need for a state, an agency that monopolizes the legitimate forces of coercion. In those few circumstances in which members of the group are likely to resort to force (when there are deep-seated disagreements and the rival factions are unable to sustain breakaway groups) altruists are as likely to resist government activity as they are to resist anything else. Since government sanctions tend to be employed against individuals, and since altruists are concerned more for the group than for themselves, coercive methods of social control will be ineffective.

At the opposite end of the spectrum of views about human nature is a world inhabited by covetous, vain and spiteful individuals. These have no alternative but to accept a powerful coercive government if they are not to exist in a perpetual state of civil disorder. Motivated by a desire for eminence over others, such people recognize few of the mutual benefits which arise from co-operation. In such circumstances the alternative to government is not anarchy but chaos.

Most debates concerning the need for government make assumptions which lie between these extreme scenarios. If people are selfish but sociable, motivated by private desires but aware of the need to co-operate in order to survive, then the relevance of government will depend to a large extent upon the strength of community feeling. The desire for goods dictates a need to construct social agreements that may be binding without being enforced if they are made in an atmosphere of trust and goodwill. This is much more likely within smallish groups of individuals who are more or less continuously interacting with one another. In this case, the need to be trusted tomorrow encourages people to keep their side of a bargain today. In the same way, it is much harder in smaller communities for selfish people to take free rides at public expense. In a larger or less coherent group, free riding can be very attractive. The consequence is drastic under-provision of generalized social benefits such as public hygiene standards and over-provision of public nuisances, such as pollution.

Thus, both stable contracts and spillovers can be produced without government if a group is small enough and stable enough to guarantee long-term interaction between its members. When a group is too large or too unstable for this, when there is no sense of community, contracts and spillovers require coercion. In this case, the only form of coercion likely to solve the problem in the long run must be administered by an agency that monopolizes the use of legitimate force. There will, in addition, be a need for some mechanism for making collective decisions. Taken together, the separate functions of making and implementing decisions comprise what we commonly think of as government.

Government, therefore, is by no means inevitable. Communities may be able to regulate themselves if they appreciate the common interest that is produced by continuous interaction. This does not require group members to hold an altruistic view of the world and can arise even among selfish people if they perceive a long-term need to get along with one another. In the absence of community the alternative to government is chaos.

3

When We Don't Need Governments

THE CASE AGAINST GOVERNMENT

I have already argued that government is not inevitable. Since much of the rest of this book is about the politics of government, however, I must take a little time to emphasize this point. I shall do this in two ways. In this section I shall look in rather more detail at the anarchist case, or rather cases, since there are at least two of them. Later in the chapter I shall look at a range of real examples of politics without government. These concern the ordered anarchy of everyday life.

The case against government is usually argued in one of three basic ways. Two of these are arguments of principle and are based upon very different assumptions about human relations. While both are arguments for anarchy, they argue for very different conceptions of anarchy. The first school of thought is essentially an argument for community and attacks government for debasing this. The second approach, adopted by 'libertarians' or 'anarcho-capitalists', is a philosophy of the radical right. Based upon a belief in the supreme importance of individual or 'human' rights (and especially property rights), this view reviles government as an inevitable violator of these.

The final argument is more pragmatic. It is a watered-down version of the libertarian view, which asserts that most government activity is not so much an infringement of rights as it is inefficient. This pragmatic case rests upon faith in the essentially efficient consequences of unregulated human interaction. Government activity is seen as disturbing natural equilibria. It is assumed to impose unnatural, and by implication undemocratic, outcomes determined by a political elite that can never be in the position to decide what is most efficient. This view has been most closely associated in recent years with those politicians who advocate monetarist economics, although it is commonly held by economists in general. In common with libertarian anarchists, they demand not the abolition of the state but rather restriction of state activity to the absolute minimum. This last argument is something to which I will return when discussing what governments do (chapter 5). In the meantime, I shall consider communitarian and libertarian objections to state activity.

Communitarian anarchy

In the previous chapter I produced different justifications for government on the basis of different assumptions about human nature. Most communitarian anarchists would stand this method on its head. Their essential argument is that government debases human nature. They do not see government producing order out of chaos. On the contrary, they see government as as being forced to control chaos. They see the chaos as caused by the destruction of communities. And they see government as the destroyer of communities. Governments, in effect, occupy themselves by clearing up social messes of their own making.

All communitarian anarchists see the fundamental human group as being something much smaller than the modern state. Many would now see it as the workplace. This means that anarchists do not need to be wildly optimistic about human nature. We have already seen, after all, that even selfish people may regulate themselves if they live in close-knit communities. Provided that groups are small enough for people to know what others are doing, and stable enough for people to value the give and take of long-term interaction, they may get by without government. Social order may be maintained because all value group membership and fear the effects of its withdrawal if they do not conform.

When We Don't Need Governments

A firm sense of community can replace most, if not all, of the functions of government. Many anarchists would also argue the reverse – that government can replace or undermine most, if not all, aspects of community. A communitarian anarchist would not deny, for example, that people who are moved from a local slum community into a modern high-rise block have a much greater need for government action if a reasonable environment is to be maintained. An anarchist would ask, however, who did the moving in the first place? Who *created the need* for more government? And the answer, of course, would be government.

Similarly, communitarian anarchists would argue that state provision of homes for the aged or welfare for the needy has the same detrimental effect upon the quality of social life. Such state action undermines the role of the community and replaces it with formal institutions. This claim should not be studied out of context. Communitarian anarchists do not suggest that the modern state should not provide welfare for the needy. A modern state without such provision would clearly be the worst of all possible worlds. The argument is rather that the modern state has created the need for such provision, causing problems that would not exist without it. While people get old whatever the social system, they are not 'problems' for a genuine community.

We face a chicken-and-egg problem. Do man's desires create a need for government, or does government condition man's desires? At a homespun level we can gain some insight into the matter by considering our own position on a range of issues. The relationship between police and rioters in recent urban confrontations is a good example. Some claim that riots are provoked by heavy-handed policing, others that firm policing is needed to subdue rioters. The police often claim that they need to be tough because the local community no longer controls its youth. Local people respond that tough policemen have undermined the community and that riotous youth is a symptom of this. A similar argument is sometimes made about the role of social workers. Some see social workers as creating and defining 'social problems' by taking over, in the name of government, some of the functions of a community. Others see social workers as agents of government, saving those who have already been abandoned by their fellows. I do not have the audacity to pronounce upon the question of whether the police cause or prevent riots, or whether the social-work industry creates or alleviates social problems. Most people, however, have views on these matters. They can use them to throw some personal light upon the relationship between government and community.

The other element in the case for government is the need to increase overall social welfare. This is not usually an explicit concern of communitarian anarchists, although they implicitly see the destruction of community by government as counter-productive and inefficient. The issue of increasing aggregate welfare by means of social redistribution takes a different form. This is because, in the complete absence of a state, private property as we know it does not exist. Thus the accumulation of private property as 'wealth' does not arise. Inequality of well-being *between* communities is usually ignored. *Within* communities inequalities are less significant because man's desires are usually considered by anarchists to be rather modest. Anarchists thus see the maximization of welfare, and the resultant role for government either as something of a non-problem or as one more problem created by the existence of government.

Libertarian anarchy

Libertarians start from the notion of the individual rather than that of the community. They are motivated by a fundamental belief in human rights, and a right is not considered to be a right at all if it can be taken away from someone. The right to private property quickly emerges as one of these inviolable rights. Immediately, of course, this creates a need for some government, since private property (as opposed to possessions) can exist only under the protection of a state. (A piece of property is more than a possession because it involves a legal entitlement. No state=no law=no property.)

Libertarians, therefore, are not true anarchists. They are opposed to *most* government rather than to *all* government.

When We Don't Need Governments

They must, for example, rely upon governments to enforce contracts, since contracts usually concern the assignment of property rights. The most wild and woolly libertarians do sometimes claim to be able to enforce their own contracts or to delegate enforcement to agents in the enforcement market. It is very hard, however, to see how permanent civil disorder can be avoided in this case.

While most libertarians approve of government as a guarantor of property rights and an enforcer of contracts, they dispute the need for government as producer of spillovers or maximizer of social welfare. Such activities will be bound to conflict with the property rights of at least one individual. Any form of enforced redistribution is obviously out, since the rights of those who lose resources are infringed. Spillovers will be produced if people want them, but those who wish to free ride should not be coerced. If the free rider problem undermines the production of valuable spillovers, then groups of individuals should devise mechanisms for clubbing together and producing them privately. They could replace lighthouses with radio beams transmitting scrambled signals, replace broadcast TV with cable TV and so on. Recognizing that some spillovers cannot be privatized in this way, libertarians conclude, when the crunch really comes, that the principle of absolute individual liberty is more important than anything else. Anything which cannot be produced by exclusive private clubs, or as a side-effect activity, will just have to be forsaken.

It sometimes comes as a surprise to people when they find two such different views of the world described as anarchy. It is certainly true that the two schools of anarchist thought attack government for almost diametrically opposed reasons. One is concerned to defend private property and one to destroy it. One looks at what groups can do for individuals, the other at what individuals can do for groups. Both, however, are united in their reliance on small, stable, groups, or communities. Both are also similar in presenting an idealized version of how the world *might* have been, of why government was not inevitable and of the damage that it has done. Neither approach has much to say about the position which most of us find ourselves in today. We are subject to governments and equipped with a set of attitudes and desires (however these might have arisen). No theory of anarchy has much to say about how we can move from this position to one in which there is no government.

One question with which we are all concerned, however, is *how much* government we need. This is the reason why I feel that theories of anarchy, and arguments for government, are important. The theories may put forward ideals, but they also give us tools that we can use when evaluating what governments do.

THE POLITICS OF EVERYDAY LIFE

Before going on to look in greater detail at what governments do, however, I want to spend some time looking at what they do not. No government can regulate every aspect of human affairs. This means that large slices of everyday life will always be organized on anarchistic lines. Nothing better illustrates the point that anarchy is not chaos than the elaborate rule book used by polite society, the fact that people stand in line when they could just as easily push in front, or the fact that you could abolish most driving laws, yet people would still stop at red lights. Everyday life is usually a model of order rather than of chaos. Yet much of it is untouched by government.

Queues

Once upon a time, long before traffic engineers were as smart as they are today with their fancy contraflow systems, I was stuck in a tailback on a motorway. Several miles ahead they were rebuilding the surface. The queue of cars was completely stationary. Most had their engines turned off, while some drivers had even got out and were talking to each other. Let me give away something about my character and tell you that I sat in my car and eyed the hard shoulder. Cars were stopped only on the roadway, and the hard shoulder was clear for miles ahead. However angry the motorists at the front of the queue would be when I came to an obstruction and wanted to cut back in, however tightly they closed ranks, I could always force my way back into the line of cars. Some aggressive driving would save me a lot of time. I'll give away something else about my character and tell you that I was still thinking about this when a dark blue 1966 2.8 Jaguar went up that hard shoulder at 70 miles an hour. All hell broke loose. Conversations stopped in mid-sentence, drivers leapt back into their seats, and there were several minor accidents as they jostled to get on to the hard shoulder. Pretty soon that was jammed solid too. The Jaguar driver and one or two others went straight to the head of the queue.

Queues are a nice example of the anarchic politics of everyday life. There's no law that forces people to wait in line, yet they act as if you'd just broken one of the Ten Commandments if you push in ahead of them.

Queueing is a convention. Unlike many conventions, it has a sensible purpose. People queue at bus stops because if they didn't, too many of them would get trampled to death the next time a number 64 with only three empty seats pulled up. A queue is a deal, and it is conditional. It says, 'I'll wait in line.' It implies, 'I won't if you don't.' If you want to test this, get together a large group of friends and feed them into the front of a hard pressed rush hour bus queue at such a rate that no one else in the queue ever gets any closer to the front. Pretty soon you'll discover just how conditional the queue is. Law and order will break down.

A queue isn't a machine, however; it makes allowances. A grumpy old lady can barge in at the front, and everyone else will just sigh and make allowances for yet another grumpy old lady. Someone in a vast hurry can charge up to the front, explain breathlessly that the end of her particular world is at hand and get on that number 64. Four or five of these in quick succession, however, and the huffing and puffing starts in earnest.

Queues, therefore, are a physical manifestation of order amid chaos, of anarchy in action. Laws don't govern queues, but norms certainly do. You will probably never get sent to prison for jumping a queue, but the informal social world in which we are all forced to exist can become pretty unfriendly. Most of the social sanctions which can be brought to bear can be at least as effective as any thing a court of law is likely to mete out for 'disorderly queueing'.

People queue because a queue solves a problem of public order. This is a collective-action problem that, as always, is more amenable to anarchic solution in a small community. We would expect to find that queueing is more prevalent in small communities than in large and alienated groups. Thus you rarely see riots at village post offices, or even on pension day. Most people are happy to wait their turn. In contrast, the *bureau de change* of a major airport at a peak period can look a little like the end of civilization as we know it. As for the London Underground at rush hour, the fact that nobody knows anyone else means that there are few rules and fewer incentives to obey them. A nine-months-pregnant mother with five screaming children to look after can be pushed out of a place on the London Underground.

Differences between nations, of course, can be even more dramatic, as a brief survey of queueing in banks can illustrate. Americans prefer high-technology efficiency, zip lines and flashing lights. There is little reliance on norms in the bastion of individual liberty, no need to rely on give and take when an impersonal system can do the job just as well. As a consequence, it is physically very difficult to barge in at the front of an American bank queue. The British like to gamble in banks. They walk into a bank and, straight away, they have to pick a winner. Not only does each queue have a different length, but also each member has a different bundle of transactions to complete. The inexperienced may rush to the back of what, to old hands, is a suspiciously short line. It turns out to contain a little old lady banking the entire week's takings from a medium-sized shopping precinct. The Irish make informal and well-camouflaged zip lines at the back of banks. This is partly to dispel any suspicion that they might be poking their noses into the business of those in front of them. It is mainly to lure unwitting foreigners into a social gaffe. In continental Europe everyone knows that anything goes.

When We Don't Need Governments

As further evidence of the highly *conditional* nature of most people's attitude towards queues, try watching a normally orderly queue under abnormal stress. The Christmas shopping rush is a good time to do this, and a good place to do it is an important city-centre bus stop. Most of the people involved will have queued at this stop before, but not all at once. Normally, all in the queue get on the next bus. During the Christmas rush the buses are nearly full *before* they arrive at the stop, while the queue is much bigger. Several buses come and go and make no impression. Standing in that queue, you will begin to feel it come alive. You will begin to feel the jostling as the next bus looms on the horizon. You will see how those grumpy old ladies who try to assert their 'rights' to barge in are tolerated much less. With luck, you may see a real scramble. This can happen very quickly. It is fascinating to watch a queue on that knife edge, when each is trying to decide whether enough of the others are still queueing to make her own continued queueing worthwhile.

The politics of driving

In Britain, the law says that everyone must drive on the left-hand side of the road. Imagine that, on some sunny day in the near future, a radical government of the dead centre decided to free the driving population of such leftist commitments, and that this law was abolished. Imagine that it was made quite clear to all and sundry that they were free to choose which side of the road they would like to use. I am willing to make a small bet that nothing would happen.

Maybe one or two more corners would be cut here and there. Maybe a few people would drive up the right-hand side of the road at 5.30 a.m. on a Sunday morning, just to see what it felt like. I doubt very much whether chaos and disaster would descend upon our road system. Those people who get their thrills from driving at 70 m.p.h. the wrong way up the fast lane of a motorway would continue to do so. If they are not deterred by the threats posed by the oncoming traffic, they would not be deterred by the threat of prosecution for driving on the wrong side of the road. Those who make mistakes and think that they are living in the United States or Italy would continue to do so. Everyone else would go on driving on the left.

The law that says everyone must drive on the left-hand side of the road is redundant. We drivers could manage that little bit of politics quite well without government. All that would be needed is the posting of a few prominent signs at the exits to international car ferry ports with the message:

> WELCOME TO BRITAIN. YOU MIGHT LIKE TO KNOW THAT MOST PEOPLE DRIVE ON THE LEFT OVER HERE, BUT PLEASE DON'T LET THIS CRAMP YOUR STYLE.

Motorists are quite good at self-regulation (sometimes). Large parts of the Scottish Highlands are served by single-track roads with passing places. Many of these are straight roads with good surfaces, on which a driver can build a good head of steam. Often two cars, going in opposite directions at a fair lick, confront each other at each end of a long straight. If there is a passing place between them, the convention is that the closer car pulls in, while the other comes straight on through. This makes sense. If they both kept on going until the car further from the passing space reached it and pulled in, they would crash head-on before anything else of interest happened. If both cars stop and fool around trying to decide which should pull in, much time is lost in process. Even if the closer driver is in a tearing hurry and doesn't want to be the one to stop, there is nothing much to be done about it. She could pass the passing place, but then both drivers would have to stop to avoid an accident. She could force the other driver to back up to the previous passing space, but no current production car can go as fast in reverse as it can forwards. This would waste time too. Only a bloody-minded driver who was simply never prepared to give way would engineer such a showdown. The 'nearer stops' convention is an elegant method of resolving the drivers' problem with little conflict, provided that each is simply concerned to get on her way as speedily as possible.

It is interesting, therefore, to observe what happens when

When We Don't Need Governments

big-city drivers hit the Scottish highlands. A big-city driver sees stopping to let others pass as a piece of chivalry. Some big-city drivers are as chivalrous as can be, but others are not. The first time that these cads hit the Scottish Highlands and the single track roads with passing places, they don't observe the convention. They run, nose-to-nose, up against the oncoming car and force it back. There is much gnashing of bumpers and many dirty looks all round. This, after all, seems the obvious course of action for any red-blooded big-city driver with no sense of chivalry. It also wastes time.

After a while the big-city driver, who may well be on holiday, mellows in the consistent glow of country life. She discovers chivalry and takes a pride in driving for the nearest passing place at the merest sniff of an oncoming automobile. The pleasure she derives from such self-sacrifice is considerable, and the born-again nice driver never realizes that her chivalrous conduct is also the most rational way to behave. She succeeds in diving for a passing place only when she is nearer to it than the oncoming car. Otherwise her chivalrous urges are thwarted. When she succeeds in giving way she basks in the waves and smiles of acknowledgement when these are forthcoming and is indignant when they are not. She goes back home never realizing that she really had no choice. In this case self-regulation just happens.

In the United States many crossroads have four-way stop signs instead of traffic lights. Everyone has to stop and each can move off when it is safe. Obviously a rule is needed to decide who should move off first when more than one of the four approaches has a car on it. This rule varies from state to state, but the Texas Driver's Code supplies one answer: 'Give way to traffic from the right.' This is consistent, unambiguous and the law. It is a rule, however, which could seriously offend a highly developed Texan sense of justice. This would be particularly true if someone were stopped facing a rush-hour queue of traffic hitting the junction from her right. It might take an hour before it was legal for her to move off. Texas drivers have largely replaced the legal rule with an alternative: 'Leave in the order in which you arrived.'

This is consistent and effective, if a trifle ambiguous. It creates no anomolies and is so widely accepted as a convention that it could be dangerous to drive according to the law at a four-way stop sign. You are the last of three drivers to stop. You happen to be in the rightmost car and you move straight off, smack into a driver who has been waiting longer and whose turn had arrived. In this case drivers regulate themselves *despite* governments.

In each of these cases a heavy dose of self-interest makes the intervention of government largely redundant, even ignored in the case of the Texan four-way stop-signs. The informal politics of everyday life is quite sufficient to do the trick, mainly because the problems are ones more of simple co-ordination than of resolving conflict. Nobody really minds which side of the road she drives on, just as long as everyone drives on the same side. Even single-track roads and their passing places, which may superficially look like settings for a showdown, turn out to present simple co-ordination problems. In such cases straightforward self-interest replaces the need for coercion.

Night driving presents rather different problems, particularly when it comes to the dipping of headlights. Here conflict is more overt. It is much more pleasant, other things being equal, to drive with your headlights on full beam. You can really see what is going on and are less likely to dent your front bumper on some meandering cyclist, riding without lights and dressed from head to toe in jet-black. It is very unpleasant and dangerous, however, to drive towards someone else's main-beam headlights. This is why dipping headlights were invented. Both the formal and the informal rules of the road demand that you dip your headlights in the face of an oncoming road user. But why do people bother, when it is much more pleasant to drive on with main beams blazing? The answers to this question once more illuminate the role of community.

In some circumstances drivers may see themselves as members of a community and thus see the need to engage in give and take. They dip their headlights because they realize that if all dip headlights, all are better off. Headlight dipping is some sort of public benefit, which all can enjoy but all must help to produce. This requires quite a broadminded view of community. Communities depend upon interaction and, in the dead of night, one doesn't interact much with the invisible driver of an oncoming automobile. Since one does not know who she is, it is not possible to know if future interaction is likely. In a small rural community, of course, or in a well defined housing development, each driver can reasonably assume that all other drivers are locals. Even without knowing the person for whom you are dipping, you may assume that you will be dealing with her again. This interpretation of headlight dipping may explain why people conform to the norm in small communities, but it depends upon a very optimistic view of each driver's sense of community when applied to inter-city highways. Nevertheless, I have seen headlights dipped on inter-city highways.

The other possible explanation depends upon the threat of retaliation. If you dazzle an oncoming motorist, she can dazzle you back. A warning flash serves to remind you of your obligations and threatens punishment if you don't conform. If you still don't dip, she can switch on her main beams and make you suffer too, with the implicit promise that she'll back down and dip if you do first. This arm's-length ritual can be observed many times on any night drive. Whether it is a friendly reminder or a threat, it is certainly politics. Whatever it is, the anarchic politics of driving is much more important than the outside chance of police action in explaining why people dip their headlights. I would be very surprised if more than a handful of motorists have ever been prosecuted for failing to dip. Once more, drivers manage without government.

Etiquette

Man developed, and with him developed civilization. From [the] first peace greeting there grew certain set salutations, certain forms of homage that bound men together in mutual protection and friendliness. Then ceremonies were created – dances in honour of the spirit of the Sun, sacrifices to some god of Fear, ceremonies in memory of the departed spirit of the dead. It is upon this foundation that etiquette and good manners are based today.

When a married woman calls upon another married woman and finds her out, she leaves three cards – one of her own and two of her husband's. If the lady of the house is a widow or spinster, she will leave only one card of her husband's. In no case does a lady ever leave her card upon a gentleman, unless perhaps in the case of illness, when a single woman or widow calls to enquire for a bachelor friend. A bachelor or a married man calling without his wife upon a married couple leaves two of his cards if the lady is out. A married man never leaves his wife's card. When cards are left, the right-hand corner of each should be turned down. . . .

(Both quotations from Lady Troubridge, *The Book of Etiquette*, 1931)

Queueing and driving well illustrate the potent influence of social norms. In order to explore these a little further we may look briefly at the subject of etiquette, the set of conventional rules of 'polite' behaviour. Etiquette and norms are definitely not the same thing. After all, members of polite society are always complaining about the manner in which new norms of behaviour have superseded the good old ways. People these days smoke in the street, tip the servants too much at shooting parties and generally behave in a fashion almost guaranteed to undermine the entire fabric of civilized life. Yet, if anything gives, it will be the old rules of etiquette, not the new norms of behaviour.

Consider the problem of opening doors. There can be no argument that, when it comes to going through doors, some generally accepted norm of behaviour speeds up matters considerably. We both stand on opposite sides of a doorway; we both step forward, stop, step back to let the other pass, stop, step forward again and generally cha-cha around. We waste time even if we don't actually crack heads. The problem of who stops for whom on a single-track road has one obvious and efficient solution. When trying to work out how to get through a door, however, there are many possibilities.

Back in the Age of Chivalry the position was crystal-clear. Two rules of etiquette resolved the problem unambiguously.

When We Don't Need Governments

Men opened doors for women. When two people of the same sex were involved, the younger opened doors for the older. (Social status was also a factor. By and large, however, people with radically different social positions did not use the same doors in the Age of Chivalry.) The feminist movement probably gave little comfort to Lady Troubridge in her advancing years. It certainly confused the position where doors were concerned. As far as I am aware, etiquette is unchanged. Men should open doors for women. Times change, however, and for a man to hold a door open for a woman is considered in some circles to be evidence of chauvinist, even porcine, proclivities. To continue to do so is not exactly to buck the trend, but it is definitely a more positive identification with the norms of a bygone age than it would have been a few years ago. Norms and etiquette are beginning to conflict when it comes to doors. When the etiquette manuals for the year 2000 go to press, new rules on door-opening will doubtless be included.

Thus much of the need for norms is practical. They serve to solve co-ordination problems and other aspects of social intercourse for which regulation is needed but coercion is inappropriate. The problem is that norms are no good if you don't know them. Etiquette functions to formalize norms and to code them as rules that can be widely and unambiguously disseminated. This solves the problem of making sure that people know what is expected in a given situation but suffers from two drawbacks. In the first place, since norms are continuously changing, the formal rules of etiquette date quickly. In the second place, formal rules tend to be rigid and therefore inappropriate in exceptional circumstances. In the Age of Chivalry even a gentlemen with no arms would have been expected to have a go at opening doors for a member of the opposite sex. This is why etiquette always seems a trifle old-fashioned and ridiculous. Nonetheless, while norms may be widely known *within* a group, one does after all need to know how to behave in one's dealings with the outside world. (Lady Troubridge lays particular stress upon the need for inflexible observance of the rules of etiquette when dealing with foreigners.)

Invitation to Politics

The other main function of etiquette is psychological. Most of us need to identify with others and with certain social groups. Adherence to group rules and norms is one of the most obvious ways of asserting this identification. The more complex and obscure the rules, the more effective they are at reinforcing group identity and excluding outsiders. This is probably why Etiquette (with an enormous capital E) is much more a preoccupation of social climbers than it is of those at the top of the tree. Someone who is interested in getting into a particular group is tempted to think that, since ignorance of group etiquette identifies outsiders, mastery of it guarantees admittance. Passing the port in the right direction does not, however, make an Oxford don.

The existence of the subject of etiquette also tends to obscure the fact that the social mannerisms of the upper middle classes are not the only things that can be thought of as etiquette. All groups have an etiquette. Anyone who has been a student will know that is considered extremely impolite to be seen in a library after 5.30 p.m., however late it stays open, or to be anything other than absolutely flabbergasted at getting a good degree. Even more dramatic examples can be culled from visits abroad, but it is as well to draw a veil over subjects such as urinating in public or eating sheep's eyes.

Pudding. This is what comes after the main course. It is not referred to as 'the sweet', 'afters' or 'dessert'.

Fork. Use fork only, if possible, for pudding – otherwise spoon and fork. These are placed along with the rest of the knives, forks and spoons in order of use on either side of the plate. They are *not* laid at the top. Never use spoon without fork.

Anne Barr and Peter York (*The Official Sloane Ranger Handbook*, 1982)

REGULATION WITHOUT GOVERNMENT

Both anarchy and everyday life represent order without coercion. One of the great weaknesses of the anarcho-capitalist position is that it is very difficult to see why the social world would not descend into chaos if enforcement were left entirely to private entrepreneurs, who would slug it out on behalf of rival clients. Communitarian anarchists, on the other hand, put their faith in the ability of communities to regulate themselves. How might such regulation be achieved?

We have already seen part of the answer to this question. Those within communities tend to honour their word and to make private contributions in the public interest because they expect to benefit from the long-term give and take of community interaction. These benefits provide every community with powerful social sanctions that can be brought to bear upon dissidents. Those who do not conform to community norms can be excluded from community benefits. Those who eat their peas with a knife will not be invited back to dinner, while those who eat babies will be cast out into the wilderness.

Exclusion from the community is a finely graded social weapon. In its most extreme form people really can be cast out into the wilderness, as they were by traditional tribes. This is virtually a death sentence, even if it does not involve explicit execution. As a punishment, exile has always been only slightly less daunting than execution. Those allowed to remain within a community are able to enjoy many of its benefits. In particular they may take advantage of indiscriminate spillovers such as street lighting, defence and public health. However, this may do a dissident little good if she is still excluded from all of the private give and take of community interaction. To be boycotted or sent to Coventry is a very severe sanction. Few of us would be capable of surviving if nobody were willing to deal with us.

There are, of course, boycotts and boycotts. You may be totally ignored by all and sundry or merely barred from your local pub on account of a spot of anti-social behaviour. You can survive being barred more or less intact, though if you like your local, you still face a serious incentive to mend your manners.

Boycotts and embargoes are the main sanctions available in international politics. In the absence of any effective international government, the international community must regulate itself along anarchistic lines. Since international trade is vital to all nations, total or partial exclusion from trade represents a serious threat. It has been used many times. Against the illegal Smith regime in Rhodesia, and against South Africa, attempts have been made at total boycotts. Military trade is often suspended with belligerent nations, while the USA has made sporadic attempts to recruit allies for trade sanctions against the Soviet Union. As we shall see in a later chapter, politics between nations is anarchy, and the international regulation of this anarchy depends largely upon exclusion.

Community sanctions may be formal or informal. We all avoid the person who washes too little, and pretty soon she gets the message. Nobody sits down and passes judgement. The exclusion just happens, and the norm of washing is upheld. Sometimes, however, social sanctions require a collective decision. If we all decide not to trade with a cheat, for example, some of us may be tempted to back down when she offers us huge sums of cash to break the embargo. We need to make, and to stick to, a collective decision to punish the dissident. Once more, we see that anarchy may need institutions, particularly if the group is too large for all to participate in decision-making. The 'community' is more than the sum of its parts, and we cannot guarantee that community decisions will simply emerge. What makes a community anarchistic, whatever its institutions, is the absence of centralized coercion.

The other main feature of self-regulation by community is socialization. This is the passing down of group norms and values from one generation to the next. Education, of course, is a part of socialization, but it tends to be the more formal and less interesting part. Explicit and tangible rules are taught to the community's younger members. A much more potent process is simply living in society. In this respect the playground is more instructive than the classroom. The shaming, the ridicule, the mysterious pecking orders, all combine to leave the new recruit in little doubt as to what is required. And, obviously, until people know the norms, they cannot abide by them.

When We Don't Need Governments

This is why when a society is broken up into different communities the school system can become a battlefield. The battle is not fought for the classrooms; these may be good, bad or indifferent. It is fought for the playground. Without the playground and everything else that goes with it, the classroom is more or less redundant. The Irish government, for example, waged a monumental war to restore the Irish language, and used the classroom as its main weapon. Young children were taught Irish and were taught other subjects in Irish. But in those areas where Irish was spoken neither at home nor around and about the language died out anyway.

The battle for the playground is why the matter of comprehensive education inflames so many tempers in England. Before the comprehensives English schools were segregated along class lines. There were middle-class state schools, called grammar schools, and working-class state schools, called secondary moderns. Working-class children who passed the 11-plus exam and went to a grammar school entered a different world. They began to be educated into a middle-class lifestyle, and their parents were not always happy with the result. Middle-class children who failed the exam tended not to go to secondary moderns. In the normal middle-class family failing the 11-plus was seen as a financial disaster, since it meant that children had to be sent to fee-paying schools. These were often of rather poor academic quality – some were little more than private secondary moderns – but they were certainly middle-class. There can have been no more forceful evidence of the power of the playground than the sight of a middle-class family scrimping and saving to send its children to an inferior, but middle-class, school.

This, of course, is why 'comprehensivization' represented such a trauma for the English middle class. In a very real sense all of its norms and values seemed threatened (or at least much more expensive). Where else but at a grammar school could middle-class socialization take place at state expense? In many English cities the situation *has* been resolved. Comprehensive schools have been sifted into those that are middle-class and those that are working-class. Order and security has thereby been restored.

The deep emotions that are stirred by attempts to tamper with the process of socialization show the strength of a community without, or even despite, government action. Whether people realize it or not, they have a very firm sense of how things are done in their community. They have some very potent weapons at their disposal to ensure that things are done in the right way. Indeed, communities can be so strong that the real problem is not how communities manage without government; it is the little matter of whether a government can have any impact at all upon a community when community and government do not agree.

4
Who is Governed?

Having argued that government is most necessary when community fails, I now want to look at what a political community might be. The short answer to this question is very simple. A community is a group of people who, more or less consciously, share common interests. As with most short answers, this one simply redefines the question. We now need to know why people might feel that they have common interests and which common interests are likely to be important to people in the real world.

A person can have almost any interest in common with others. There is a community of people who are 7 feet tall and have an interest in banning the construction of low doorways. There is a community of seasoned drinkers who would like all bars to be forced to open twenty-four hours a day. In addition to all of the single interests that people might hold in common, there are countless permutations and combinations of these. Each combination defines groups with clusters of shared interests. Thus the community of seasoned drinkers who are 7 feet tall is particularly concerned with the height of pub doorways.

In addition to the sharing of interests, communities have two other important properties. The first is *stability* and the second *interaction*. Both of these are crucial elements in the argument about why community and government may both do the same job. It is the stability of a group that enables its members to take a long-term view of why they need to get along with one another, of why they might be able to solve collective-action problems among themselves. Thus a group of people who come together once and once only (the passengers on a city-centre bus, for example) may see little point in making short-term individual sacrifices for long-term gain. A group of people who regularly get together, say the market-day passengers on a regular but infrequent rural bus service, know that the sacrifices they make now may be repaid in the future. Thus our rural bus passengers may be quite happy to wait for a latecomer, to refrain from smoking, to help each other with their bundles of shopping and so on. The city-centre passengers get on, sit down, complain to the driver if she hangs around 'needlessly' and smoke their heads off if not restrained by a by-law enforceable in the courts. Stability encourages the pursuit of long-term interests, since the community will be around in the long term. It thus encourages *reciprocal action*. At the heart of why a community may replace government lies the fact that communities allow people to engage in collective action. And they do this by providing the stability which allows for long-term give and take.

Community interaction is obviously crucial because if there is no interaction, there is no reason for people to involve themselves in reciprocal action. Thus the same stable group may all have common interests, yet they will not be a community if they don't interact. Those who live on a modern housing estate may well fit this description. Such people may form a potential community, yet never actually deal with one another. The physical environment of a community may have something to do with this. One housing area may be a street of terraced houses, for example, with everyone facing everyone else and meeting in the street on the way to shops. Another may be a high-rise block of apartments built so that everyone looks out away from each other and so that each is likely only to meet the people next door. Many modern housing developments have omitted to include places such as local shops and pubs where locals can meet. This provokes immediate complaints about long treks for the groceries but also causes more fundamental problems for the development of communities. The places in which people do get together, the large shopping and entertainment centres, are shared by many people with varied interests and hence offer no focus for community interaction (The development of the notion of *community architecture* reflects the realization of the importance of such factors.)

The general social structure can also affect community interaction. The most often quoted example of this is the emergence of the nuclear family. When the basic family unit extends to only two generations, parents and their dependent children, the scope for interaction is far less. When the family spans several generations, to include grandparents and grandchildren, and brings in more distant relations, uncles, aunts, cousins, in-laws and so on, the scope for interaction is obviously much greater.

The importance of stability and interaction can be seen in the typical laments of those who mourn the erosion of community. We hear that people don't talk to each other as they used to, that they don't do so much for each other, that the turnover of the population is much faster (people don't stay as they used to). We hear all sorts of folk stories of how in the good old days when Mrs Jones went into labour she had only to bang on the wall and the neighbours were in to help, while the people at the end of the street phoned for an ambulance and next-door-but-three looked after the little ones. Alternatively, we hear horror stories of people who now die in their homes, while nobody notices for three days. Whether such stories are myth or reality, they certainly illustrate what people *expect* from community, and it is what they expect that is important.

While all communities share common interests, stability and interaction, some interests are clearly more important than others. Thus in this chapter I want to look at certain types of interest that seem to play a particularly important part in holding communities together. Three broad types of interest always seem to be at the forefront of community relations. These are 'ethnic' interests, such as race, language and religion; 'class', or economic, interests; and interests relating to nationality or culture.

ETHNIC INTERESTS

Race is usually the most immediately obvious of these. It is certainly the hardest to change. People who are in the same racial group are quite simply in the same racial group, although this does not automatically mean that they share common interests. Shared interests arise in practice because different racial groups tend to be treated in different ways by the rest of the population. In part this is because racial groups often share distinctive cultural values, but this raises a chicken-and-egg problem. Do distinctive values provoke different treatment, or does different treatment reinforce the identity of the racial group and lead it to develop distinctive values? I will return to the role played by cultural values. Meanwhile it is clear that many examples of racial prejudice are based not at all upon the values of the victim but merely upon her race.

However mistaken people's views of racial differences might be, these views can generate racial communities with distinctive common interests. Prejudice may not even be shared by those who nevertheless behave in a racially conscious manner. A prime example is the housing market. If the residents of a solid white area are all in fact unprejudiced but perceive others to be prejudiced, they may still practise racial discrimination when a black family moves in. The 'non-prejudiced' fear that others, who they think are prejudiced, will want to leave the area. They fear that their community will be eroded by this and, of course, they may fear that house prices will consequently fall. They too leave the area, not because they are prejudiced themselves, but because they fear the effects of the prejudice of others.

This is a variety of panic or craze and is a good example of a collective-action problem that, unsolved, leaves all worse off. Another racial version is the old 'Would you let your son marry a white woman?' problem. The answer is often, 'I'm not prejudiced myself, but others are. I don't want my son to marry a white woman because everyone else will give them a tough time.' The doting parents may or may not really feel this way. They may or may not be right about the prejudice of others. It hardly makes any difference whether they are rationalizing their private prejudice or are genuinely fearful. Either way, racial discrimination is reinforced, even created where none before existed. Prejudice, or the fear of prejudice, can be self-fulfilling. If Eskimos are belived to make poor racing drivers, they will not be given the chance to race. The absence of successful Eskimo racing drivers will then confirm what people 'always knew'.

In short, as long as racial groups are distinctive, it is possible to believe (or to believe that others believe) distinctive things about them. Even if these beliefs are absolutely wrong, they can serve to give the victims common interests where none before existed. If a group is treated as if it were different, it can become different. Mistaken beliefs can therefore be self-fulfilling.

Language is another factor that draws communities together, although it is easier to change your language than your colour. Moreover, language discrimination, though not prejudice, is inevitable. If you cannot understand somebody else, then communicating with her becomes considerably more difficult and unlikely. Interaction is restricted and community necessarily more difficult to establish. In this sense, a common language is almost bound to draw people together and to distinguish them from others.

Language minorities within a state will inevitably tend to be discriminated against, at least in terms of language. Whether this discrimination is felt to be significant will depend upon the extent to which the language community shares other common interests, since language is closely related to nationality and culture. Thus French Canadians are not French Canadians simply because they speak French and live in Canada, even if this is the most convenient way of telling them apart from everyone else. The majority of French Canadians would continue to share common interests even if the whole world woke up tomorrow speaking only French and living only in Canada. Whether these common interests would ever have been recognized without the language issue, of course, is another matter.

Religion can be treated on two levels. It is something that defines a group of believers, and it is an activity. Conventionally, when we think of religious minorities and religious discrimination, we think of prohibitions on the *practice* of religion, on the activity involved. Freedom of religion tends to mean freedom to practise rather than freedom from discrimination because you happen to belong to a group of believers. (Nowhere is this distinction more stark than in Northern Ireland, where there is undoubtedly freedom of religious practice and undoubtedly religious discrimination.) However, communities of interest can arise from both religious practice and religious affiliation. Obviously, infringements of freedom of religious practice create common interests among practitioners, although even these are not always clear-cut.

The greatest problem arises because religious freedom involves both the freedom to engage in practices that are internal to the group of believers in question and the freedom to engage in actions that affect the outside world and that may well conflict with the desires of others. Many religious groups, after all, seek to impose religious standards upon non-believers. A sect may want to ban divorce, contraception, homosexuality and abortion or to force shops and businesses to close on holy days. It may even feel that its freedoms are infringed if it is forced to live in a society where such things go on. Any attempt to impose religious standards upon the outside world, however, may well provoke opposition from others and thereby provide the sect with common interests and a sense of community.

Problems can also arise when religious practices that are wholly internal to the group conflict with general social norms, even with laws. Examples include conscientious objection to military service, the central role of illegal *ganga* in Rastafarian belief, the refusal of a number of sects to allow their children's lives to be saved with blood transfusions, the desire of Sikhs to wear turbans rather than motorcycle crash helmets and the intensive isolation and indoctrination of new converts to the Moonies. When internal religious practice conflicts starkly with social norms, everyone else in society tends to feel that she has a right to intervene. Very rarely is society sufficiently tolerant of religious practice to allow it to conflict with the laws of the land. Yet the laws of the land are not absolute and immutable, and often they simply reflect the religious beliefs of a single dominant group. This situation is very evident in the Irish Republic, where a number of fundamental Catholic beliefs are enshrined in the law. These include opposition to abortion and contraception, and in 1983 there were moves to enshrine the prohibition of abortion in the Constitution. In an overwhelmingly and devoutly Catholic population (recent survey evidence suggests that 87 per cent of the population goes to church at least once a week, while only 2 per cent never goes), this is not a greatly divisive issue. Nevertheless, those religious groups that are more tolerant of abortion in certain circumstances do have their freedom curtailed.

Religious discrimination arises in a way very similar to racial discrimination. There is no need to repeat those arguments here; it is enough simply to say that real or imagined cultural differences may prompt different, and quite possibly discriminatory, treatment. In the same way, discrimination may even be practised by those who have no prejudice themselves but fear the effects of the prejudice of others. Thus some Protestant employers in Northern Ireland refuse to give jobs to Catholics because they are prejudiced themselves. Others may do so because they fear the effects of the (possibly imagined) prejudices of their work force. Either way, discrimination persists. As a consequence, the distinctive interests of the two communities are reinforced.

As was the case with language, religion is a matter that almost guarantees the stability and interaction of communities. Places of worship constitute focal points, while people change their religion only rarely. Religion thus provides all of the ingredients for the successful development of community, and provides them in abundance. Religious communities have always been strong enough to operate both without government and in outright defiance of it, the most obvious example being the power of the Catholic Church in a number of Eastern European countries. For new arrivals religion can also serve as a way into a new local community. One of the first things that people often do when they want to establish themselves in a new environment is to make friends at church.

Of the three 'ethnic' characteristics, race is the most immediately obvious and immutable, yet it is also the trait that has the least inherent potential for drawing people together into a community. If race combines with other 'ethnic' cleavages or with cultural and economic factors, its effects will be reinforced. Otherwise the existence of a racial community depends upon the way in which one racial group is treated by others. The existence of linguistic and religious communities depends only upon the existence of different languages and religions.

NATIONALITY AND CULTURE

Nationalism is as potent a force as religion. The two, taken together, account for a significant proportion of the atrocities that are committed in the names of great causes. Yet nationality is a most elusive idea, one that tends to run like sand through your fingers just when you think that you are getting to grips with it. It depends much more upon how people feel about things than upon what they do, say or look like. Nations need not be defined by religion, language, race or any other observable characteristic, although they may be. While nations tend to have homelands, they are not even defined by where people are born. The worldwide Jewish nation existed for hundreds of years during which few Jews were born in Israel, and a Bedouin is a Bedouin wherever she may have been born. It is for these reasons that I am combining my discussion of national and of cultural communities. In the last analysis it is culture that defines a nation.

Consider the Scots. Consider why most Scots feel themselves to be Scottish, as opposed to British or English. They speak more or less the same language, have the same racial characteristics and a similar blend of religious beliefs. Scots speak with an easily identifiable accent, so that a Scot is recognizable the moment that she opens her mouth; but then so is a Cockney, A Brummie, or a Geordie, yet London, Birmingham and Newcastle are not nations. At the end of the day we Sassenachs are simply forced to agree that the Scots are different because they think differently. They share a set of values and beliefs that combine to make them view the world through different eyes. They share a distinctive national culture. Yet even this still merely redefines the question. We need to know what is *national* about a national culture as opposed, for example, to a religious or an ethnic culture. We need to know why the Scots share values and beliefs that distinguish them from the rest of us. Part of the answer relates to the fact that they have a shared history.

Now, 'history' is a nice short word that means an awful lot more than most people think. Most people think that history is what happened. But who knows what happened? For the most part history is an *interpretation of the past in terms of the present*, and what a nation shares is a *version* of history. Each version of history selects particular events and gives them special significance. What is surprising, when you begin to look at the history books of different nations, is the huge differences that exist between two versions of the same set of events. Even the British and the Americans differ over the dates of what the Russians call the Great Patriotic War 1941–5 and the Irish call the Emergency. What is clear is that nations cherish their own versions of history and that many nationalists set great store by events that seem to others to have taken place an awfully long time ago. Most people who come afresh to modern Irish politics simply cannot comprehend why 'Remember 1690' is still such a potent slogan. But the Battle of the Boyne is, quite simply, one of those events selected by conflicting national groupings as significant within their conflicting views of history.

We still need to know why such beliefs and values endure so tenaciously over long periods of time. To understand this we need to know how they are transmitted from one generation to another. I have already touched upon the process of socialization when discussing how communities may regulate themselves by making social obligations clear to all members. This process seems to me to be the one of the least understood in politics. We know, of course, that young children pick up a lot of things from their parents, from their schools and from their peers. Which input is the strongest, and what happens when they conflict are other matters. The child of two of today's liberal parents goes to school and within weeks horrifies them by making racist remarks picked up in the playground. Modern teachers feel that discipline breaks down because parents are less strict than they used to be. Little Susie comes home from school believing that everything teacher says is the gospel truth, whatever her parents tell her.

With regard to the things that define national groups, however, all of these aspects of socialization tend to reinforce one another. We need not worry too much about our lack of knowledge about how socialization works if all of the ways in which it appears to work are moving things in the same direction. Distinct national groups tend to have distinct, and highly reinforcing, processes of socialization. Whatever the precise process, beliefs and values will be more enduring and distinctive if they are passed on coherently within the group.

This, of course, is why separate sectarian education systems can be blamed for preserving the conflict over nationality in Northern Ireland. It is not so much that schools can, on their own, change beliefs. The problem arises when every aspect of socialization reinforces the same beliefs. Schools, and especially peer groups, can be potent parts of the socialization process. Mixing children together in their formative years may not solve communal conflicts, but it can certainly help. This is also why those who wish to preserve the cultural distinctiveness of the two communities wish to preserve parallel education systems.

A political culture, therefore, is characterized by a shared view of history. However, the process of socialization that transmits this also conditions people in many other ways. This conditioning, even over utterly trivial matters, also differs between cultures. Once it exists, it serves to make cultural groups even more distinct.

Once more, Northern Ireland provides good examples.

Ulster people do not have their religious and national affiliations tattooed on their foreheads. Yet even a newcomer learns very quickly that there are all sorts of little ways of telling whether a new acquaintance comes from the Catholic or the Protestant community. Haircut, dress, some speech patterns and the notorious aspirated 'haitch' (as in 'Haitch Blocks') all combine to make predicting someone's religion a relatively accurate process. This is true even if you don't know the name, address or school of the person concerned, (each of which is usually sufficient in itself). Some Catholics are no doubt called Stanley, play cricket and talk about Londonderry. If you met such a person in Belfast, however, you would be prudent to assume him a Protestant. It's not always quite as easy as this, but it's rarely impossible to pigeon-hole people.

In short, national culture is extremely pervasive, while differences between cultures can be comprehensive. Most of these differences are symptoms rather than causes of national antagonisms, but they certainly serve to reinforce them. The fact that the French eat frogs' legs while Italians eat blackbirds does not *cause* British antipathy to foreigners (this has much deeper roots). There is no doubt, however, that frogs and the French are closely related in the minds of most Britons.

ECONOMIC COMMUNITIES

Economics is all. So, at least, it would seem from the way in which politics is conducted in most Western systems. One of the more persistent phenomena of the twentieth century is the emergence of economic policy as the main issue with which politicians concern themselves. Political parties tend to represent socio-economic interests, while elections put one interest or another supposedly in the driving seat. Modern Britain is held to be a class-conscious society, and the fundamental definition of class is economic. Yet do economic interests create communities? More crudely, are classes communities?

In the introduction to this book I stated clearly that I would be concerned predominantly with the things that people want, as opposed to those that they need. This is one of the points in my argument at which this crude distinction confuses more than it clarifies. The immense importance of advertising in all market systems is evidence enough in itself that people can be made to want things that they don't need. The converse is that they may need things that they don't want. (All smokers need to give up smoking; few want to.) This discrepancy between conscious wants and unconscious needs is often described as the problem of false consciousness. In one form or another it forms the basis of most fundamental critiques of the capitalist system.

Much of Marxist theory, for example, depends upon a clear distinction between classes and communities, classes being groups that share *real* interests, whether these are consciously felt or not. Capitalist society, by obscuring these real needs, is held to prevent genuine communities from forming and acting in the best interests of all their members. On the contrary, false 'needs' are inculcated and communities thereby created which bolster, rather than erode, the power of capitalism. More determinist versions of Marxism see contradictions within capitalism that inevitably unfold to expose the real interests of workers. This creates real class-consciousness (and hence community), which leads to the overthrow of capitalism. Indeed, more Machiavellian revolutionaries sometimes support the election of reactionary governments that highlight these real interests by means of repressive measures. Many Marxist see social democracy as a form of 'repressive tolerance' that uses modest reform to reduce conflict and hence obscures real interests. Nearly all versions of Marxism lay heavy stress on the development of 'real' class-consciousness, though there is some debate over whether or not this can take place before a revolution.

The notion of false consciousness is both potentially persuasive and impossible to handle within conventional notions of scientific practice. I do not, however, regard the 'unscientific' nature of the concept as evidence that theories that use it are either useless or wrong. I will, as usual, take the easy way out by concentrating on conscious desires, although I feel bound to qualify this discussion with a very clear reminder that I am talking about capitalist society as it actually is rather than about society as it might be in a range of quite different circumstances.

Having got that off my chest, I am free to remark that on the face of things there is nothing in the conscious interests of economic groups in Western societies that necessarily leads them to become communities. Yet many such societies, and Britain in particular, are highly class-conscious. In practice, such consciousness seems to arise because there is a high degree of economic segregation in many aspects of social life. Such segregation arises in housing, at the work place, in the educational system, in leisure activities and even in religious practice, with different denominations tending to be the preserve of different economic groups. If someone leaves school at 16, races pigeons and is a Methodist, we expect her to come from an economic group different from that of a squash-playing, Anglican university graduate. None of these distinctions is absolute, of course, but they represent strong tendencies which significantly colour our expectations.

Some of this segregation is an inevitable consequence of our economic system. Housing and educational segregation are obvious examples. Common interests are forced upon people, whether they be council tenants, owner-occupiers or unemployed teenagers. Other aspects of this economic segregation are the product of socialization. Thus it is traditional rather than inevitable that the working classes tend to gamble on greyhounds while the middle classes tend to gamble on the performance of the Stock Exchange.

Given such segregation, arising for all sorts of reasons, interaction within economic groups is likely to help the conscious realization of common interests. Coherent interaction is more likely when economic groups are segregated. It is well known, for example, that workers in large factories tend to be more 'militant' than those in small factories, where segregation is less complete. Similarly, those who are segregated in municipal housing tend to conform to a more consistent political pattern than do their economic peers dispersed elsewhere. Indeed, it is usually argued that the emergence of the 'working class' during the industrial revolution happened not as a result of the development of new machinery but because this new machinery tended to be installed in factories. Factories concentrated and segregated workers in a way that cottage industry did not and thus helped to develop class-consciousness.

If economic communities develop because groups of people are inevitably thrown together by the economic system, such communities could conceivably be as large as the system itself. Is the working class in Britain, for example, a collection of local communities of working people, or is it something more than this? Clearly, occupational interests can extend far beyond a local community, a fact made obvious within capitalism by the development of the large national and multinational corporations with which many workers must deal if they wish to improve their pay and conditions. This provides an impetus for the development of a wider consciousness of economic interests. (This impetus, arising from a seemingly inevitable tendency towards monopoly, was seen by traditional Marxists as one of the crucial auto-destructive aspects of capitalism.) As a consequence, it makes sense to represent economic classes as 'two-tier' communities.

Much of the practical reinforcement of community feeling comes from local economic segregation, partly inevitable and partly traditional. Thus if the workers for a particular employer all tend to live in the same area, crucial reinforcement is provided. If they are segregated from others with different interests, this process is intensified, as can be seen from the very strong class loyalties that have developed in isolated coal-mining communities in both Britain and the United States. Local class communities are in turn united by certain broader economic interests. Larger communities emerge when these interests assert themselves.

The continual day-to-day reinforcement of class interests is more likely at a local than a national level, however, while the process of socialization also tends to be local. Moreover, at a national level other factors may tend to obscure common interests. Such factors include bases of community that we have already discussed – race, religion, nationality and even language.

Once more, the classic example is Northern Ireland. Few could deny that day-to-day life for Catholic and Protestant workers in Belfast is very similar, or that Catholic or Protestant workers have much more in common with each other than with their middle-class co-religionists. Despite this, common interest has only occasionally been felt by the two religious components of the same economic class. Working-class racism in Britain and the USA is a similar phenomenon. Thus the extent to which a broader class-consciousness develops to extend beyond the local community depends a great deal upon the ways in which economic and other interests interact. (I have already mentioned that the 'dilution' of class-consciousness by other interests, such as race and religion, is a perfect example of false consciousness.)

This process does not stop at national or even state boundaries. Economic interests are global, and one of the practical manifestations of this is the multinational corporation. Whatever might be possible in theory, there is little doubt in practice that international class-consciousness is at a low level of development. After all, one of the standard reactions to high national unemployment is to restrict imports to protect domestic jobs and thus to export a problem that will show itself in higher unemployment elsewhere. One very powerful reason for this is the fact that governments operate, and solutions to problems are thus sought, at state level. In theoretical terms, there is no reason why economic classes should not be international. In practical terms, they are not.

To summarize, economic interests structure both local and national communities. The reinforcement of local class communities tends to be unremitting and inevitable, a simple consequence of the everyday facts of economic life. The reinforcement of national communities of class interests tends to be sporadic and much more critically dependent upon the overall organization of society, both in economic terms and in terms of other potentially conflicting interests such as race, religion and nationality. A community has consciously felt common interests. The possibility of false consciousness therefore means that the community to which

Invitation to Politics

people may feel that they belong may not in fact reflect their real needs.

THE BOUNDARIES OF GOVERNMENT AND COMMUNITY

The boundaries of government are drawn upon maps and marked out on the land. This has the great advantage of being unambiguous. Wherever you care to stand, you will be under the jurisdiction of some government or another. Not only this, but you will only ever be under the ultimate jurisdiction of one government. Since governments control a monopoly of legitimate coercion, there cannot, by definition, be two or more governments with ultimate jurisdiction over the same people. Situations in which two or more governments attempt to enforce jurisdiction over the same people are, again by definition, wars.

Communities must communicate and interact. Until recently this has tended to mean that communities must be compact. It has never, however, meant that there need only be one community in one geographical area. Two or more close-knit communities can easily share the same area, even if each refuses to deal with, or positively avoids, the other. (In a fascinating recent study, one author has shown that Catholics and Protestants living in the same area of Belfast use different bus stops, post offices, shops and so on, taking quite circuitous routes to use their own services rather than those of the other side.)

Even when parts of two communities coexist in the same area, it is very unlikely that both will be confined to precisely the same boundaries. Figure 1 shows a simple world peopled by four communities, the triangles, the squares, the circles and the oblongs. You will see immediately that even a very simple world produces complex problems. All shaded areas contain between two and four communities in various combinations.

Governments govern communities when communities cannot govern themselves. We must recognize, however, that

Who is Governed?

the boundaries of government can never correspond with the boundaries of community. Look again at the simple world in figure 1. Where, if anywhere, are the 'natural' boundaries of states if these stop short of a single world government? The white areas could be self-governing, since they contain only

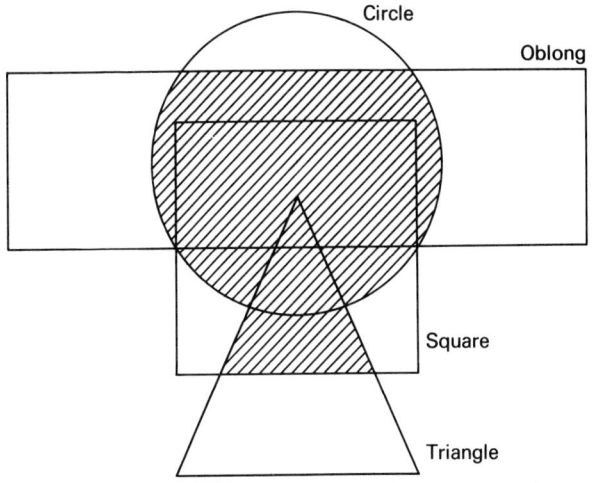

Figure 1 A simple world with four communities

one community, but they also exclude large numbers of that same community. If the area of any single community were chosen, this would include some members of all other communities. If each possible combination of communities were taken as defining the area of a state, four communities would need many governments, and even then several states would be split into two physically separate portions. In short, the scope of government and community can never correspond, because of the geographically interlocking nature of communities and the need for government jurisdiction to be unambiguous.

The fact that there is no ideal fit between government and community does not mean, however, that we should not do our best. Some solutions are clearly better than others. Look at figure 2, which shows another Earth. Once more, this presents a complex system of interlocking communities, but the solid line does seem to make sense as a boundary between

Invitation to Politics

Figure 2   Another Earth

governments. Only community B is divided. Such a boundary certainly does not guarantee the success or stability of government in either 'country', of course. These will depend upon the nature and salience of the interests involved and upon many other things. On the face of it, however, matters are likely to be worsened by any other boundary.

Boundary-drawing problems bake some of the hottest potatoes in politics. Ireland, Israel, Nigeria, Germany and many, many more examples testify to this. The speed at which atlases become out of date even these days is quite remarkable, yet actual changes of political boundaries represent only a tiny fraction of all of those rumbling disputes that persist over centuries and periodically erupt into anger and violence. While it is impossible to generalize about boundary disputes, many of these have the basic structure outlined in figure 3.

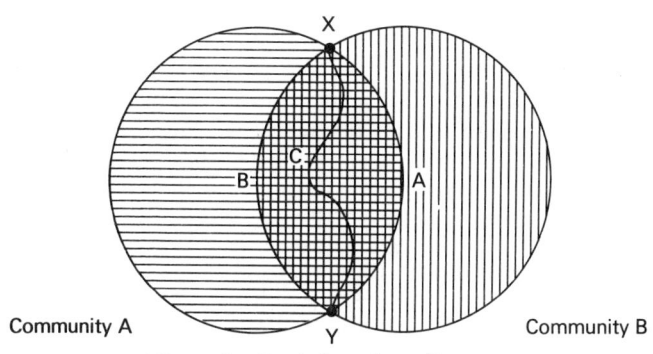

Figure 3 Basic boundary dispute

Two communities, A and B, overlap. The area inhabited by community A is horizontally shaded, and that by B vertically shaded. The area XBYA is inhabited by both. If each community wants its 'own' government, one community at least will be disappointed, and the area of overlap will be in contention. The dispute will concern how, precisely, a line may be drawn between X and Y. Community A would like the line XAY, community B would like the line XBY and any line between these (such as XCY) represents a potential compromise. If both communities feel very strongly, there is no 'natural' solution to the boundary dispute, which will be hotly contested. 'Natural' boundaries, such as rivers or mountain ranges, may come to the rescue (XCY might be a river), though such 'natural' boundaries often tend also to delimit communities themselves. At the very least, natural boundaries can be defended militarily and may as well represent face-saving solutions when neither side feels that it can back down in public.

In practice, things are never so simple. Many communities, for example, are completely overlaid by others. This is the case with the Northern Ireland Protestants, given the natural boundary presented by the shores of the island of Ireland. Crudely, this situation looks like that in figure 4. The Protestants are community B, a local majority within its 'own' area, but a minority within the natural boundaries. The Catholics are community A, a majority within the natural boundaries, but a minority within the territory of community

Invitation to Politics

B. If the two communities cannot coexist, there is no stable solution to the problem, as Ireland knows to its cost. It may be tempting to think that a state can be defined around the boundary of community B's territory, but fifty years of instability in Northern Ireland illustrate the consequences of this.

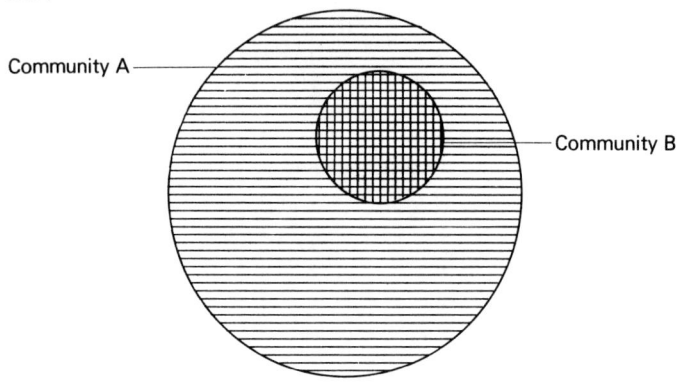

Figure 4   A community within a community

The partition of Ireland into Northern and Southern Ireland did, in fact, attempt to delimit the territory of Northern Protestants. Inevitably, the North also encompassed a substantial minority of Catholics. Worse, the actual border between Northern and Southern Ireland was drawn so as to include as large a portion of Catholic territory as possible while preserving a Protestant majority. This is why it is proclaimed a gerrymander by Irish republicans. This is why substantial portions of Northern Ireland have substantial Catholic majorities and have become almost impossible to govern in the face of either active resistance or passive non-co-operation from the local community. The problem facing Northern Protestants is that if the boundaries of their state were redrawn to exclude those areas with a Catholic majority, the remainder would probably be too small to remain a credible and viable state. As if that were not bad enough, it would still contain a substantial, and growing, minority community.

Who is Governed?

A similar situation can be found in Israel/Jordan on the west bank of the river Jordan, in Bangladesh and in the Biafra. It is no accident that each location is a perennial member of that long list of the world's trouble spots. If each community is prepared to fight to the death, there really is no natural solution to the boundary-drawing problem. This is why, in recent years, there has been some support for the notion of 'consociational' government. In such circumstances each side accepts some set of natural boundaries and concentrates on constitutional arrangements that protect the position of the minority community. This is the logic of the attempts at 'power-sharing' and constitutional guarantees in Northern Ireland that have so far failed because neither side can agree on 'natural' boundaries. It is a solution that has met with some limited success in Belgium, where the political power of both Flemings and Walloons is enshrined in the Constitution. In this case there is more, though by no means absolute, agreement upon the 'natural' boundaries of the state.

The matter of who ought to be governed, therefore, is usually insoluble on the basis of general principles. It is in practice solved by practical politics, almost inevitably violent. This is because the boundaries of government define the area within which one state controls a monopoly of legitimate force. As we saw in the introduction, legitimacy is an elusive notion in practice, while the matter of who has monopoly of force, legitimate or not, can be resolved conclusively only by a battle.

5

What Governments Do

We have already seen that there are many things that must be done by government if they are to be done at all. These include the provision of services such as national defence, public hygiene and pollution control. Public debate over such matters tends to concern whether we want a particular service at all. If we decide that we do want it, we must decide how much we want it. In a world of scarce resources we cannot have everything we want; we must make choices. If we look around this world, however, we always find that governments produce such things if they are produced at all. Arguments that defence, public hygiene or pollution control should be hived off to the private sector are made only by those who want nothing to do with government of any sort.

On the other hand, many things can be produced quite easily without government. In France, for example, government-owned companies make cigarettes and even run casinos, despite the fact that such simple pleasures can be provided by any enterprising businesswoman. Nobody suggests that such things must inevitably be produced by government. Rather it is argued that, for one reason or another, they are better produced by government. When the public and private sector present clear alternatives, public debate tends to concentrate upon how rather than upon whether the relevant services should be produced.

A large part of government activity can be found between these extremes, between cigarettes and public health, between gambling and national defence. Services such as personal health care or education can be provided *in part* without government. Arguments in favour of government intervention in such matters are more complex. Governments may take a broader view of the costs and benefits of a particular service than would a private producer, attempting, for example, to provide the social benefits of a healthy and educated population rather than healing or educating only those who are willing and able to pay. Something such as educating your children, which may seem on the face of it to be an essentially private activity, has very important public consequences. No isolated parent or schoolmaster thinks much about these but, taken as a whole, the social benefits of an educated *population* are profound.

Debate over such matters is invariably intensely ideological. It concerns how far we should be prepared to look for the public consequences of individual action. Every action is rather like dropping a pebble into an infinite pool. It creates ripples, and these never stop, though they tend to diminish as they move away from the point of impact. We must decide, at some point, to ignore them. Those who are intensely individualistic in outlook tend to be hostile to government action because they ignore the ripples sooner. They tend to see only very limited social consequences of individual action. Those who set individual action in a broader context can usually see more justifications for government activity.

As well as taking a broader view of the social consequences of individual action, governments can be more efficient than private operators at producing things. They can avoid the costs of competition, such as advertising, duplication and over-capacity. They can have access to better information. Doing many different things at once, they bring a range of talents to bear upon a problem. People who oppose this justification for government activity tend to focus upon the well-known inefficiencies of bureaucratic decision-making and the efficiency gains which they believe to result from private competition.

Whatever governments do, however, they do distinctively. This is because whatever else governments do, they monopolize the source of legitimate coercion. It is this monopoly, after all, that is the key to arguments for government in the first place. All discussion both of how much and of what governments should do, will depend upon the role of coercion in one context or another. Different forms of legitimate coercion, however, produce different types of government activity.

The most direct use of coercion involves regulation and enforcement. Force, or the threat of force, can be used to modify the behaviour of individuals. This can be done in order to achieve ends which include the enforcement of contracts (people can be made to honour their promises), the reduction of negative spillovers such as pollution (polluting factories can be closed down) and certain forms of redistribution (land can be expropriated and given to peasants).

A more indirect use of force relates to the production of goods and services by government. When governments produce goods they usually depend upon coercive powers of taxation to raise revenue. Force is one stage removed as a means to the end. The British are not conscripted into their army in order to provide national defence; this would be direct regulation. However, a volunteer army is financed by compulsory tax payments. Taxpayers are given no option on these and can ultimately be hauled off and thrown into jail for failing to pay them.

Governments also plan, innovate and co-ordinate. Plans may be adopted voluntarily by the population, particularly if they are consistent with self-interest. Nonetheless, a government plan is always a potentially coercive policy. In this sense it is rather different from a plan that you or I might produce. We could, after extensive research, decide upon the perfect pay norm to solve the country's economic problems. Nobody would take any notice, however, even if we were famous economists. Yet when government publishes a voluntary pay norm, the fact that it is voluntary does not obscure the fact that it could easily be turned into a compulsory pay policy. In this case coercion looms in the background, even though it is not explicit.

Thus the various general goals of government may be implemented by various means; each is characterized by a different role for force. We start our more detailed discussion with the least overtly coercive, that of planning, co-ordination and innovation.

GOVERNMENTS PLAN, CO-ORDINATE AND INNOVATE

Co-ordination without conflict

The most obvious need for co-ordination arises when there is no conflict whatsoever in the population but a collective decision must be taken. Thus motorists must decide which side of the road to drive on. They do not really care *which* side this is, as long as it is the same side for all. A small group of drivers can easily solve this problem for itself. A larger group needs some institutional means for making a collective decision.

The problem is one of setting norms and standards, and it is very important. Nuts must fit bolts, steamships must give way to sailing boats (or vice versa) and a pint must be a pint must be a pint if people are to know what they are buying or selling. When there is absolutely no conflict whatsoever, as in the case of driving on the left (or right), government can simply take a decision for the benefit of all. More frequently there is limited conflict that is overwhelmed nonetheless by the need for some co-ordinating rule. This is the case with rights of way for steamships and sailing boats. Steamship owners may well see the need for some rule but prefer it to be 'sail gives way to steam'. Once the decision is taken, however, all have an incentive to observe it. The fact that a government with potential coercive power promulgates such a rule gives it added authority.

The most important aspects of co-ordination often concern technical matters. Not only must plugs fit sockets, but also some types of plug are safer and more efficient than others. Government co-ordination here may be welcomed by all, since most care little what sort of plug they use, as long as it is safe. The same general argument applies to things like colour televisions or satellite broadcasting systems, radio frequencies and so on. Certainly one important function for specialist government departments is the setting of standards to solve co-ordination problems.

This is one type of problem which a free market is unlikely to solve without help, although the market leaders in an oligopoly may set their own standards. Without government regulation, however, oligopolistic producers will tend to set conflicting standards in order to 'tie in' their customers. An obvious recent example can be found in the competing VHS and Betamax systems in the video cassette market. Razor blades provide another dramatic example. Once a blade was a blade and would fit any razor. But the big guns in the market decided, quite deliberately, that this was no good. New razors were designed so that one company's razor just would not take a competitor's blades. The most expensive examples of this can be found in computer software, where one manufacturer's software rarely fits another's system.

Government planning and co-ordination of this type helps to increase social productivity in areas of little conflict. It is characteristically *government* activity both because of the capacity of norms to become laws if conflict should arise and because some forms of innovation and research may present collective action problems. This role for government arises only when the group is large. Small groups can usually solve their own co-ordination problems.

Co-ordination and conflict

Governments may also inform collective decisions that involve quite high levels of conflict. Obvious examples concern the management of the economy. In any complex society it is difficult to predict the collective consequences of a large number of individual decisions. I gain a huge pay rise, and so does everyone else. Will I be better off as my wages outstrip inflation? Will I lose out as wages disproportionately increase inflation and my real income declines? If everyone wins a 10 per cent pay rise, will they all fare better, or worse, than if they win a 50 per cent pay rise, given, in each case, the consequent rise in prices? No individual has enough information to decide this in isolation. Government research and planning may provide the answer, and an 'ideal' pay norm may be discussed and published. People may not abide by it – a problem to which I will return more than once in this book – but simply knowing what this norm might be at least enlightens their decision-making. This explains one aspect of the role of technical specialists, such as economists, in the machinery of government. Using their models of society, such people can try to tell the population of the consequences of their combined actions. Governments, by centralizing expertise, may inform decisions. (The fact that no two experts can ever be found who agree with one another rather undermines this point in practice. The principle, however, is sound.)

There is no guarantee, of course, that government feedback on the consequences of individual decisions will improve collective decision-making. Indeed, naive behaviour by government may have the opposite effect. Predictions can be self-fulfilling. Petrol shortages, for example, can be created simply because they are forecast, as motorists rush lemming-like into an auto-destructive spree of panic buying. Sophisticated governments, on the other hand, can 'talk down' interest rates, predicting their fall and hence causing it as borrowers hold back and lenders compete for business. Canny governments may therefore lie in pursuit of what they see as the public interest, denying real shortages, for example, in order not to exacerbate them. And governments *always* deny that they are even thinking of devaluation, long after they have decided to devalue. Disinformation, therefore, can be as valuable as information.

One fairly recent example well illustrates the effect that this type of information or disinformation may have on collective decisions. During the energy crisis of the mid-1970s, speed limits on many of Europe's roads were reduced in order to conserve petrol. A side-effect of this was a significant reduction in the number of deaths and serious injuries from traffic accidents. The fact that there were fewer fatal collisions was a well-known consequence of lower speed limits, but detailed information on this was never publicized. When the energy crisis was officially deemed to be over, speed limits were raised once more, with little public comment.

It would not be difficult, as a result of careful research, to quantify precisely how many people are annually sacrificed on the roads in order that speed limits may be a little higher. If this information had been publicized and public opinion on the matter tested, the result might well have been lower speed limits. Instead of effectively asking people, 'Do you want speed limits raised or not?', the question could have been, 'If speed limits are raised, (say) another 500 people will die on the roads each year. Do you want speed limits raised or not?' Possibly people would have decided that 500 lives a year was a small price to pay for the pleasure of driving a little faster. The explicit nature of the decision, however, would have given it a very different character.

Thus even in circumstances of conflict, and even in cases that involve quite stark redistributions, government can make the consequences of decisions explicit. If taken seriously, this information can have an important conditioning function. It may even help to solve collective-action problems. Once everyone is aware of the anti-social consequences of a particular action, social pressure may get to work on the dissidents. Smokers are definitely on the run these days, for example. This is largely as a result of government publicity campaigns, which are clearly having a long-term impact on the huge social costs (especially borne by the health service) of this particular vice. In part the publicity has dissuaded smokers directly. More significantly, non-smokers have gone on to the offensive. They are now much less prepared to suffer the public spillovers of smokers' private pleasures. Finding themselves in an increasingly hostile social environment, smokers' incentives to quit are greatly enhanced.

Co-ordinating many decisions

So far I have considered decisions only one at a time. A much more serious problem of social choice arises when a number of decisions are related. In such cases a series of decisions may need to be co-ordinated. It is quite possible for a set of decisions, each taken in isolation from the others, to be quite incompatible. Without any central co-ordination, this will happen when people separate the crucial matters of what they want to buy and what they want to spend.

We can all agree, for example, that helping the aged is a good thing. Asked the simple question, 'Do you want more help for the aged?', we would answer, 'Yes.' We probably also agree that paying taxes is unpleasant. Asked the simple question, 'Do you want to pay more taxes?', we would answer, 'No.' We agree to do more for the aged but not to pay the necessary taxes.

This problem is greatly exacerbated when different people want different things, *even if they are prepared to pay for them*. Imagine the population to be split into three equal groups. Group A wants to help the aged at a cost of £100 million and is prepared to pay the extra taxes involved. Group A is not, however, prepared to pay £100 million to help the young. Group B wants to help the young but not the old. Group C wants, *and is prepared to pay for*, more help for both young and old. If each decision is taken in isolation, there is a serious co-ordination problem, as can be seen from table 1.

Table 1 An incoherent majority decision over three related issues

	Decision 1 Help the old?	Decision 2 Help the young?	Decision 3 Increase taxes by £100m or £200m?
Group A	Yes	No	£100m
Group B	No	Yes	£100m
Group C	Yes	Yes	£200m
Majority decision	Yes	Yes	£100m

Taken together, the three groups will agree to help both young and old but not to pay for this. Each group on its own has a perfectly consistent and coherent set of preferences relating to three separate decisions. Taking all groups together, however, their collective preference is inconsistent.

Only if all three decisions are presented as a package can a coherent collective decision be taken (on the basis of more information about how each group feels about things than I have provided).

Thus one of the most important things that a government does is to develop consistent policy packages. The prime example of this is usually its annual Budget or Finance Act. We have just seen that wanting things and wanting to pay for them are two matters that clearly require co-ordination. The annual Budget is a book-balancing exercise designed to settle the matter of how much will be borrowed, and how much raised in taxes, to pay for how much expenditure on what. Given the vast scope of most modern governments, this is a monumental exercise.

As a mere mortal who often has trouble balancing a cheque book or paying three bills at the same time, I am amazed that such an exercise is even remotely possible. It is hard to conceive, even when you try, how one would go about estimating the cost of running the health service next year. That must then be added to the cost of the education system, of defence, of unemployment benefit (having guessed how many will be unemployed) and so on. This grand total must be offset against expected income from taxes (having guessed how much people will spend and earn), from borrowing (having guessed interest rates) and so on. This mind-boggling task is, of course invariably the full-time job of an entire government department, the Finance Ministry or Treasury. This department tends to be the hub of any Civil Service, and it is not hard to see why. As long as collective decisions are taken about raising taxes and spending money, something like a Treasury will be needed to ensure that decisions are presented in packages that produce coherent outcomes.

Most of the planning, co-ordination and innovation discussed here could be performed by an institution with access to centralized information and authoritative analysis. This aspect of what governments do is not, therefore, an argument for government as such. Once governments exist, however, they will be better suited than most agencies to plan, co-ordinate and innovate in this way. Quite how crucial is the potentially coercive nature of government planning is very hard to determine. At one end of the scale we have the pay norm, which is voluntary just as long as it is observed but is made compulsory as soon as it is not. On the other hand, governments advise people about hygiene standards, even though all know that going to bed without brushing their teeth will never be against the law.

GOVERNMENTS PRODUCE GOODS AND SERVICES

One of the main justifications for having a government in the first place is the collective-action problem. There are many public benefits that people can enjoy, whether or not they contribute. Selfish consumers take free rides. In a group that is too large for free riders to be dealt with by informal social pressure, they will have to be coerced. One very common method of coercion involves governments in financing the production of publicly valued goods and services, using its powers of taxation.

In practice, very little in this world is pure. There are very few purely public benefits, and there are even fewer private activities with no public consequences whatsoever. In extreme cases we may devise ways of preventing free riders from consuming almost anything. (If I am obsessed with excluding others, I can build a minefield around my lighthouse.) Conversely, the 'private' tuna and onion sandwich that I have just eaten keeps me alive, taints my breath and generally has some limited impact on the people around me. All of this means that there is no easy distinction to be made between the public and the private domain. One shades into the other.

Thus if we see a role for government in the production of certain goods and services, there is no 'natural' limit to what we might want to see governments do. (They may even go into the business of producing odourless tuna and onion sandwiches in order to conserve the stock of untainted breathing air.) In the absence of any clear natural criteria, the issues of what, and how much, governments should produce become matters of intense political contention, especially

Invitation to Politics

once it is accepted that they should produce at least a little of something.

If we think about the public consequences of private action in a little more detail, however, we see three basic circumstances in which government may be important. In the first place, some of these spillovers are overwhelmingly matters of public concern. The light from lighthouses and the health from public hygiene precautions are obvious examples. These things are valued almost entirely for their spillover effects. We might think of them as 'pure' spillovers. They are the public consequences of individual actions when the individual actions themselves are of no consequence. Pure spillovers tend to be available to all if they are available to any. This means that the private benefits to any individual would never make a voluntary contribution towards the costs worthwhile. There is thus an undiluted free rider problem. It is difficult to see how these goods can be produced at all if they are not financed by government.

In the second place, there are goods and services that can be produced and consumed privately but have significant social implications. Personal health care and education are obvious examples. These spillovers are sufficiently large to be matters of major public concern. Yet the private benefits involved mean that such activities would take place even without government. In this case, private production quite possibly produces insufficient spillovers of the right sort. The need for government involvement in these 'hybrid' goods is not to get them produced in the first place but to get them produced *in certain ways*.

Finally, there are goods that are consumed privately but produced in ways that have public implications. This final category can obviously be extended to include almost everything. Consider cosmetic surgery. Now I might think that my huge hooked nose is a major disfigurement of my otherwise even and not displeasing features. I decide to change it, and enjoy browsing through catalogues of alternative noses, choosing the one that will make me a star. You may agree with me about my face and sympathize with my desire for cosmetic surgery. That odd-looking growth above my moustache would have to be spectacularly horrible, however, before people would decide that removing it was in the public interest. In this sense, cosmetic surgery is a very private good. It might seem attractive to leave it to the private sector. Yet, while doctors are engaged in cosmetic surgery they are not curing the seriously ill. The *very existence* of private cosmetic surgery has public implications.

I shall therefore look separately at those goods that are valued *only* for their spillovers, those hybrid goods that have both public and private implications and those 'private' goods whose manner of production is nevertheless a matter of public concern. I do this for the sake of clarity. It is important to remember, however, that these are not discrete alternatives. They are merely useful stopping points upon a continuum that stretches from the most purely public to the most purely private forms of production and consumption.

The production of public benefits as the spillovers of private action can involve modifying people's behaviour (as is the case with pollution control) or actually constructing things (as is the case with defence). This is a useful distinction, although we should not labour it. After all, most of the hardware involved in defence (the nuclear submarines, the cruise missiles and the backfire bombers) is only hardware. Most items of hardware are physical and tangible, private goods in the sense that people can be excluded from them. Thus, if I were rich enough, I could afford a nuclear submarine, a cruise missile or a backfire bomber of my very own. It is not the submarine that is a valued spillover but the defence that it provides.

More generally, if certain spillovers require the construction of capital equipment, it is the co-ordination and deployment of the equipment that actually provides the public benefit. In this sense there are no public *goods* (if by such we mean tangible products). There are only public *services*. The cruise missile site in my front garden, trained on my neighbour's dog and ready to fire if the dog fouls my footpath, has purely private benefits. The cruise missiles aimed at the nation's enemies, supposedly deterring them from attack, defend us all.

Nonetheless, some pure spillovers do require the provision of social capital while others do not. In the former case collective-action problems reduce rather conveniently to problems of raising the necessary money. I shall therefore consider these first, returning at the end of the chapter to look at the public consequences of regulating private behaviour.

Producing pure spillovers

There is no collective-action problem at all when a particular spillover is the result of private actions that are profitable anyway. Good examples are art and innovation. In these cases the benefits to a single individual are sufficient in themselves to justify the effort, regardless of free benefits to everyone else. As a hyper-rich paranoid, I may even install missile sites in my back garden in order to deter the enemy. I would reap a sufficient return on my investment simply from their protection of *me*. Protecting the rabble would be an unintended side-effect, however much they might welcome it.

In all other circumstances the problem of how to produce spillovers, put very crudely, boils down to the problem of financing goods that cannot be sold in the normal 'pay-as-you-use' manner. This is the ultimate justification for taxation, and raising taxes is without doubt one of the main things that governments do.

I have so far assumed agreement over whether public services are to be applauded or deplored. This has no doubt provoked many squirms of irritation among those who do not agree that cruise missiles and backfire bombers are the best ways of defending the nation. Some such people have even tried, as yet unsuccessfully, to pay taxes on condition that their tax payments are not used to purchase the necessary plutonium. This controversy arises from the fact that some of the public consequences of private action are optional, while others are not.

Optional spillovers. Governments often produce things, such as public broadcasting, that are optional, yet available to all. They then face an acute version of the problem of deciding who, and how much, to charge. First, they must decide whether or not to charge non-users, who after all have indicated that they do not value the service provided. Second, they need to decide who, precisely, the users are. This is a particularly tricky problem once we recognize that many things, such as art or literature, provide possible benefits for those who are not the *direct* consumers.

Britain, in common with many other countries, has a national broadcasting service. Radio and television programmes broadcast by the BBC are available to everyone with access to a receiver. Despite this, the programmes are optional. This distinction may be hard to take if your nextdoor neighbour turns up the sound for *Top of the Pops* to such a high level that it shakes the very foundations of your existence. Nevertheless, no one can force you to watch *Top of the Pops*. If you don't like it, you can switch it off. This point is much more than a minor consolation for a few fuddy-duddies. It affects how we feel about what governments do in two crucial respects.

In the first place, when governments produce optional spillovers they can monitor patterns of use. This information can help them to decide how many people like what is being provided. Optional public goods can thus provide *consumer feedback*. When services are provided free, consumer feedback is limited to information about those who like or dislike the service in question. When charges are made, some information about how much people like things is provided. The more someone is prepared to pay for something, the more she can be presumed to like it. Feedback is obviously crucial if we are trying to increase social welfare, since it is one very important way of finding out if we are succeeding. Thus if the whole world switches off *Top of the Pops* within five minutes of the first broadcast, we may be forced to conclude that this programme is of little perceived value. We may even decide that *The Eurovision Song Contest* is a much more efficient maximizer of social welfare.

In the second place, when governments produce optional spillovers, we feel rather differently about taxation than we do when we have simply no choice but to take what we are

Invitation to Politics

given. Taxation is coercive, but this leaves open the question of who should be coerced. One possibility is to force consumers to pay for what they use, even when they cannot be prevented from using it. When a spillover is compulsory, like defence, all consume. The problem becomes whether we should produce it at all. When goods are optional, like broadcasting, the question becomes whether non-users should be forced to pay.

Television provides a good example of the problem of funding an optional spillover. The first British broadcasting station was operated by the British Broadcasting Corporation, a public agency. At that time, before the age of video games, video-recorders, personal computers, cable and Viewdata, domestic TV sets were not useful for anything but receiving broadcast television programmes. When the only broadcaster was the BBC, it was reasonable to assume that anyone using a television set was watching BBC TV. There could be little dispute that, if anyone should pay, at least these people should.

Those who did not have television sets might have felt rather hard done by had they been forced to pay as well. They would probably not have been impressed by the argument that they too derived benefits from the BBC, even though, to a limited extent, this was true. After all, actors, producers, journalists and newsreaders were kept off the streets, where they might otherwise have committed all sorts of public nuisance. Entirely new cultural forms emerged, leading eventually to such national institutions as *Top of the Pops, The Generation Game* and *Fawlty Towers*. Such benefits would probably have been seen as too limited and intangible to be worth much to non-viewers. Government took the decision to tax only those with television sets, using the TV licence system.

When the commercial television network (ITV) started broadcasting, a few bright sparks argued that they shouldn't have to pay the BBC licence fee if they watched only ITV. They received short shrift from the government. The grounds for this were that the service consumed was broadcast television in general, and that the BBC was an integral part of this. The briefest exposure to US broadcast television confirms the view that the existence of a national television network run on non-commercial lines increases the quality of *all* television. This includes that of the commercial channels that are forced to compete with it for audiences.

A broadcast television signal is a very good example of a pure spillover. The broadcaster simply cannot direct the signal only at subscribers. This causes a technical problem of enforcement, a problem that is much greater now that people use television sets for purposes other than receiving broadcasts. Taxing ownership of TVs, with either a one-off sales tax or an annual fee, taxes people who might not be consumers of broadcasting. Given this, users must be identified, so that evaders can be penalized. Hence the famous Post Office detection vans.

These detection vans are a most interesting phenomenon for those of us who are interested in government. Indeed, they are almost unique. Nearly all public benefits produced by government are either discriminating (so that governments can choose to charge users) or undiscriminating and compulsory (so that all are charged whether they like it or not). There are rather few examples of undiscriminating but optional spillovers. A public park is optional, but it can be fenced off. Clean air is undiscriminating but not optional. It is just as well that there are rather few of these goods. The detector van solution is expensive and tedious. The arts, the physical environment and other aesthetic goods do, however, provide clear examples. In most of these cases governments take the easy way out and make everyone pay. This is much simpler than sending out aesthetic detector vans, designed to identify closet culture vultures.

Thus when governments produce optional spillovers they must balance two conflicting considerations. They must raise money by taxation, and the easiest method is to tax all, including non-users. This is likely to upset, if not outrage, non-users. On the other hand, taxing users only is not feasible if they cannot be identified. It is in the nature of many spillovers that users do not need to identify themselves before they consume.

When governments resort to taxing all for optional benefits, they often appeal to a whole range of ways in which even those who choose not to consume get value out of the good concerned. Consider opera.

I hate opera. In my more extreme moments I object to contributing towards any form of public subsidy for this awful 'artform'. This is despite the fact that, without such subsidies, opera might possibly collapse. Opera lovers pay for their pleasure when they buy tickets, but they do not pay the full price. Some of this comes out of my pocket. When governments subsidize the arts in this way, using agencies such as the British Arts Council, they do so because 'the arts' are seen to provide cultural benefits for all, even those who do not directly consume them. Those who advocate such subsidies do so in part because they consider that art makes the world a more civilized place. A work of art is seen as good for society as a whole, not just for those who look at it. This raises the very fundamental question of how, in the broadest sense, we can put a value on anything.

The narrowest possible view of the value of a good looks simply at the enjoyment of the direct user. A slightly broader view looks at more indirect social benefits, such as the civilizing function of the arts, but there are still further components to value. In my more moderate moments I mind less about subsidizing opera, for two main reasons. The first, if I am feeling *very* mellow, is that opera gives me a vicarious pleasure. I would still hate to be locked in a room with a performing opera singer, but I rather like the idea of opera going on just as long as I don't have to listen to it. I think of it as a 'good thing', and I like to have it around even though I never expect to enjoy it. In the second place, I like to have the option of going. Who knows, one day I may grow up. Someone may write an enjoyable opera. As a matter of fact, I'm even prepared to pay a little for this option. In such mellow moments I would be rather disconcerted if the nation's opera suddenly collapsed. I would feel a sense of loss for something that I never intended to use, but nevertheless liked to retain the option of using. Vicarious consumption and option values are spillover effects that are impossible to see or to monitor. They cannot conceivably be financed on a 'pay-as-you-desire-pleasure' principle and must thus be paid for by everyone if they are paid for at all. Yet these intangible components of value are often crucial to aesthetic goods.

One of the things that many people want from government, for example, is conservation both of historic architecture and of beautiful countryside. Perhaps the starkest example can be found in the desire of many people to preserve tracts of wild and deserted countryside, even wildernesses. Few people are likely to enjoy such places directly. Many just like having them around and having the option of using them. In the United States (where many people are surprised to find a higher proportion of land in public ownership than anywhere outside the Soviet Union, China and Canada) there are many public agencies designed to safeguard the vicarious satisfaction and option value that Americans get from their wildernesses. There is a Wild and Scenic Rivers Act and a Wilderness Act. There is a whole cluster of public servants, in agencies such as the US Forest Service and the US Bureau of Land Management, whose job it is to ensure that places such as White Cloud Peaks or Hell's Canyon remain as empty as possible and *therefore* can be vicariously enjoyed by as many as possible.

In short, there is an enormous range of possible social benefits that arise from many goods that appear, on the surface, to be optional. Wildernesses are perhaps the most extreme example, since the whole point about wildernesses is that they are valuable only if they are not used very much. At the other extreme is television, an optional good available to all and privately enjoyed by many. TV can easily be financed by users, provided that they can be identified. The cultural spillovers of TV for the rest of society (be they good or be they bad) are donated by TV viewers as free gifts.

Betwixt TV and the wilderness we find goods such as opera, intensely enjoyed by some but probably not enjoyed by enough people for users to finance the full cost. So opera is subsidized by government. This may be because opera-goers are needy people who require government handouts, although this is not a conclusion that you would be likely to draw should you loiter outside Covent Garden. The more usual justification is that opera is good for us all, even those of us who don't like it. This, the codliver oil theory of opera, is but one example of the general European trend for 'high art' to be subsidized from the public purse and for television to be paid for by viewers. All optional goods particularly illustrate the ideological nature of the search for the indirect public benefits of private action, for it is these benefits that must be invoked in order to justify coercing those who have opted not to consume.

'Compulsory' spillovers. Many spillovers are compulsory in the sense that, if they are produced at all, they must be consumed by everyone. Defence is the classic example. Once one is defended, all are defended. A more mundane example is street lighting. Once a particular street is lit, it is lit for all who use it. In an extreme case it would, I suppose, be possible to bathe our streets in infra-red light and to sell infra-red night sights only to those who were prepared to pay. It is, I am quite sure, much cheaper and more convenient to use the old-fashioned visible part of the spectrum and to concentrate upon solving the problem of raising the money for a compulsory spillover.

Compulsory spillovers face governments with a different set of problems. In the first place, since nobody chooses to consume, consumer choice does not provide a feedback mechanism. Since no option exists, the pattern of demand does not help governments to evaluate their success. Governments must therefore make decisions on a different, and possibly less responsive, basis. In the second place, since all consume the good, the 'pay-as-you-use' principle cannot apply. Taxation must therefore be raised on a more general basis. This has the important consequence that compulsory goods are potentially more controversial. People are made to pay for what is produced, whether they want it or not. Worse, those who do not want what is produced must not only pay for it, they must also suffer it. Public debate is thus likely to focus as much upon the desirability of the good in question as upon how to raise the money.

What Governments Do

No distinction is absolute, and the distinction between optional and compulsory public benefits is no exception. As we have already seen when discussing state-funded opera, even the performing arts can be construed to provide 'compulsory' benefits that extend beyond those who happen to be present at performances. In practice most spillovers have optional and compulsory components. A public park is optional in the sense that nobody is likely to be forced at gunpoint to promenade in it. It is, however, compulsory in the sense that when the land is used for a park, it cannot be used for an airport or an art gallery. Opera is optional in the obvious sense but compulsory in the sense that I can escape the broader cultural effects only if I emigrate to Philistinia.

This lack of a clear-cut distinction between goods that are optional and those that are not stimulates another type of political debate over government activity, that concerning the relative weight that should be attached to the optional and the compulsory aspects of a given good. Thus opera-lovers justify *my* subsidy of *their* private pleasure by claiming that having opera around is good for me. I deny this, or reply that such intangible and slight benefits are not worth the money. Disputes of this nature are quite common. Every year irate inhabitants of remote country cottages object to paying a sewerage charge when they are not connected to a main sewerage system and often have to pay privately for their own sewerage. The agency concerned usually makes a reduction in the charges to take account of this but may insist upon some payment for removing rainwater from the city streets that even a cottage dweller is forced to walk from time to time. Policing and public order, things that might seem to be universally valued, are of relatively little use to those with no property to protect.

The debate over how great a weight should be attached to compulsory aspects of spillovers is, once more, ideological. It tends to reflect broad cultural attitudes, so that collectively minded groups tend to emphasize indiscriminate social benefits, while the more individualistic tend to emphasize personal decisions and opting out. Thus opera is paid for by opera-goers in one society and by public subsidy in another.

Within a given society, however, one of the most obvious features of compulsory goods is that they can polarize politics dramatically. As soon as people disagree over whether some compulsory service is a good or a bad, someone is bound to be very unhappy. Either the service will be produced, in which case those who hate it will be furious, or it will not, and those who love it will be mad. It is a moot point whether people get madder when frustrated by not having something that they want and are prepared to pay for or when forced to consume and pay for something that they hate.

Nuclear arms, defence in general, the EEC, US gun control and Northern Ireland are all issues that arouse intense passions. They do so precisely because the policies involved are compulsory. In each case those who lose the political debate are forced to suffer something that they detest. It is almost always this type of issue that polarizes the views that people have of their government. When opting out is impossible dissidents have a real incentive to change things.

Governments produce 'hybrid' goods and services

So far we have been talking about goods and services that are valued only for their public consequences. Education, transport and personal health care, however, are examples of 'hybrid' services. Only an ostrich could claim that these services have no spillover effect on others, even when they are produced for and consumed by individuals. The social benefits arising from health, education and transport systems are much more than merely incidental side-effects of private activity. The spillovers are so important that if they are not produced in sufficient measure as a result of private transactions, then this is a matter for serious public concern. The quality of education, health and transport in any system has a direct effect upon overall well-being. These collective consequences stretch far beyond the transportation of your weary carcass from A to B or your encyclopaedic knowledge of molecular physics. If nobody could get from A to B and no one had even heard of molecules, the world would be a poorer place.

What Governments Do

Unlike pure spillovers, certain aspects of hybrid goods and services can be produced failing either a government or a sense of community. For this reason it may be tempting to think, since private transport or health services can operate without (or even despite) government, that governments produce these things because they maintain a doctrinaire hostility towards private enterprise. The problem, however, is that private production of these services at best generates public benefits only by accident and almost always in short measure. At worst the private production of services such as transportation generates all sorts of negative spillovers, such as pollution, road deaths and high energy consumption. Government intervention in the production of hybrid goods may well be necessary in order to guarantee the generation of valuable spillovers or to control negative ones rather than leaving these matters to the vagaries of the market.

This problem pushes hybrid goods to the forefront of public debate. The clear importance of both the public and the private aspects of their *consumption* makes it easy for people to construct arguments in favour of both public and private *production*.

In addition to this, many hybrid goods are 'staples', things that people simply cannot do without. Since we must all consume health care, transport and education in the course of a normal life, the matter of whether these services are equitably provided is obviously very important. Equitable provision of such staples involves redistribution if there is unequal ability to pay. Either redistribution may be accepted as an inevitable consequence of the equal provision of health care and education, or it may be an end in itself. Indeed, equal provision of staples is one way of achieving redistribution. It has always been true, of course, that those most opposed to redistribution tend also to be those most opposed to the government provision of staple services. Hybrid goods are thus ideologically controversial, and intense debate over the role of government in their provision is a common feature of nearly all political systems. Certainly, throughout Europe one of the easiest ways to classify political parties is to consider their policies on matters such as health care, education and public transport. These three policy areas tend to be among those things that do change with a change of government.

The public aspects of most hybrid goods are so important that only the most ferocious advocates of the free market claim that no education, health care and transport should be provided by government. Governments everywhere provide some of these, so that the distinction between the things that in theory are public benefits and those that in fact are provided by governments can easily become blurred.

Mass transportation provides one of the best examples of a hybrid good, since many of the possible public consequences are easy to identify. The benefits clearly extend beyond those who use it. Few owners of private cars would dispute the value that they get from a public transport system that they rarely use. This value becomes starkly obvious during the public transport shut-downs, when roads become clogged with cars half-full of people who normally travel by train or bus. People who live on commuter routes also benefit from more efficient road use, as do employers who lose fewer hours through the lateness of employees and so on. Private transport has many negative spillovers. Cars pump poison into the air, kill innocent pedestrians, consume scarce energy and stand rusting by the roadside when not in use. Any reduction in these spillovers that might result from increased use of mass transportation would provide a public benefit.

Casting the net a little wider, the option value of public transport can be considerable, even for those who never use it. I drive a car and almost never use local buses. I would be most upset, however, if the local bus system collapsed. Not only would the roads clog up with former bus passengers, but also my car may break down one morning or the price of oil may go through the roof. I like the option of travelling by bus. When the chips are down, I should be prepared to pay something for this valuable option. After all, I cash it in all the time. I run a rather older and less reliable car, at lower cost, than I would be able to get away with if I were forced to rely upon my car because there was no public transport.

Casting the net wider still, efficient transport is an essential part of our social and economic infrastructure. Thus cheaper transport may mean more trade, and more trade may be good for us all. Many of the surges in economic performance that countries sometimes experience can be tracked, one way or another, to developments in transport technology. It is certainly true that the industrial revolution, for example, was vastly accelerated by the development of fast and efficient rail transport. This enabled greatly improved access both to the raw materials and to the markets needed by manufacturing industry.

If the effect of any private activity is to cause ripples in an infinite public pool, then hybrid services such as transport make big ripples that extend a long way. While there is no *inherent* reason why mass transportation should not be provided by the private sector, many important spillovers will not be guaranteed by private production. The social efficiency of mass transportation, for example, tends to depend upon high levels of use. The level of use will depend, among many things, upon relative price levels. Yet commercial companies may see private advantages and higher profits coming from high prices and low levels of use. In the extreme case a commercial mass transportation company might be running at a bare profit, yet be able to generate more custom by dropping prices and running at a loss. This is obviously something that no private company can do indefinitely. Such a policy might, however, increase the public benefits arising from mass transportation.

In practice few mass transportation companies, public or private, operate at a profit. This may be because they are all badly run. It is such a universal phenomenon, however, that it seems likely that there is no combination of price, volume of use and level of service that produces a net profit. In the case of railways the story has usually been one of initially high private profitability, followed by a steady and long-term decline into debt. In those cases where governments have not stepped in and run railways at a loss (and they are now run at a loss nearly everywhere) the railway system has more or less crumbled to nothing (as it has in the USA). These days it takes a quite spectacular faith in the power of the market to believe that a major railway system could be run for private profit. Yet loss-making major railway systems may well be socially cost-effective once all of their indirect public benefits have been considered. (There is no guarantee of this, of course, but it is certainly possible.) If governments do not intervene, therefore, these public benefits will be put at risk.

The huge losses recently made by all major airlines, public and private, suggest that history may repeat itself. Already big private operators are unable to survive without a cartel (IATA), without government protection of their main routes from rivals, and without huge government subsidies to the aircraft construction industry.

The potentially huge public benefits of mass transportation may be guaranteed either by subsidies paid by government to private producers in exchange for operating uneconomic services or by taking mass transportation directly into the public sector. If subsidies are paid to private compaies, some form of government regulation will obviously be required in order to ensure that the money is used appropriately. Thus either by subsidizing and regulating or by producing directly, government provides spillovers that are enjoyed by many. Since these benefits extend beyond those who actually use public transport, it may be necessary to finance the costs that arise on a basis broader than charges to users. General tax revenue may need to be deployed in this direction.

All of this means that when the fares are set for a nationalized railway system, for example, rail users cannot be expected to pay at levels that will cover all costs. If fares did meet costs, running railways could be a profitable business. History has shown clearly that it is not. Since fare income will be less than costs, a loss will be made, and this must be made good by government in the form of a subsidy. The subsidy can be thought of as underwriting the public service elements of rail transport.

This is precisely the system used for British Rail. When British Rail's budget is set, it includes a substantial government grant to cover loss-making but socially valued services. In exchange local branch lines and other services that would be axed by any business executive concerned only with profits are kept open. In most cases the costs are very well known. This makes it a straightforward political decision to spend, say, £30,000 each year keeping the Chuddington Flyer in operation. The general social benefits to Chuddington may be hard to quantify. At least, however, we know what they cost us, and we can use this to form some idea of whether we are getting value for money. The debate over public transport is thus relatively straightforward, since costs and benefits can be estimated relatively easily. The debate in 1982 over the running of the London Transport system, for example, was well documented with complex cost-benefit calculations. These included estimated levels of congestion and traffic accidents, as well as fares, taxes and so on.

In the case of transport, direct spillovers to individual non-users can be easily identified. In the case of health care, however, things are more tricky. Spillovers tend to be more general and less tangible.

Public health provision against infectious or contagious diseases helps everyone, including those not directly affected. Curing your typhoid helps me if it reduces my risk of infection. This risk is a very pure spillover affecting all, even the Royal Family. (In 1861 Prince Albert died of typhoid.) A risk, however, can be a very intangible thing, especially once effective public health provision over a number of years has kept a particular disease at bay. Such health care is invisible.

The option value of health-care is also critical. I may be as healthy as healthy can be, yet still derive some comfort from knowing that help is available should I need it. As well as this, the medical research and development which goes on even while I am healthy will help me when I fall sick. Thus at the same time as I pay for my health-care option, I am also making an investment. More generally still, we all derive benefits from living in a society with a healthy population. We do this directly because of higher levels of production and general well-being and vicariously because of the way in which the suffering of others makes us feel uncomfortable.

Education is another commodity that is clearly delivered to individuals as a private good. Just as there is a flourishing market in private health care, there is a flourishing market in private education. Yet, if anything, the public spillovers from education are even less tangible than those from health care. We all get old and frail, but childless couples and single people may well have decided never to have children. They will consume far fewer direct benefits from education than a couple with ten kids, yet they will still get enormous value from living in a society with an educated population.

If one of the key elements that has traditionally fuelled public debate over hybrid goods is the extent of indirect benefits to non-users, the second major aspect of the debate concerns the efficiency of government as a producer. When a government produces a pure spillover such as defence, government efficiency simply cannot be compared with the eficiency of a private producer. This is because a private producer is never inclined to produce pure spillovers. The question of comparison does not arise.

When governments produce hybrid services, however, the fact that these are delivered to individuals for their direct consumption means that some aspects of the service may be provided by the market. The temptation then arises to compare the 'efficiency' of government with that of the market. And this opens the way for opponents of government to focus upon any apparent inefficiencies of state provision.

Government provision of private goods may be less efficient. However, one of the fundamental justifications for the state as producer of health care, education and transport is that the market does not provide all of the social benefits that are inevitably involved in these. It may be the case that the service delivered to direct consumers is less efficient when government is the producer. This may, however, be because direct benefits are deliberately or implicitly sacrificed in order to maximize the social benefits which are, after all, the justification for government action in the first place. This need not always be true. Government may be better than the private market even at producing private goods. Alternatively, bureaucratic decision-making may inadequately replace market feedback as a means of allocating resources, without providing any social benefits. The point, however, is that it is simply not valid to assume that because an organization such as British Rail makes a 'loss' it must therefore be inefficient. British Rail may be inefficient, but if it were run as efficiently as possible in order to maximize the indirect social benefits of rail transport, it *ought* to make a loss on its direct income and expenditure account. Such a loss, therefore, is not directly relevant to any evaluation of British Rail's efficiency.

This is a difficult problem. Central government subsidies to British Rail were, in 1982, of the order of £900 million. This helped to maintain a rail network of 10,400 miles. However, the Serpell Report, published early in 1983, claimed that closing the 'most expensive' 80 miles of track would save a quite disproportionate £100 million each year. It further claimed that a 9,000-mile network would require a £700 million public subsidy, while a 6,000-mile network would need a £500 million subsidy. The only way to eliminate the need for a subsidy would be to close everything save the main lines from London to Cardiff, Manchester and Newcastle, some commuter routes and the goods lines on which coal is taken to power stations. The remaining 1,400 miles of track could make a 'profit' in the narrow sense of covering direct costs with charges to direct users. No attempt was made in this report, however, to publish an analysis of the more indirect costs and benefits of British Rail. On the contrary, most potential social benefits were dismissed out of hand. This report, therefore, does not help us very much, although it does rather nicely illustrate the quite drastic conclusions that can be reached about hybrid goods if social costs and benefits are ignored.

No one can deny that such narrowly based cost-benefit analyses should take place. They serve, after all, to tell us how much the indirect social benefits of hybrid goods are costing us and enable us to decide whether we are getting value for money. That is all they do. It is preposterous to conclude that hybrid goods are inefficient simply because they make a loss using this narrow interpretation of costs and benefits. Nobody expects the army to make a profit, but all like to know how much it is costing us, so that we can decide whether it is worthwhile. The public service component of hybrid goods such as transport is in exactly the same position. At the end of the day, we may even decide that the last 80 miles of track is worth £100 million a year, just as we have decided, presumably, that much larger annual expenditures on nuclear weaponry give us value for money.

The real problem with the claim that governments provide hybrid goods less efficiently than the private sector is that the criteria for measuring efficiency are unclear. Even if the scope of social benefits can be agreed, these may be so intangible that they are impossible to measure in any precise sense. (We can *understand* the value of a local rail line to a rural community, but can we *measure* it?)

Once more, this problem applies equally to hybrid goods and to pure spillovers such as defence. It is just that with a service such as defence it seems so obvious that people regard it as inevitable. The fact that some aspects of hybrid goods can be provided by a private market makes it tempting to apply market criteria of efficiency to all aspects of their production. In the same way that nobody knows how to measure whether we get value for money from defence, or whether defence spending is efficient, nobody knows how to measure the value of public transport. This obviously undermines any judgement about efficiency, since it becomes difficult to decide whether the public sector is succeeding at what it sets out to do.

If we agree, for example, that personal health care has far-reaching implications that are insufficiently provided by a private health market, we should not automatically denigrate a state health service if it seems to serve direct users less well than could an alternative private system. Indeed, the health 'market' provides some very good examples of the ways in which a 'rival' private health market can exploit the very public sector to which it claims to be superior. Doctors need very expensive training. Only those who have paid full cost price for private education from the age of 5 until they qualify can claim that their training has received no state subsidy. This is very rare in Europe and uncommon in the United States. Full-cost education for doctors, full-cost medical research and so on would make private medicine much more expensive than it is at the moment. In addition, of course, private practitioners are under no obligation to take on those difficult and possibly loss-making cases that do not appeal to them. The state sector has no such option. In short, the efficiency of private and public health services cannot be compared not only because the public sector does many things (such as research and training) that are general public benefits but also because public health services typically subsidize private ones.

The third element in most public debate over hybrid goods concerns responsiveness. As we have seen, one of the potential benefits of markets is that they provide consumer feedback. Since many hybrid goods can be delivered to their direct consumers on the basis of market competition, the loss of feedback when they are provided by government frequently appears to be a matter for concern. At least, it is often argued, the private education market offers consumer choice. This enables consumers to make it clear what they want and forces producers to be responsive to this. If parents want tough discipline and rote learning, they can go somewhere in the private sector and buy it. They do not need to have modern methods stuffed down their (children's) throats if they don't want them.

This is a complex argument with a number of elements. 'Consumer sovereignty' is usually lauded for three reasons. The first is that choice is something that people value *in and for itself*. The second is that choice enhances efficiency, if we measure efficiency in terms of people getting what they want. When people want different things, more will be happy if they can actually have different things. The third argument relates to markets. It is that consumer choice forces producers, who want as big a market as possible, to be very sensitive to consumer preferences, as well as producing as efficiently as possible in order to cut costs and hence to lower prices.

Only the third argument relates directly to the responsiveness of the public and private sectors, since choices of educational system can be offered within the state sector. This does not imply selective education (a matter that is sometimes dressed up as choice by its advocates). It does imply having a range of different educational products on offer, something that is anyway available in most cities with a number of schools, each with a different character. We have already dealt with the intractable difficulties of comparing the productive efficiency of public and private producers who have very different objectives. Consumer choice, however, can be introduced into the public sector.

This is why governments sometimes try to simulate market feedback within the state sector. A good example of this is the 'voucher' system for education. Rather than being allocated to a particular school by educational bureaucrats, parents receive 'education vouchers' and use these to choose their children's school. The intention is to keep state-sector schools on their toes rather than letting them relax into that comfortable inefficiency that arises from monopoly control of any staple good. Great care should, however, be taken when evaluating simulations of the market within the state system. It should always be remembered that one of the justifications for government provision in the first place is shortcomings in the market.

A classic example concerns school desegregation in the United States. The main argument for desegregation is, of course, that educational segregation by race is a bad thing in itself. It promotes racial disharmony, even hatred. It can underline, even exacerbate, inequalities. And the social costs of racial tension in the USA are patently enormous. The social benefits of desegregated education cannot be achieved by free consumer choice. The point of desegregation is to reduce prejudice in the long term. Yet short-term choices may well be dictated by those very prejudices. This particular set of public benefits is destroyed by consumer choice, whether in the public or in the public sector.

To summarize, hybrid goods such as health care, education and mass transportation mix public and private benefits in significant measure. As a consequence, debate over the proper balance of public and private benefits is likely to be intense. This problem is exacerbated by the fact that private benefits tend to be direct and tangible, while public benefits tend to be indirect and intangible. Furthermore, since the demand for

What Governments Do

hybrid goods may appear to present a choice between public and private production, there is a tendency to measure the efficiency of the public sector against that of the market. In fact, justifications for the involvement of the public sector usually depend upon a decision to include wider social benefits in the calculus. This means that the two modes of production cannot be compared using any simple criterion.

Governments and private goods

Almost no activity is purely private in the sense of having no spillovers at all. So far we have concentrated on the social consequences of consumption, but the way in which a good is produced can have major public consequences. My desire for a gas-guzzling limousine accelerates the depletion of global energy reserves. My desire for cosmetic surgery diverts doctors from saving the sick. My desire for gold reinforces the South African social system. Even a good that has very few consumption spillovers, a bar of chocolate, for example, may be produced in a way that has important collective consequences. These may provide a justification for governments moving into private production.

Most Western governments produce private goods. Nationalized industries often compete with the private sector in the markets for road, air and sea transport. Government banking facilities compete with private banks. Many European governments run nationalized automobile, aircraft, oil and steel companies. As well as competing with the private sector, many governments retain monopoly control over electricity, gas and water supplies, telephone lines and refuse collection. Government's role in private production may thus be as sole supplier in a given market or as one among a number of competitive producers.

'Natural' monopolies. Some goods appear positively to invite monopolistic production. A good example is a local system of telephone lines. Each line supplies a private telephone service to a consumer. Telephone lines clearly can be run on a private basis, and run profitably, as they are by the Bell Telephone system in the USA. Local telephone lines, however, are ugly,

though most of us are prepared to put up with their ugliness in exchange for the service they provide. Two parallel sets of local telephone lines would probably be intolerably ugly and would certainly be immensely wasteful. With ten competing sets of local telephone lines, the sun would filter through to us only in the middle of summer. The social costs of competition in the telephone line market are thus extremely high. More important, however, two private producers can compete with one another only if they each produce the entire system. Ten producers may compete only if ten entire systems are produced. This is quite different from the private market in, say, telephone handsets. Rival producers in this market need produce only as many handsets as they can sell. Each competitor does not need to supply the entire market before she can compete, which is the case with 'natural' monopolies like telephone lines, cable TV lines, electricity, gas and water supplies, sewers (though not septic tanks!) and so on. It is beyond dispute that telephone lines can be more efficiently provided by a single monopolist than by a number of competitors who would simply duplicate resources. Natural monopolies have the property that competition is inevitably wasteful.

The distinction between goods and services that may be natural monopolies and those that are not has a fundamental bearing on the role of government within the private sector. This is because it determines the nature of feasible consumer choice. For goods such as private telephone lines, it is infeasible to offer consumers a choice by simultaneously making available a range of rival systems. For many private goods, such as transistor radios (or even telephone handsets), the simultaneous provision of alternatives is the normal method of offering choices. This means that normal free-market competition simply does not arise as a possibility for natural monopolies. The fact that such goods will be produced by either a public or a private monopoly obviously changes the balance of arguments for or against government action. This is because many of the arguments against government (in terms of the beneficial effects of competition, choice and so on) cannot be deployed when the alternative is a private monopoly.

This situation is further complicated by the fact that many natural monopolies involve supply systems of one sort or another and thus either have strategic importance (such as telecommunications) or are staple goods (such as sewerage or energy). In each case a producer monopoly is obviously a matter of public concern, particularly if it is in private hands. Such monopolies will almost inevitably be regulated by government in order to prevent any abuse of their position.

A private company that monopolized power supplies could, for example, wait for the depths of winter and then raise the price of power to extortionate levels. (This would be genuine extortion, since consumers would face a choice between paying or freezing.) Power costs would bear no relation to anything other than the monopoly position of the supplier, and it is inconceivable that this would not be seen as a matter of public concern. Government action and natural monopolies of this sort are thus inextricably intertwined, although the need for government regulation does not automatically imply, of course, that government should be the direct producer.

Indeed, a rather different type of competition can be introduced into a private market in natural monopoly goods. However, this form of competition will need to be administered by something like a government. We have seen that producers of natural monopoly goods cannot simultaneously offer consumers a choice. Competition can be conducted, however, on the basis of fixed-term monopoly contracts. Rival producers can tender for a contract to produce the natural monopoly for a set time. After this time the contract is put out for tender again. But who administers this process? Indeed, who is the contract with? The answer, of course, is government.

This is the situation that exists in the case of commercial television broadcasting in Britain. Each area has a regional commercial TV station in a monopoly position. These monopoly contracts are reallocated once every few years by a government-sponsored body, the Independent Broadcasting Authority (IBA). Many contracts are renewed each time they come up, but some are not. The threat of competition from rival bidders is thought to keep the broadcasting companies on their toes.

A similar system is envisaged in Britain (and already exists in the USA) for cable TV lines. The US model is for local councils to license local cable operators. (The councils have planning control and could prevent the operators from stringing their cables.) The actual cable system itself is almost invariably a monopoly. Competition for the monopoly licence is conducted by rivals offering a bewildering range of extra services and stating the prices that they will charge consumers. The councils may bring in specialized private cable consultants. Ultimately, however, a public authority offers the monopoly contract to a private operator.

Deeply involved in laying down the terms and conditions of such contracts, governments inevitably become a crucial component even of the private production of natural monopolies. The net consequence is that government often becomes the actual producer because if the regulation of natural monopolies is in any way stringent, private production may become unprofitable. In this case governments must produce if anyone is to produce at all.

This is the worldwide position with respect to postal services, for example. The postal service of any country is a natural monopoly, provided that the service is seen as something that needs to extend to every single part of the country. The British Post Office is one of the nation's largest employers, and it would be staggeringly wasteful to duplicate the entire business for the sake of having two rival producers rather than a single monopolist. If public benefits are seen in having easy and cheap postal deliveries to every address, the contract for a private postal monopoly would be very restrictive. It would include the obligation to deliver letters speedily to remote islands and other difficult destinations. Such deliveries would almost certainly never be cost-effective, at the sort of price that any one would be prepared to pay, in the private sector. While private businessmen would no doubt love to have a contract to deliver bundles of business mail between the city centres of London and Manchester, none would probably be prepared to take on the whole public service contract. Given the natural monopoly character of the postal system taken as a whole, direct government production is the only answer. I know of no national government that does not run its own postal service.

Perhaps the most important point of all, however, is that there may be very little real difference between a heavily regulated private monopolist and a government, at least when each is viewed from the perspective of the consumer. There is certainly very little to choose between the Bell Telephone system in the USA and British Telecom. In such cases, whether or not the government is the actual producer tends to be the result of a combination of historical accident and the overall ideological climate. Thus the comparison between Bell and British Telecom can be extended to cable TV, electricity and gas supply, refuse collection and so on. For each of these natural monopolies, the US solution tends to be government franchised private production and the British solution to be direct production by government.

Governments mop up the spillovers of private production. Apart from natural monopolies, governments may take over the production of certain goods when they consider the social consequences of their private production to be unacceptable. Almost anything can be considered a production spillover if we are prepared to cast the net wide enough. The entire social structure of most Western states is a product of the system of private production. I will limit this discussion, however, to more direct spillovers from private production, since these are quite enough to be going along with.

Obvious production spillovers include competition costs, such as advertising and bankruptcy, as well as disruptive variations in the levels of price, supply, quality and safety. Other potential costs of private production include the tendency of unregulated markets towards monopoly and a tendency for private producers to suppress technological innovation if this will harm profits. (Radial car tyres and stainless steel razor blades were both much more durable than the products they replaced. They were not introduced as soon as they might have been, however, because private producers feared that this extra durability would reduce corporate profits.) The most avid buyers of new patents are large private companies, which put very few of them into production.

A further cluster of social spillovers from private production is related to activities that have irreversible consequences. While some social costs are borne by the community here and now, others are stored up for the future. Natural resources can be depleted; ancient buildings can be demolished and lost for ever; beautiful environments can be destroyed irrevocably. These costs are no less real because they are not immediately obvious.

A very clear example concerns the activity of independent producers in the first American oilfields. Wildcatters raced around discovering oil here, there and everywhere, thereby creating periodic gluts and famines. One consequence was a dramatic variation in the price of oil. Another was a very rapid depletion of exhaustible reserves. Once a new well was discovered, its private owner had an incentive to pump it dry as quickly as possible. Since no wildcatter was big enough or strong enough to wait out a glut until the price rose, each was caught in a vicious spiral of increased production and falling prices. In this particular instance the disorderly market was not stabilized by government. Standard Oil did the job for it, becoming the world's largest company in the process. Indeed Standard Oil's monopoly control of the oil market made it more powerful than most governments, a situation which provoked the first-ever anti-trust legislation in the USA.

In this case the time scale was short. In many cases the costs of private production are born by future generations. Such costs are now evident in many of the West's inner cities. Private manufacturers, on straightforward cost-benefit grounds, have continously preferred developing green-field sites to rehabilitating nineteenth-century city-centre factories. The result has been a progressive degradation of the inner-city environment. We pay the price today for decisions taken over several generations.

In all of these cases private production has social costs that are a matter of public concern. In most of these cases government may either regulate private activity or take it over completely. In some cases the consequences of regulation may render private production unprofitable and make direct government action inevitable, a situation quite clearly evident in examples ranging from inner-city land through the protection of ancient monuments to the husbandry of natural resources.

Take, for example, a particularly important historic building that is hopelessly expensive to maintain. As it is set on a valuable city centre site, its private owners want to demolish it and build a shopping precinct in its place. The irreversible loss of this building is considered too great a production spillover to ignore. Yet this building will deteriorate into a ruin if it is not maintained. With no profits, the private owners do not want to maintain it. In order to maintain the public benefit of this old building, either the private owners must be subsidized *and regulated* or the building must be taken over by a government agency.

Thus in many ways governments may be socially more efficient than private producers. They may innovate, conserve, stabilize and maintain safety or quality when private producers would not mop up their own spillovers. There is, however, a potential price to pay that is very similar to the one faced by governments when they produce hybrid goods. They lose consumer feedback. The pattern of consumer demand in a competitive market tells producers what people want. Remove consumer choice, and even with the best will in the world it becomes more difficult to identify consumer preferences. This problem is faced by any monopoly, be it private or public. If profits depend upon how well producers make what people want, and if producers want to maximize profits, then they have a strong incentive to make what people want and to make it well. Governments, when they act as producers, are not concerned to maximize profits. The profits of private monopolists do not depend on how well they please their captive market. In either case the feedback system breaks down. This does not mean that public or private monopolists are necessarily unresponsive to their clientele. It is just that they are not forced to respond by market pressures.

Any producer concerned to respond to consumer demand has only to listen. Consumers express their feelings by complaining, as well as by the act of consuming. After all, monitoring consumer satisfaction by looking at patterns of revealed demand is a very *indirect* way of going about things. An increase or a fall in demand can occur for all sorts of reasons. If the demand for untipped Gauloise cigarettes falls, is this because consumers now prefer tipped cigarettes, because they are giving up smoking, because they have less money to spend, because these particular cigarettes are declining in quality, or what? All sorts of deductions can be made by trained marketing economists, who look carefully at sales data. The alternative, of course, is to ask the consumers. Gauloises are made by an agency of the French government. The problem of responding to the desires of smokers, however, is precisely the same as if Gauloises were made by a private producer.

It is crucial for governments to be able to receive and respond to consumer demands if they move into the business of supplying any type of good. Opponents of the Soviet Union are fond of imagining bizarre deliveries of shiploads of toilet paper to remote parts of Siberia. Few of us know whether such scatalogical horror stories are actually true, but they are clearly plausible in the complete absence of consumer feedback. Toilet paper sales are not the only method of discovering where this important commodity is needed, however. The example says more about popular views of the responsiveness of the Soviet government than it does about its efficiency as a monopolistic producer.

Yet responsiveness is not as easy to develop as it might seem. The great advantage of the market as a mechanism for revealing demand is that markets depend on money, and money is a scarce resource. It can therefore be assumed that a consumer is prepared to spend most money on the things she most wants. Simply asking people about what they want is unlikely to solve this problem. We all like to moan about the postal service, the railway system, the nationalized gas company, and so on. We like to moan because, facing a monopolist in control of a staple good, we have no other method of expressing our dissatisfaction. Some of us moan more than others. Indeed, some who are very fed up moan less than others who are only a little unhappy. Moaning, in short, is not a scarce resource. Even the most well-meaning producer imaginable can face a daunting task sifting through a welter of moans to sort out her most pressing problems. Some yardstick is needed for comparing one moan with another.

In addition to money, time and energy are scarce resources. Governments that are concerned to respond to consumer demands may well decide to take more notice of those that cost large amounts of time and energy than of those that are more sparing. Using time and energy as yardsticks, a government might assume that the person who devotes most time and energy to a particular complaint is the most concerned. On this principle, medical services could be directed towards those areas with the longest waiting lists, transport services to those with the largest bus queues and so on. In practice, as we shall see in chapter 8, 'How Governments Decide', all yardsticks are imperfect and often unfair. Money is no exception, so the important point to remember is that market feedback on consumer satisfaction, based as it is on money, can be replaced by alternative methods that are potentially as good. The extent to which they operate as well in practice is obviously a major topic of public debate.

Finally, consider the productivity of government as a private producer. The key arguments here have already been made in the section on hybrid goods. All monopolists tend towards inefficiency, and government is no exception. The problem is compounded for government because of the absence of a single clear-cut criterion, profit maximization, against which to judge performance. Other criteria are less easily quantified. Even a highly profitable multinational enterprise knows that certain local operations may run at a loss, yet will contribute to the profitability of the overall system (because they provide valuable tax losses or back-up facilities in the event of production failures, because they deter strikes elsewhere in the system, or whatever). A highly profitable multinational enterprise, however, has a global balance sheet on which this contribution is ultimately recognized. The contribution of a loss-making nationalized industry to the British economy is clearly much harder to quantify. The important point to remember is that government acts as producer because of social considerations broader than those that would be applied by the private sector. Similarly broad criteria must be used when assessing productivity.

To summarize, when governments produce private goods, market feedback must be replaced by receptiveness to demands in order to determine consumer preference and by a clear specification of objectives in order to provide a criterion for assessing efficiency. The processing of such demands and the specification of such objectives are important aspects of what governments do.

Governments can be market leaders. When governments produce private goods, they do not always act as monopolists. Sometimes government agencies compete with the private sector. They usually do this in order to force private producers to behave in certain ways.

The most obvious examples of such market-leading behaviour, practised by all governments from time to time, can be found in international currency markets and interest rates. Governments often want to move or to lead the market in a certain direction. They can do this by acting as buyer or seller in the market, forcing interest or exchange rates up or down as a consequence. Even when a currency market is 'freed from regulation', central banks, such as the Bank of England or the US Federal Reserve Bank, 'smooth' market fluctuations by buying their own national currency when its value is falling or by selling when the price is rising. Central banks are effectively arms of government, subject ultimately to government control. They maintain large reserves of gold and 'convertible currency' that are run down when they want to buy national currency and built up when they want to sell. Exchange and interest rates are simply too important to the economic strategy of any government to be governed entirely by market forces. Even those governments that sustain a fervent belief in market forces acknowledge this and intervene

What Governments Do

from time to time in order to help market forces along. In addition to this, the notorious vulnerability of markets to panics and crazes can be counteracted by a government that behaves in precisely the opposite manner to private speculators.

Governments can intervene in other private markets to affect price, quality, supply, innovation and many of the other factors that we have already considered. They do not even need actually to intervene. A threat is often sufficient. This is because a threat from a single competitor can significantly move a market. Thus if I am speculating in silver by forcing the price up as a result of buying and hoarding, a single producer offering silver at a lower price can foil my plan. I may react before she sells a single bar. A government prepared to make trading losses in the cause of broader social considerations can have a dramatic effect on a free market.

All this relates to one of the most elusive production spillovers of them all, private competition. Oil companies, for example, know this to their cost. After all, they can be sitting around making super-profits as a result of not competing too hard with one another, when along comes Cosmic Gas. Cosmic Gas opens filling stations that sell petrol at below the market rate. Before the big oil companies know what has hit them, there are huge queues of cars outside Cosmic Gas stations. The big companies must either lose business or lower their prices. After they have lowered their prices, it turns out that Cosmic Gas has produced the valuable spillover for all petrol consumers of lower prices throughout the system.

When a particular market is in the grip of a cosy cartel and competitive forces are at a low ebb, government can inject competition if none emerges naturally. The normal procedure in such a market is for new private entrants to be bought off by the cartel. Government, by resisting this, can force prices down throughout the system.

The best possible evidence of the effect of a single dissident competitor upon a market ruled by cartel is, of course, the drastic reduction of all transatlantic airfares brought about by a certain Mr Freddie Laker. Pan Am, British Airways and

TWA passengers, as well as those of Laker, reaped the rewards. It is not necessary for governments to sit around and wait for Freddie Lakers in situations such as this, however; they can become Freddie Lakers themselves.

Governments can have similar market-leading effects upon quality. The private car market, for example, produces much of its low-quality output because motor manufacturers see no profits (or even see losses) in higher quality. Thus nearly all cars are very easy to burgle, mainly because their door locks are very poor. Much better locks could be fitted at little extra cost, but motor manufacturers refuse to do so. A state-owned car company could, by forsaking some profit, put this and many other quality problems right, forcing private manufacturers to follow suit or lose business. In a similar way, government-owned high-technology companies may force the pace of industrial innovation or provide low-cost backing for risky ventures.

In each case governments lead markets by forcing the private sector to abandon policies that maximize profits at the expense of social efficiency. In each case governments do this by bringing cut-throat competition back into those markets in which the cutting of throats has given way to the shaking of hands.

Government production redistributes wealth

When governments sell goods or services below cost price, the bulk of the deficit is met by taxation. Taxes must be raised on some basis or another. They may be raised *progressively*, on the basis of ability to pay. They may be raised *regressively*, on the basis of relative powerlessness in the decision-making process (or inability to pay). I should make it clear at this point that I am using the terms 'progressive' and 'regressive' taxation in a sense rather different from that used by some other authors. I refer here to the actual amount of tax paid, not to the tax rate. It is the amount, *not the rate* of what people pay and receive that produces redistribution. (A universally applied 100 per cent tax rate would be highly redistributive!)

It is impossible to be absolutely certain about the

redistributive effects of the public sector. In order to do this we would need to make statements about what life would be like if the public sector did not exist. These days this would involve some pretty mind-stretching assumptions. Some purists leave the matter at this. They shelve the question of public-sector redistribution because it can never be definitively answered. This is not a very useful attitude. We can say quite a lot about the different types of redistribution that different types of public production and taxation are likely to stimulate. Even if we can rarely quantify, we can at least see the direction in which things are going.

Nevertheless, we still face huge problems, particularly when we are dealing with spillovers. Finding out how much people pay is not too difficult. Finding out how much good they get out of things is another matter entirely. In principle, spillovers affect all equally. In practice, all will not feel equal effects. You should know by now that I hate opera. As a matter of fact, I am not too fond of ballet either. I don't hate ballet, but it leaves me cold. Yet in others ballet can inspire feelings akin to Beatlemania. I could live next door to Sadler's Wells and not lift a finger to see *Swan Lake*. Others would travel from the Outer Hebrides. So who gets what out of state-sponsored ballet?

It would be silly to pretend that we can make no estimates at all of the incidence of public benefits. Some, after all, are straightforward cash payments, such as welfare benefits. Others, such as health care and education, at least have direct users who can be monitored. (Though never forget that the whole point of public endeavour in such fields is to generate indirect social benefits that can rarely be measured.)

Consider health care. Now, we know from medical research that the poor are much more likely to fall sick than the rich. Contrast unskilled workers and professionals in Britain. Unskilled workers are about three times as likely to get ear diseases, bronchitis and fractures. They are about twice as likely to contract heart diseases, digestive diseases, mental illness, arthritis and rheumatism. If all paid the same for a health service that was then used by those who needed it, redistribution from rich to poor would clearly take place. (As a matter of fact, it is also well documented that take-up of health benefits is lower among the poor than among the rich. Redistribution is thus less marked than it might be.)

In general, however, we can say that if tax payments rise more steeply than the benefits derived from government production, then they redistribute from rich to poor. If tax payments rise more slowly than benefits, then tax-financed government production redistributes from poor to rich. This happens when taxes are used to subsidize expensive pursuits such as opera or supersonic travel. If only the rich can afford to fly Concorde, then subsidizing Concorde tickets from general taxation makes the rich better off, as the poor pay some of their costs. In contrast, if everyone enjoys public television about equally, then subsidizing this on the basis of progressive general taxation redistributes from rich to poor. The rich pay more for the same pleasures.

Since taxes redistribute in this way, the rich tend to oppose the use of progressive taxation to finance high levels of government activity. The poor tend to favour this. Furthermore, since different goods and services provide different benefits for rich and poor, each sector of the population tends to favour some goods more than others. Progressive taxation thus causes disputes not only over how much governments should produce but also over which goods should have highest priority. The familiar left-right-wing spectrum in the politics of most European states is defined by views not only on the scale of government production but also on its nature. The right, while opposed to many forms of tax-financed government expenditure, is nevertheless in favour of high levels of public provision of defence, of public order and sometimes also of expensive capital infrastructure such as airports or nuclear power plants. The left tends to have contrary preferences.

In many countries a significant proportion of taxation is raised on a local basis. Local taxation often has a regressive effect, usually involving the exploitation of a city by its suburbs. All cities have limits. City governments provide goods and services and partially finance them by levying local taxes on those who live within city limits. Those who live in suburbs, outside city limits, can use many city services without paying. Suburbs therefore need to produce fewer services and hence to raise lower taxes. Suburb dwellers are usually richer on average than city dwellers (being able to meet higher housing and transport costs), so this process redistributes from poor to rich. It can even become a vicious circle whereby high taxes encourage those who can afford the costs to move to the suburbs and leave fewer, poorer, people in the city to pay a higher share of the same tax burden.

The main alternative to local or national taxation is inflation. When a government prints new money at a rate that is faster than economic growth, all money becomes worth less. This new money can be used to pay for government production in a manner that amounts to a tax on old money. It is a progressive tax, since people who have more money pay more than those who have less. This situation is complicated by the fact that *money is not wealth*. Many rich people (for example, big property owners) may well have less money than many poor people (for example, retired people living on the income from a nest-egg). It is well known that people on 'fixed incomes' are hard-hit by inflation. It is less commonly realized that, apart from this, inflation is a method of taxation that redistributes more systematically than most of the alternatives.

Governments that finance budget deficits by printing 'too much' money are in effect using inflation as a redistributive tax. This is probably the reason why it becomes a matter of so much public controversy. No politician claims that inflation is a good thing. To do so would be rather like advocating murder or devil worship. Some politicians, however, clearly think that it is worse than others. I am quite certain that it is no accident that those who oppose inflation most vociferously tend to be those most hostile to redistributive taxation (that is, those on the right of the spectrum). In contrast, those most prepared to tolerate inflation as an acceptable price to pay for other benefits tend to be those on the left who are also in favour of progressive taxation to finance high levels of government spending. Some have certainly argued that inflation has had a more dramatic redistributive effect, from rich to poor, than any other aspect of what governments have recently done in modern Britain.

Thus when governments either finance production or produce things themselves, they are able not only to solve collective-action problems caused by spillovers and to attempt to increase social welfare by increasing social productivity, but they can also redistribute. In many cases when governments increase the size of the public sector, they do so quite explicitly in order to redistribute. In other cases redistribution happens inadvertently. In some cases, redistribution is inadvertently perverse, operating in the direction opposite to that intended. This may be either because benefits are very unevenly distributed (as with Concorde) or because taxes are regressive (as is sometimes the case with local rates on property in Britain).

While many of the problems that tend to justify government can be solved by tax-financed production, some cannot. Many collective-action problems, such as pollution control, depend much more upon regulation for their solution. It is to these that we now turn.

GOVERNMENTS REGULATE

The need for regulation is one of the fundamental justifications for government. Indeed, it is the most fundamental, in the sense that all, save communitarian anarchists and a few anarcho-capitalists, favour *some* government regulation. The need for government production tends to be rather more contentious. While regulation can fulfil nearly all of the objectives that a government might have, it may not always do this in the most palatable manner.

Redistribution by expropriation

Progressive taxes may be used to fund public services and thus to redistribute in an indirect fashion. Expropriation, however, can be used to redistribute very explicitly. Expropriation raises a neat theoretical paradox. As we saw when discussing anarchy, there is a real sense in which private property cannot exist without government. If something is my property, it is legitimately mine. When something is in my possession it is simply under my control, legitimate or otherwise. If you dispute my ownership of my possessions, we can roll up our sleeves and settle the matter with a good old-fashioned show of strength. If you dispute my property, I must either appeal to abstract principles of justice or go to the law. If you dispute my principles of justice, the law enforced by government is my only recourse. In the absence of communal agreement over the principles defining private property, government allocation and enforcement is the only answer. Yet what government giveth that can it take away.

Direct and unconcealed redistributions of property by governments, using their powers of expropriation, are rather less common these days than they used to be. This process was most dramatically in evidence during the colonial era. When Elizabeth I of England conquered Ireland, for example, she attempted to restore stability by starting a plantation movement. Land ownership was simply taken away from the Irish lords and reallocated to English and Scottish settlers. Some Irish lords preserved and cherished the ancient titles to their land, but these were as worthless as if some twentieth-century bureaucrat had stamped 'cancelled' across the top in red ink.

The modern equivalent of this process is a socialist revolution. One of the fundamental components of any socialist conception of revolution is the annulment of the traditional set of property titles. This is an explicit recognition of the fact that property flows from the state, and that fundamental changes in the state may involve fundamental redistributions of property. When the ideology of the revolution is nationalist rather than socialist, such expropriation and redistribution tends to affect only that property which is owned by foreign nationals.

Coercive expropriation without compensation, and the subsequent redistribution of property by the state, is thus a traumatic process, tending to reflect a revolutionary transformation in the system of government. Expropriation with fair compensation, however, can mean almost anything. Some would argue that there can be no such thing, on the grounds that a fair price is one agreed by both buyer and seller, so that no expropriation would be needed. This might be true in a free market, in which the market price is affected by no single transaction. Such a situation rarely obtains, however, when governments take things into public ownership.

Consider an extreme example, involving an airport. This needs a new runway, and the government must buy the land. As it moves into the market for this land, of course, the price of land begins to rise. Once nearly all of the land has been purchased, one landowner attempts a piece of extortion. The land is worth £1,000 per acre as farmland. The price drifts up to £5,000 an acre as the government buys heavily. The extortionist demands £5 million for the final 10-acre site, which belongs to her. Is £1,000, £5,000 or £500,000 the 'fair' price for an acre of land in this context? The market price of the land is £1,000 per acre, since the market price must be the price at which the land can be disposed of to buyers in general. It is not, however, the price at which the seller will voluntarily part with the land, because there is one buyer who really needs that particular land and who can be put on the rack for it. To say that £500,000, is the market price of this 10-acre site is like saying that the market price of insulin is £1 million an injection, because that is what a diabetic millionaire would pay to save her life.

In a case such as this few would deny that the government should ultimately expropriate the land. If compensation is paid, it may be either at £1,000 per acre, the market price of farm land, or at £5,000, a price that would in fact be paid by government voluntarily. It is difficult, however, to construct an argument for compensation at a higher rate than this.

Expropriation with compensation is not always unwelcome. Sometimes the 'market' price can be 'too much' to pay for a complete take-over. There are two reasons for this, both of which have been particularly exploited by multinational companies involved in the 'expropriation' of a subsidiary by a host government. In the first place, the market price of a company's shares usually depends upon a restricted number of shares being on the market at a given time. Any attempt to sell the entire company could flood the market and depress its share value. Owners who want to sell are often delighted to be expropriated with compensation at market rates. In the second place, some multinational subsidiaries make unrealistically high paper profits because they are used as tax shelters. This may well increase their apparent value but is of no use to the expropriating government, which obviously does not need a tax shelter.

Expropriation with compensation is thus a complex matter, since the concept of a fair price is impossible to define in the circumstances. Thus the one firm statement that we can make is that the precise level of compensation will always be a serious bone of contention.

Regulating spillovers

Governments may use direct coercion to reduce negative spillovers such as pollution. My car pumps a nasty collection of poisonous gases into the atmosphere. Automobile exhaust is so dangerous that a good way of committing suicide is to shut your garage door and to remain in your car with the engine running. My car pollutes more than the air. Countless thousands of acres of beautiful countryside have been buried under concrete in order to provide the roads that my car needs if it is to be of any use to me. Many innocent pedestrians have been slaughtered on those roads.

If I am honest with myself, I can be in no doubt that driving my car is an antisocial act. If I am justifying this antisocial behaviour to myself, I take comfort in the fact that there is little that I can do about the problem. If only I quit driving and take to the pavements, no one will notice any drop in the level of pollution. No fewer children will suffer brain damage from lead poisoning. No fewer roads will need to be built. I am a good driver, so no fewer innocent pedestrians will be slaughtered. No isolated individual can make a significant contribution towards the prevention of pollution.

Running cars that use lead-free petrol costs more than

running cars that use the old-fashioned poisonous variety. Even if lead-free petrol were available in every filling station, I would have little incentive to buy it. When only I burn lead-free petrol, it makes no noticeable difference to the environment, so why should I pay more for the privilege? Only if everyone were to burn lead-free petrol would it make a difference. Then all, even motorists who must pay more for their pleasures, would be better off breathing cleaner air. A government that banned the sale of poisonous petrol would reduce the negative spillover of air pollution, to everyone's advantage. This course of action has, indeed, been taken recently by the US government.

This is precisely the sort of problem that a community could solve on its own if it were small enough and coherent enough. Social norms would emerge to regulate antisocial behaviour by individuals. Each member who wanted to remain in the group would conform with these or be excluded. Regulation provides the clearest example of the interchangeable roles of government and community. Government coercion is often most needed in those areas of social life where enlightened self-restraint, if it worked, would do the same job.

In the case of lead in petrol, where there is widespread agreement on the 'goodness' of the good, low cost and only a very gentle redistribution, few would object to government coercion. A more effective way of reducing exhaust pollution, however, would be to install expensive catalytic converters in all car engines. If all drivers were *forced* by government to fit their cars with these 'cat crackers', as they are in California, they might well feel that the costs did not merit the direct individual benefits. This is because, in the absence of regulation, drivers have been able to reduce their private costs by forcing society to pay for some of their spillovers. (They would certainly not pump exhaust gas into the car, if the atmosphere were unavailable to receive it.) Forcing people to pay for their own spillovers is one of the main ways in which government provides public benefits by regulation.

Such actions may cause intense anger among those who

What Governments Do

have grown accustomed to regarding their ability to dispose of spillovers freely as an inviolable right. Motorists and dog owners are notorious examples of this phenomenon. Any proposal to close British parks to dogs, on public hygiene grounds, is met by howls of indignant and self-righteous protest by dog owners. The 'right' of dog owners to dispose of canine excrement in public places appears to be a part of the British way of life. It is defended vociferously by people who would be horrified and outraged if I were to decide to economize on my plumbing and use public parks for the same purpose myself.

In most cases, including that of pollution, government regulation also produces some redistribution. All non-polluters are made better off, and the general level of wellbeing in the system is increased, at a direct cost to former polluters. If redistribution is not intended, it can be reduced by combining regulation with subsidies. These may reduce the scale of redistribution involved to a level at which everyone is better off than she was before.

The classic example is a factory with a dirty chimney. The factory pumps dirty smoke into the air, forcing local residents, who gain none of the benefits, to pay some of the costs. The total cost of this dirty air to local residents is greater than the cost of treating the pollution at source. It would actually be cheaper for them to club together and pay the factory owner to treat her waste products than to sit there passively and let the smoke settle on their washing. If a government steps in and forces the factory owner to treat her smoke, she is worse off, while the residents are better off, than before.

One alternative is for government to pay the factory owner to treat her smoke, collecting the money in taxes from local residents. Everyone may then be better off, although the residents are worse off than they would be if no tax-financed subsidy were paid. A second alternative is for governments to penalize polluters rather than to subsidize or regulate them. Thus if polluting companies are charged penal taxes, this amounts to some form of compensation for the indirectly affected taxpayer. Those who suffer the pollution have to pay less in taxes for the same public budget. This is actually quite a common situation. It is used, for example, by the regional water authorities in Britain, which load water rates against companies with high levels of undesirable effluent and reward those who treat their own.

Moral regulation

We have our clearest view of the way in which government replaces community when governments regulate morals. Government intervention in such matters as drug-taking, pornography and under-age sex is sometimes justified in terms of the protection of the individuals concerned from themselves. This paternalist attitude is, however, difficult to limit logically to 'moral' issues. The belief that certain activities stunt growth or even kill does not result in the abolition of tobacco smoking, motor racing or free-fall parachute jumping. Some other criterion must be appealed to in order to limit the scope of government regulation of our personal lives, and this is usually some indirect notion of public interest.

Mrs Mary Whitehouse would want pornography to be banned in Britain even if it could be shown conclusively that it reduced, rather than increased, the number of sexual assaults. She would want it banned because she sees pornography as undermining traditional values, a function that others imagine to be performed by mind-expanding drugs or homosexuality. Such activities are seen as antisocial in the sense that they undermine a sense of community by subverting the conventional norms of behaviour. These norms, in the last analysis, are part of what holds a community together.

Moral regulation brings our discussion of government almost full-circle. We began by looking at the ways in which governments replace communities. We end by considering the ways in which governments protect communities, providing legitimacy and reinforcement for their moral values. This is why government regulation of private morality is inherently conservative, although it is a matter in which conservatives may be supported by revolutionaries. With the benefit of hindsight, the crumbling of an old regime often seems to be accompanied by an age of moral decadence. The coming of the revolution is marked by a 'reign of virtue' that helps to consolidate a new-found sense of community. One of the first things that Castro did when he came to power was to close Havana's many brothels.

WHAT GOVERNMENTS DO

Governments plan, governments produce and governments regulate. The latter two functions, the justifications for government itself, are interchangeable to quite a considerable degree. Many of the things that governments do can be done either way. Thus broadcasting, a matter of obvious public concern, may be taken over by a public broadcasting service or regulated by a public broadcasting authority. Both models exist side by side in Britain, with the BBC and IBA, and both can be made to do a very similar job. The telephone service can be state-run or state-regulated, and the results can be very similar.

One final example quite clearly illustrates the choice between regulation and production that must be made by any government. It concerns litter. When you drive along country roads, throwing sweet papers and beer cans out of the car window, you do so because you cannot be bothered to pay the small cost of taking them home. If we all dump our spillovers out of the window, we all soon pay the price with a littered environment. In a small community social pressure will constrain litter bugs. Even the most wanton of these will look over their shoulders before dumping their cans on the street, for fear of being seen and censured. When community breaks down they become more brazen, caring less about what others think, while others think less about it anyway.

Government may step in and clean up the environment by regulation. Littering can be banned and large penalties imposed for non-compliance. In practice, litter laws are difficult to enforce. Nasty though litter is, few think of it as nasty enough to warrant major expenditure on the detection and punishment of offenders.

The alternative is for government to produce a litter-free environment more directly. Litter bins can be left around to reduce the costs of not littering. People can be employed to go around picking up and disposing of all those beer cans. Regulation costs money. It may even cost as much as actually producing things. Thus it may be cheaper to pay refuse disposal operatives than to set up a litter police.

The choice between regulation and production may, therefore, be an economic choice. Most commonly, however, it is ideological. Basic justifications for government action usually depend up taking a broad rather than a narrow view of social costs and benefits. The narrow view tends to emphasize regulation. Individual welfare is seen as the fundamental unit of analysis. Government is seen as necessary to control the direct charges on individual welfare that may be caused by negative spillovers from other individuals. Negative spillovers invite regulation by government. A broader view takes the group as the fundamental unit. It sees positive ways in which group endeavour may be rewarded if only collective-action problems could be resolved. This puts government in a potentially more active role, producing social benefits on behalf of the group.

Thus regulation rather than production tends to appeal more to those on the right. This is probably because regulation is usually justified in terms of the protection of individual rights from violation. Production, on the other hand, tends to involve taxing people for things that, as individuals, they may not want, whatever the social benefits. Thus those on the right prefer to regulate strategic industries rather than to nationalize them. They prefer to regulate pollution or environmental protection rather than to allow government a more active role. And so on.

For those on the extreme right, who may claim that they are not much in favour of regulation by government, this process takes place beneath an interesting camouflage. The far-right solution depends upon a dramatic extension of the scope of private property rights. Pollution may thereby be attached by giving people 'air rights', noise abatement by giving people 'silence rights' and so on. Of course, the more rights people have, particularly the more rights to things as intangible as silence or the atmosphere, the more they will involve government in attempts to enforce them. This increase in the scope of private property rights dramatically increases the scale of government regulation, albeit by the back door. A government that enforced 'only' property rights might be a very big government indeed if property rights were dramatically extended.

In conclusion, we can at least be confident in asserting that the ways in which governments do what they do will depend crucially upon the way in which they look at that infinite pool. Those who see individual actions as causing relatively few ripples will be inclined to regulate in order to limit their effects. Those who see more ripples travelling further will be more inclined to let governments take over the whole pool.

6

Making Collective Decisions

Robinson Crusoe did not need to make collective decisions, at least until Man Friday appeared on the scene. After this Crusoe adopted the all-too-familiar technique of deciding what to do, then generally bossing poor Friday around. However, when three or more people interact, and when none is a dictator, they will often need to decide what to do. In small groups this process may be informal. In larger groups, even those that do not have governments, a set of decision-making procedures and institutions may well be needed.

All collective decision-making presents serious problems. Most of us forget these when we 'talk things through' and look for a 'consensus', when we vote, when we use vetoes or when we use any of the other methods for making social choices that we usually take for granted. Yet all social choice mechanisms are beset by paradox and inconsistency. Most important of all, none is very good at identifying a *collective* choice that is more than simply the *collected* choices of all.

The precise technique used to make a decision can greatly influence the final result. This means that differences between techniques are much more than mere technical matters. Choosing a technique for making social choices is not just something for the political technicians who fine-tune our system. We all know that changing the electoral system, for example, can dramatically affect party politics. New parties may emerge that offer us choices that have never before been presented. Old parties may die. The electoral system is, however, but one example of a social choice mechanism. Such mechanisms, whether they are selection committees or mass meetings, fundamentally affect most aspects of our daily lives.

Three very serious matters conspire to make it almost impossible to identify the collectively preferred solution to a particular problem. In the first place, we tend to give little thought to the possibility that the *collective preference may often differ from the collected preferences of all*. It is quite possible, as we saw when we looked at the collective-action problem, that the sum total of a collection of individual decisions is not the same as the decision preferred by the group as a whole or even that preferred by each of its individual members. In the second place, there is the problem of how to take into account the fact that some people feel more strongly than others about particular issues. If, for example, 2,000 people violently oppose, and 2,500 people vaguely favour, the building of a new pressurized water reactor, how can we take their relative strengths of feeling into account? Should we build the reactor or not? Finally, there is the often ignored but immensely important practical problem that any system for taking collective decisions can generate serious paradoxes.

IS THE COLLECTIVE WHOLE MORE THAN THE SUM OF THE INDIVIDUAL PARTS?

Collectively people often want something quite different from that which each wants individually. This, after all, is one of the justifications for government in the first place. Everyone wants to dump her litter; no one wants pollution. Everyone wants health; no one wants to pay. A binding collective decision can help to solve this problem, but the manner in which a decision is taken determines quite how collective it is.

Consider the members of a trade union who face a decision over whether or not to strike in support of a pay claim. Now, the purpose of the union in the first place is to enable the relatively weak individual members to take effective collective

Invitation to Politics

action against a relatively strong employer. The threat of strike action represents their most potent collective bargaining chip. Without a union the bargaining strength of individuals is so low that they will never win concessions. Each person, however, might rather not go on strike, regardless of what the others did. Not striking when the others struck would enable the non-striker to gain a pay rise without short-term loss of earnings. Not striking when the others didn't strike either would safeguard the individual's job. A lone striker would be an easy target for the employer to pick off. This is a classic collective-action problem, and the decision to strike is thus essentially a collective decision. There has been much talk in recent years about the relative merits of secret and public ballots on strike decisions. Much of this discussion has missed the point about the collective nature of the decision to withhold labour. If someone is prepared to strike only if everyone else strikes too, the knowledge of what everyone else is prepared to do is a key component of her decision. This knowledge is automatically made available by a public ballot but not by a secret one. There is a real question mark over whether collective decisions taken by secret ballot are genuinely collective, once it is accepted that the collective whole is more than the sum of its individual component parts.

In addition to the problem of distinguishing between the collective preference and the collected preferences of all, there is the rather more ethical matter of whether individuals ought to be held responsible for their contributions to group decision-making. If I vote to go on strike, for example, should I not be held partially accountable for the collective decision? Accountability is the other side of intimidation, and the possibility of intimidation is much stressed by those who argue for secret ballots. Historically, of course, it is the reason why secret ballots replaced public voting in national elections. With the broadening of the franchise, too many new voters were too dependent upon their employers and patrons and could not resist pressure to vote as they were told. More recently, the possibility of corrupt practices and the purchase of votes by candidates has provided a powerful argument for

Making Collective Decisions

the secret ballot. The interesting thing, however, is that only one side of the case is usually presented.

Secret ballots and 'democracy' are seen to go hand in hand, while organizations that use public voting (most notably trade unions) tend to be portrayed as undemocratic. If we desire to take genuinely collective decisions, however, the case of the secret ballot can be argued both ways. The recent debate in Britain over the use of secret ballots in trade union decision-making is thus more ideological than it may superficially appear. The introduction of secret ballots in trade unions could undermine that ability to take collective decisions which is part of a trade union's very reason for existence.

Secret ballots are especially advocated when strike decisions are to be taken. This case is usually made on the grounds that strikes are less likely when the decision is taken by secret ballot, and therefore that strike decisions taken by a public show of hands must be less democratic either because of intimidation or because they do not reflect the wishes of the whole membership. In fact, decisions to strike are less likely when using secret ballots rather than a show of hands, even with unanimous participation and no intimidation, because of the collective nature of the decision. The use of secret postal ballots takes this one stage further. At least when secret ballots are used at meetings, preferences and decisions can be discussed before and after the vote, and some knowledge of the views of others can be absorbed. This is not a part of postal voting, which really is no more than a method of collecting the preferences of all.

In general, the distinction between a collective preference and the collected preferences of all has two components. One is practical and one rather more mystical. The practical point is that a person's preferences are often *conditional*. Thus I may choose to go out to the pub if I know that my friends have chosen to go too and that my enemies have chosen to stay at home. Otherwise, I will choose to stay at home myself. A jolly evening in the saloon bar is thus the result of a conditional decision and is more difficult to achieve if we all choose in isolation. This is a practical problem, since people

Invitation to Politics

could in theory be offered conditional choices. In practice conditional choices are hugely difficult both to present and to process.

Returning to the matter of trade union reform, many are for or against this policy, 'other things being equal'. 'Other things', however, are rarely so obliging. Trade union reform may provoke intense conflict if it is opposed by a significant proportion of the population. Many may favour reform but only if it does not provoke conflict. They may not consider the price of conflict to be worth the benefits of reform. Their preferences are thus conditional. Faced with a simple choice between reform and the status quo, they very much like to find out what everyone else thinks. If the group of voters is too large for them all to choose together, two possibilities remain. The first is to break the large group into a series of small groups and to take a representative decision, a possibility that I shall consider at some length in the next chapter. The second is to hold a conditional ballot. Conditional ballots, however, look very different from those to which we are accustomed.

Figure 5 shows an example of a possible conditional ballot

Select only one option		Two hypothetical results			
Question: Would you favour a restriction of trade union power:		A		B	
		Voters (%)	Cumulative (%)	Voters (%)	Cumulative (%)
(a) In any circumstances?	☐	8	—	20	—
(b) If at least 10% of other voters agreed?	☐	8	16	5	25
(c) If at least 20% of other voters agreed?	☐	8	24	5	30
(d) If at least 30% of other voters agreed?	☐	8	32	5	35
(e) If at least 40% of other voters agreed?	☐	8	40	5	40
(f) If at least 50% of other voters agreed?	☐	8	48	5	45
(g) If at least 60% of other voters agreed?	☐	8	56	20	65
(h) If at least 70% of other voters agreed?	☐	8	64	5	70
(i) If at least 80% of other voters agreed?	☐	8	72	5	75
(j) If at least 90% of other voters agreed?	☐	8	80	5	80
(k) If at least all other voters agreed?	☐	8	88	5	85
(l) In no circumstances?	☐	12	100	15	100

Figure 5   Conditional referendum on union power

on trade union power, together with two hypothetical results. The simple choice normally presented to voters is contained in the first and last options, (a) and (l), which are unconditional. The remaining options (b) to (k), offer conditional choices. They thus provide some of the richer information needed to enable collective decisions to be more collective by allowing each to express a view that takes into account the views of others.

Assume that the matter will be decided by a simple majority. In this case result A would mean that trade union power will not be restricted. While 56 per cent of voters are in favour of change, *if at least 60 per cent of all voters favour change,* the conditional criterion is never satisfied. While 80 per cent favour change, if 90 per cent of all voters favour change, for each option that has majority support the percentage in favour is always less than the percentage required by that majority before their votes can be taken as valid. Without this information on conditional choices, reform might well have been selected. Some voters might have wrongly believed that many others were also in favour. Imagine that the 56 per cent who favour reform *on condition that 60 per cent of all voters favour reform* actually believed that more than 60 per cent were in favour. Confronted with a simple yes/no choice, they would have voted yes. The conditional social decision thus differs from the outcome of unconditional choice.

Result B, on the other hand, produces change if conditional choices are used. There are 65 per cent of voters who favour change if at least 60 per cent of all voters are in favour. The conditional criterion is satisfied. Once more, the unconditional choice might have been different. Voters might have underestimated the number of others in favour of change, and voted no as a consequence.

As far as I know, conditional ballots such as this are used nowhere. There are several reasons for this. In the first place, you will by now have realized that they are complex to specify and complex to interpret. In the second place, they are suitable for policy decisions only when the status quo is a possible alternative. This is because no choice may satisfy conditional criteria, a possibility that means that conditional choices would be difficult to use for selecting candidates or representatives. In the example I have just been citing, this would not matter. If no alternative satisfied conditional criteria, no restriction of trade union power would result, and this would be entirely appropriate. There would be no mandate for it. If, however, the same system were to be used to select public representatives, no representative might satisfy the criteria. The consequence would be that no representative would be selected, and this might undermine the whole point of representative democracy. In the third place, the example I have used uses a single conditional criterion only, the number of other voters favouring change. Many choices may be conditional on a whole range of criteria. Trade union reform, for example, may be favoured if x per cent of other voters are in favour and if y per cent of union members are in favour and if z per cent of employers are in favour (or if p per cent of voters, q per cent of union members and r per cent of employers, or . . .). Several conditional criteria can provide extremely complex problems, increasing both the difficulty of presenting and interpreting the choices and the chance that no outcome will satisfy the specified conditions. Nevertheless, conditional choices may be appropriate in certain circumstances, and the fact that they present problems is no reason to ignore them altogether.

The second, and more mystical, part of the distinction between collective choice and collected choices concerns the extent to which there may be a *collective will*. If such a thing exists, it may differ even from the collected conditional choices of all. In essence, this problem concerns the question of whether a group of people can have a collective mind. It is a matter that is one of the traditional preserves of political philosophers, into which I would trespass only at great peril. Being something of a coward, I leave it to the philosophers. I pause only to draw it to your attention and to point out that when the contents of a collective mind differ from the contents of the minds of the individual members of the collectivity, it will be very difficult for anybody with less than infinite wisdom to find out what the collective mind is actually thinking about.

HOW DO WE MAKE DECISIONS IF I HATE SOMETHING MORE THAN YOU LIKE IT?

When I hate something more than you like it we face a tricky decision-making problem. It is easy enough for me to convince you that I hate opera; I have probably already done this. I face a much greater problem if I want to make you realize just *how much* I hate opera, yet we must both confront this problem if we want to balance my hate against your love. It is a problem that is greatly compounded when we are trying to balance the desires of an intense minority against those of an apathetic majority. While few would deny that there are circumstances in which the minority will should prevail, there is no foolproof, 'objective' method of comparing the different intensities of feeling experienced by different people about the same thing.

In the real world, of course, a number of yardsticks are used. We have already seen that markets use money to allocate resources, on the grounds that those who want things more will be prepared to pay more money for them. Money, as well as being a medium of exchange, is a *numéraire,* a commonly valued commodity in short supply that can be used as a yardstick. Other examples of *numéraire* goods include tobacco in prisons and sweets in a children's playground. Money has one great disadvantage as a *numéraire*. It is unevenly distributed among the population, and this means that it is difficult to distinguish those who do not want something from those who cannot afford it.

An alternative *numéraire* or yardstick is time. Everyone has twenty-four hours available in her day, seven days in her week and fifty-two weeks in her year. (Some live longer than others, of course, but this is a *relatively* unpredictable and random matter.) Using time as a yardstick, we could assume that people must want the things that they devote most time to. More ambitiously we assume that if I devote more time to confounding the production of opera than you do, I hate it more than you. This potential solution to the problem of comparing intensities has many drawbacks. I may be a

Invitation to Politics

sluggish sort of person with no strong feelings about anything. You may get worked up about almost everything. You may therefore feel more strongly about opera than I but may devote less time to it because you feel even more strongly about other things.

One thing, however, is certain. Straightforward voting on issues will not capture any of that richness in a decision-making problem that is produced by variations in the intensity of voters' feelings. Yet such variations are an essential component of the decisions we face. This richness is added to the decision-making process, at least in theory, by a combination of pressure groups and the trading off of interests, and I will return to these matters in chapters 7 and 8. For the moment it is sufficient to note that no social choice mechanism is very good at capturing intensity and that no one can argue that majority decisions are necessarily the same as those that are most preferred.

PARADOXES OF VOTING

All voting systems are beset by paradox and inconsistency. No voting system can simultaneously fulfil a set of very modest demands that we might reasonably expect any system for making social choices to satisfy. A simple example makes this clear.

Some time ago a private property developer asked for planning permission to develop some vacant land in front of my house. This is the largest remaining green-field site in central Liverpool, about 1 square kilometre in area. Liverpool City Council at the time comprised three parties, none with overall control. Any two needed to form a coalition in order to vote any proposal through the council. All three parties felt differently about the development of this large and unusual riverside site. One party wanted to see council housing built on it. One party wanted to turn it into a public park. The third party wanted to allow it to be developed by private contractors. The full preference orderings for the three parties were as follows:

Making Collective Decisions

	Party A	*Party B*	*Party C*
1st choice	Council houses	Park	Private houses
2nd choice	Private houses	Council houses	Park
3rd choice	Park	Private houses	Council houses

You may care to amuse yourself by identifying the parties, but the Planning Committee had to decide upon its priorities. The decision they took depended upon two things. The first was the sophistication of council members, which we can safely assume to be low. The second was the order in which the alternatives were presented for discussion. If council housing had been presented first, it would have been rejected by a coalition of parties B and C, each of which preferred something else. Once council housing had been rejected, the run-off between private housing and a park would provoke parties A and C to combine and choose private housing. On another hand, if a park had been presented as the first matter for decision, it would have been rejected by a coalition of parties A and C. This would have resulted in a run-off between council and private housing. Parties A and B would have combined to choose council housing. This problem, however, was a three-handed monster. If private housing had been presented first, it would have been rejected by parties A and B. The park would have won the run-off with council housing, since it was preferred by parties B and C. (You may be interested to know the actual outcome. The private developer's planning application forced the issue, and was rejected. As I write this, I can watch the riverside site being transformed for the 1984 European Garden Festival, after which it will become a public park.)

The paradox here is quite clear. Any of the three outcomes might have been selected. Which outcome was in fact selected depended upon the order in which the alternatives were considered. Every outcome that was selected was such that a majority of voters preferred an alternative. (Thus the park won in this case, yet parties A and C each preferred private houses.)

This particular example has been carefully chosen to make my point as strongly as possible, but it is by no means unique.

One of the few genuinely important insights added by political scientists to our understanding of politics is a little theorem that proves beyond question that every conceivable system for taking social decisions falls foul of one or other of five modest conditions that most reasonable people would want to impose on any decision process. This theorem was developed by Kenneth Arrow, and the modest conditions are as follows:

(1) *Unanimity*. Taking two of the possible choices on offer, if one choice is such that nobody prefers the other, the 'unanimously' preferred choice should be selected.
(2) *Non-dictatorship*. Nobody should be in the position of being able to impose the outcome she prefers when all others prefer an alternative outcome.
(3) *Transitivity*. The decision rule should be such that if it selects outcome A over outcome B and outcome B over outcome C, it does not select C over A.
(4) *Range*. All possible preference orderings of the choices on offer should be open to the participants in decision-making. The decision should not depend upon people holding certain views.
(5) *Independence of irrelevant alternatives*. When individuals choose between two alternatives, the outcome depends only upon their preferences relating to these alternatives and not upon how they feel about a third ('irrelevant') possibility. Thus if individuals are asked to choose between outcomes A and B, the decision rule should take account only of their relative preference between A and B and not of how they feel about a third outcome, C.

All of these conditions are eminently reasonable. After all, who could want a mechanism for making social choices to ignore outcomes that all preferred, to give dictatorial power to a single individual in the face of otherwise unanimous opposition, to make inconsistent choices, to work only when people preferred certain things or to be upset when an irrelevant option was thrown into the discussion? (This last condition sometimes confuses people. Consider the following example, however. You go into a Chinese restaurant and are offered a choice between two set meals, the A Special and the B Special. Your group chooses the A Special. The waiter then tells you that a new meal, the C Special, is available. In the light of this, your group changes its mind and chooses the B Special. The reason for this condition is that there is often a near-infinite number of things that are not on offer. Your choices between those that are on offer should not depend upon these.)

Arrow proved definitively that no social choice mechanism can avoid all of these pitfalls at the same time. The Liverpool example that we have just considered shows how the majority voting can produce inconsistent (or intransitive) social choices when we allow all possible methods of ranking the solutions. It cannot deliver consistency and range at the same time. Paradoxes of voting, however, are legion.

One of the more notorious of these is the plurality, or 'first-past-the-post', electoral system used in British and American elections. Imagine that three groups in a constituency prefer three candidates, thus:

Table 2   A Technicolor Paradox with plurality voting

	Percentage of voters	Preferences for candidates		
		1st preference	2nd preference	3rd preference
Group A	45	Ms Blue	Ms Mauve	Ms Pink
Group B	30	Ms Pink	Ms Mauve	Ms Blue
Group C	25	Ms Mauve	Ms Pink	Ms Blue

The first-past-the-post winner is Ms Blue, with 45 per cent of the votes. A majority of voters, however, prefers either of the other candidates by a 55–45 margin. (This is a violation of the independence criterion. Faced with a simple choice between Ms Blue and Ms Pink, the group prefers Ms Pink to Ms Blue. If a third, 'vote-splitting', candidate enters the fray, the group now prefers Ms Blue to Ms Pink. As a matter of fact, it also prefers Ms Mauve to Ms Pink, even though Ms Mauve never comes close to winning.)

Every voting system that has ever been devised, or ever could be devised, falls foul of one or other of Arrow's simple proscriptions. Some people have attempted to deny the importance of this result by attacking one or another of the five as irrelevant. Unfortunately for them, it has by now proved that any one of the five criteria can be dropped and still no conceivable voting system can simultaneously satisfy the remaining four. The absolute inevitability of voting paradoxes, I am afraid, is beyond dispute.

The literature in this field tends to be rather technical and intimidating. In order to satisfy yourself about its conclusions, however, you may care to amuse yourself by trying to devise a voting system that satisfies all criteria. (You will be in good company. This very endeavour was one of the many obsessions of Charles Dodgson, alias Lewis Carroll.) You will almost certainly fail, but if you should happen to succeed, patent your system. You have a brilliant career in political science in front of you.

HOW SHOULD COLLECTIVE DECISIONS BE MADE?

All methods of making collective choices must deal with the problems of distinguishing between collective and collected preferences, of intensity of preference and of paradox. No method can tackle these successfully, but these problems do impose standards against which any system can be judged. The arguments in this chapter must be set in context, however. At the end of the day, politics is about making collective decisions and taking collective action, and formal decision-making rules are only a part of this process. The existence of communities, for example, is a much more important factor. Since communities are characterized by common interests, formal collective decision-making mechanisms (if they are required at all) will process individual preferences that reflect the commonality of these interests. Paradox may not be rampant, therefore, because in practice only certain preferences are likely to be found in the population. Community interaction may enable genuinely

Making Collective Decisions

collective interests to be identified. Even different intensities of preference may be accommodated with the give and take of a stable community. When communities are large they may require inflexible decision rules, of course, but few social decisions are likely to be taken as a result of the inflexible application of a single rule. This is one of the most powerful arguments against direct democracy, and I will return to this in the following chapter. Most decision-making structures have several tiers, and problems that emerge at one level may be resolved at another. Indeed, as we shall shortly see, one of the main arguments for *representative* decision-making is precisely that the problems discussed in this chapter would result in an intolerable political process if inflexible formal decision rules were the only method of aggregating individual preferences.

Nevertheless, this chapter has shown that formal rules are important. In certain circumstances, the precise rule in question can influence the result. When new constitutions are written, for example, much thought is given to the decision rules imposed. Thus it has been argued that the emergence of Nazi Germany was made more likely because of the electoral system and decision-making process laid down by the Weimar Constitution. In the same way, de Gaulle insisted upon a new constitution before he 'rescued' France from its problems in Algeria. The Fifth Republic replaced the Fourth, and one of the most significant differences between the two constitutions was the electoral law that governed the choice of public representatives. In Britain the general elections of 1951 and February 1974 each produced decision-making paradoxes by which a party with fewer votes than a single rival actually 'won' the election. (The 1951 'winners' governed the country for four years.) More recently intense ideological disputes within the British Labour Party have surfaced as disputes over the rules for selecting both party leaders and parliamentary candidates. Nobody imagines that these debates are really about the rules. Everybody knows that they concern the rules because the precise rules adopted determine the result of a much deeper ideological conflict.

The argument that all methods for making collective

decisions are inevitably imperfect is not meant to depress you. It is instead intended to add some perspective to the often heated and usually misguided debates that take place over precise decision rules. We must, after all, take social decisions and this simple need overwhelms all others. Given this, we need to be aware of the problems involved, to remember that no method is perfect and to place little faith in formal rules.

7

Where Decisions are Made

DIRECT OR REPRESENTATIVE DECISION-MAKING?

The problem of *how* to take collective decisions is closely related to the problem of *where* they are taken. In all but the smallest of groups it will be impossible for everyone to get together and decide what to do. Presenting conditional choices to large groups may help, as we saw in the last chapter, but this technique is usually impractical. The main alternative is to break decision-making down into a series of stages. Each stage can then represent a small-group decision and may possibly be more 'collective' as a result. Each small-group decision may be seen as 'representing' that group, and these decisions may then be aggregated into one that 'represents' all groups. Whatever method is used for making social decisions and wherever decisions are made, however, one simple fact of life links them all. At the beginning of the process there will be a wide range of individual views. At the end of the process there will be one social decision.

This is why nearly all models of social decision-making have the same shape when they are viewed from a distance. That shape is a pyramid. This pyramid shape will be familiar to all. Whether you are the member of a company or a trade union, a pressure group or a government, a university or a crime syndicate, you will be aware of a decision-making hierarchy. Now, a high position in this hierarchy may not necessarily confer status or other benefits; all may be equal in every other respect. However, the process of boiling many

Invitation to Politics

preferences down to a single decision usually involves a system with several tiers, each operating with groups of a manageable size. If you want to understand any organization in which you participate, you need to have a picture in your mind of this decision-making hierarchy, and this picture will almost always take the shape of a pyramid.

Organizations *are* different, of course, and these differences become obvious when we approach our picture a little more closely. Pyramids are constructed in different ways. Many are rather like a Chinese puzzle. Lots of little decision pyramids must be cunningly assembled into a single whole. Some must be constructed from the bottom up, others from the top down. Some have broad bases; some have narrow bases. The universal pyramid shape, however, is a product of the fact that all decision-making systems select one choice from many.

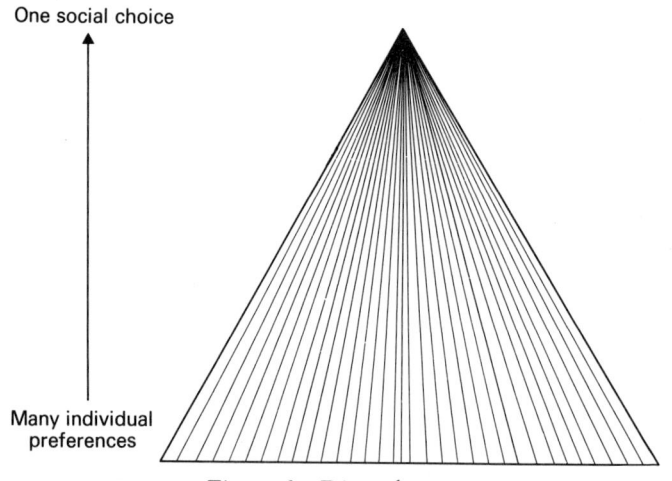

Figure 6   Direct democracy

Nowhere is this more apparent than with the simplest model of them all. This is the one that describes direct democracy and consists of the single pyramid shown in figure 6. The puzzle in this case is not to assemble the model but to discover whether it even vaguely resembles anything that can be found outside the smallest of groups in the real world. In small groups, of course, this single-stage decision-making process is very common and reflects decision-making without institutions in which all get together and decide the result. In large groups this model reflects what happens at a binding referendum. Everyone casts her vote, and the totals of votes cast decide the result. In each case we have a model of direct decision-making.

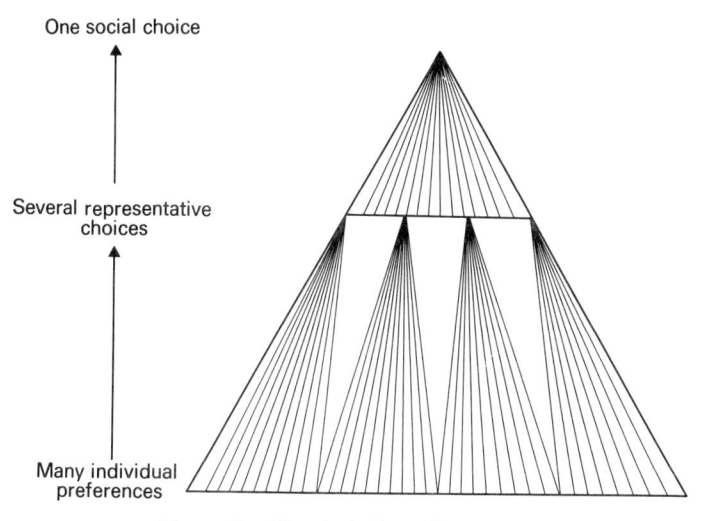

Figure 7 Simple indirect democracy

In most large groups, however, decision-making takes place in several stages. This is indirect decision-making and is modelled by first arranging a neat base of smaller decision pyramids and then topping off the model with a single, larger, pyramid that covers all of the points of the lower pyramids. This is shown in figure 7. In this case each pyramid presents a social choice problem. Different pyramids may present different problems that may well be solved in different ways. I am writing these words in front of a television set on which there is coverage of the annual delegate conference of the British Trades Union Congress. One delegate after another moves to the rostrum to speak, contributing a decision-making process that aggregates the

Invitation to Politics

preferences of many unions. Yet many of the delegates have been chosen in quite different ways. Some have been elected, by a range of different systems, while others have been selected. Delegates representing tiny unions may know many of the members well. Delegates representing huge unions have arrived at the conference as a result of a complex and often impersonal selection process within that union. This is probably entirely appropriate. It may well make good sense to organize decision-making differently in different types of unions and to process the views of their delegates by yet other methods. Indirect decision procedures make such flexibility possible. Thus a complex indirect decision model may look like that in figure 8.

All indirect models of decision-making have two key characteristics. The first is the use of decision units that are

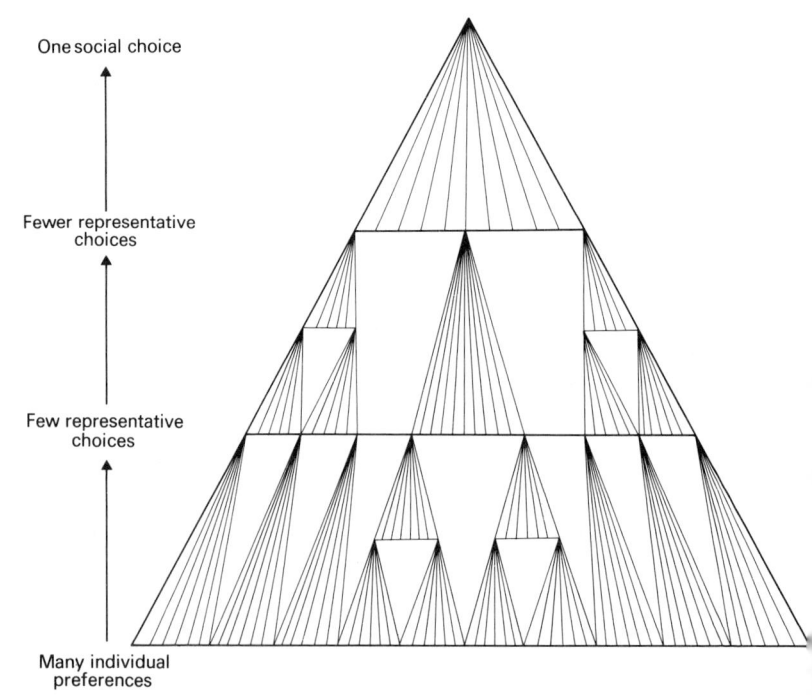

Figure 8   Complex indirect decisions

Where Decisions are Made

smaller than the whole group. The second is decision-making in a series of stages. In contrast, direct decision models represent whole-group, one-stage social choices.

DIRECT DECISION-MAKING

In the age of information technology 'direct democracy' is making something of a comeback. Instant polling via two-way cable television is already with us. At the moment this is confined to the entertainment industry, adding spice to quiz shows and popular current affairs programmes. Silicone Valley has, however, provided a technology that may revive interest in a 'populist' method of making decisions that is particularly susceptible to the types of problem we discussed in the previous chapter. These problems have not previously had much practical significance, since direct decision-making has never before been a practical proposition for large and complex groups.

One of the main reasons for this has traditionally been the inconvenience and expense of regularly polling the views of the whole population. The costs are huge. They fall upon individuals, who must drag themselves out into the windswept night in order to cast their votes and may rapidly get fed up with the whole process. They also fall upon the community as a whole, which must pay the direct price of organizing polls, counting votes and so on. Moreover, organizing polls takes time, and some decisions cannot wait. Providing the population with all of the information necessary to make good decisions not only takes time and money but also makes demands of voters that they may not be prepared to accept.

A good example of such problems can be found in the referenda that have recently been held in Britain. Both the Scottish referendum on proposals for a devolved Assembly and the national referendum on renegotiated terms for the British membership of the EEC consumed huge amounts of time and money. The EEC referendum in particular demonstrated that even if all voters are sent information on the issues at public expense, and even when those voters are confronted with the novelty of their first chance to participate in a direct national decision, levels of public interest and information can still be low. The country would grind to a halt if every public decision had to be taken on this basis.

Thus the main reasons why direct decision-making has rarely been used have been practical ones. Political theorists and many practising politicians regard this as just as well, however. The superficially 'democratic' façade of a system that lets *everyone* decide on issues is difficult to demolish. It is tempting indeed to equate majority rule with democracy, yet the two are by no means the same thing. The difficulties arise, however, because the most powerful objections to direct democracy tend to be rather technical.

The most important of these objections are based upon acute versions of the problems that we discussed in the previous chapter. They include the problem of taking account of different strengths of feeling on the same issue (and hence of what to do about intense minorities), the problem of finding a genuinely collective preference (as opposed to the collected preferences of all) and problems of inconsistency and paradox. I discussed a further objection when looking at justifications for having any government at all. This concerns the problems that may arise when related issues are considered in isolation rather than as part of a package. Direct democracy offers few solutions to these problems, while indirect systems at least offer some scope for the correction of the worst paradoxes.

In the first place, indirect systems break decision-making units down into smaller groups. A smaller group of decision-makers can function more easily as a collectivity rather than as a collection of individuals. Collective preferences and conditional choices may be easier to identify, since it is much easier to find out how the other members feel. A smaller group that has some idea of what the collective preferences might be is also better placed to spot paradoxes when they arise. These may then be corrected. Finally, a smaller group may be better placed to develop ideas about the relative strength of feeling of its members.

Where Decisions are Made

Most people, I am sure, will intuitively sympathize with this argument. Many may have already come across it in one form or another. Even when a small group does have formal procedures, people can step back from the outcome and say, 'This is not what *we* really want.' Because a small group can have a sense of 'we', if you like, it can see a paradox when it arises. Those who have voted in a large group decision may be disappointed with the result but may reluctantly agree that it must be what 'they' wanted. This may not be true at all, but a larger group offers no scope for judging the decision against a commonsense feel for the situation. When you lose out as a result of a small-group decision you may be sad, but you will accept that the result reflects the group's feelings. When you lose out in a larger and more formal process, you often feel frustrated that somehow the decision does not really reflect what all want together.

In addition to exaggerating the disadvantages of large-group decision-making, direct democracy is a one-stage process. Decision processes that have several stages offer more scope for problems and paradoxes to become apparent and, possibly, to be corrected. Indirect systems allow for several stages of input into decisions. As we shall shortly see, pressure-group activity and the trading of one policy against another at least offer an opportunity to take account of intensities of feeling and collective preferences. These processes operate at the second stage of a two-stage process and have little role in a direct democracy. In practice, logrolling and pressure groups may have the opposite effect, distorting decisions and creating paradoxes of their own. Their precise effect can be estimated only by getting down to cases. Direct democracy, however, necessarily has far less 'play' in it. It will inevitably be more rigid than indirect democracy, and rigid systems always run the risk of generating paradoxes.

In addition to exaggerating the problems associated with all systems for making social choices, direct democracy provides less scope for making integrated decisions about a range of issues. We have already seen that one of the functions of a legislature is to enable packages of related decisions to be formulated and, in particular, to enable the development of

Invitation to Politics

budgets. If all issues are put directly to electors, the consequent decisions may be quite incompatible, even if each elector is perfectly consistent. We saw in an earlier chapter, for example, that voters may want to increase help for the old and the young, yet wish to pay for only one of these things. Direct democracy tends to bypass this integrating stage and thus is more likely to result in incompatible bundles of collective decisions.

None of the theoretical objections to direct democracy is in any way mitigated by the arrival of cable TV or electronic referenda. Indeed, there is a further objection that arises from the cheapness of electronic decision-making. One of the things that governments do is to replace markets when they either fail or are inefficient. We have already seen that governments need some form of feedback mechanism in order to do this effectively. They can get this feedback by using alternative *numéraire* goods such as time and energy. They may take willingness to devote time and energy to a matter as an indicator of concern. This is one of the conventional justifications for the role of pressure groups. In addition, when even voting takes some time and energy, it is reasonable to assume that those electors who care least are among those who do not bother to vote. Their views therefore are effectively given less weight. If voting were effectively freed of any costs, however, *apathetic* majority rule could become even more likely. Even those who cared little about the result might sit in their armchairs and press buttons on the remote controls of their TV sets. Their views would weigh as much as the views of those who were at least prepared to get cold and wet. Electronic democracy would thus serve to exaggerate the faults of direct democracy by reducing the time and effort required to participate in decisions, making it even more difficult to take account of varying intensities of preference.

Once more, I suspect that most people realize this intuitively. People do not take what they see on TV too seriously and, I am sure, would feel uneasy about the genuine representativeness of decisions taken on the basis of TV polls. Such polls are an interesting enough way to sound out opinion, fly kites and bounce ideas around, but would you really feel happy if people took binding collective decisions from the comfort of their armchairs? I suspect not. The great danger of such polls is that they are seductive, yet it is hard to put your finger on quite *why* you feel uneasy about them.

If the current leap forward in information technology makes direct democracy a cheap and viable possibility, the superficially attractive case 'Let the people decide' will be hard to answer. The statement that the people should not decide looks suspiciously like an elitist judgement that the people are not fit to decide. I hope that I have shown that this is not the case. The distinctions involved, however, are both subtle and open to abuse or over-simplification by self-interested politicians.

Half-way between direct and indirect decision-making comes the referendum. Very few political systems use referenda for collective decision-making as a matter of course, although a partial exception is Switzerland. The normal position is for referenda to be used in certain circumstances, the most common of which is constitutional change. New constitutions are often put 'directly to the people' by means of a referendum. This is an obvious expedient, since an old constitution is presumably being replaced because it is unsatisfactory. It would be difficult to argue, therefore, that it should lay down the rules for settling on a new one. In the same way, amendments to existing constitutions often require a referendum. This is the case, for example, In Italy and Ireland, though not in the United States. In such cases constitutional referenda must usually produce a qualified majority (such as two-thirds or three-quarters of voters or the electorate) rather than the simple majority (50 per cent plus one) that is often considered sufficient for lesser decisions.

There are three reasons for preferring a qualified majority for constitutional change in particular and for direct democracy in general. The first is that all constitutions are intended to be inherently conservative. They are intended to preserve a set of 'rules of the game' that enable the game to continue in the face of short-term pressures for change. If the rules can be changed too easily, it becomes almost impossible to be sure about what the game actually is.

In the second place, qualified majorities are intended to provide some protection against the oppression of large intense minorities by an apathetic majority. This protection may be maintained in the cause of social efficiency or out of respect for the rights of the minorities involved. If there is a two-thirds majority for some issue, this means that there are twice as many in favour as against. The minority must feel twice as strongly about the issue than the majority before social welfare is reduced by qualified majority rule. With a three-quarters majority, the minority must feel three times as strongly. With a simple majority, on the other hand, the minority need only feel 1 per cent more strongly for a socially inefficient solution to result. If we take a constitutional matter such as freedom of religion, and then take an aspect of this such as religious education in schools, it might well be the case that those in favour of compulsory religious education feel much more strongly than those against it. Yet those against may form an apathetic majority. They may vote to abolish religious education in a referendum on a constitutional amendment. The sense of loss felt by the intense religious minority as a whole may well, however, exceed that of the majority taken as a whole. The requirement for a two-thirds or three-quarters majority for constitutional change reduces the chance that this might happen. Those in favour of religious education may feel just as strongly, of course, even if they are only a 20 per cent minority. But at least the chance that the strong feelings of 40 per cent of the population may be frustrated is reduced by qualified majority rule.

Unfortunately, the reverse problem is now introduced. An apathetic *minority* can, with qualified majority decision-making, block changes that are intensely desired by a majority. Intense minorities are thus protected against changes that they oppose but are not helped to introduce changes that they want. Thus qualified majority rule can work only when there is a status quo, as is the case with constitutional change. There is a good chance that nothing will be approved by two-thirds of the population (say if 55 per cent favour one thing and 45 per cent another). When decisions must be taken and there is no status quo – for example when we select representatives or must respond to a totally new situation – then qualified majority rule is ineffective.

Finally, qualified majorities are felt to be less susceptible to paradox, although this is true only if the status quo is regarded as better than most alternatives. The paradoxes generated by qualified majority decision-making tend to result in the retention of a status quo that few people want when there is a disagreement over what to replace it with. For example, imagine that we want to reform the system of local government. Ninety-eight per cent of the population agree that the current system is hopeless. This group, however, splits evenly into those who want local government abandoned altogether and those who want it greatly strengthened. Qualified majority rule would produce no change, the outcome desired by only 2 per cent of the population. The remaining 98 per cent may even have this outcome at the bottom of their list. Thus all justifications for the use of referenda with qualified majorities tend to be conservative, since they greatly increase the chance of retaining the status quo.

Apart from the ratification of constitutional change, referenda can be used for the direct decisions on more mundane policy matters. The position here is far less clear-cut. No country other than Switzerland uses referenda as a matter of routine for a range of policy decisions, although many US local authorities must put all proposals for public borrowing directly to their electorates. Most policy referenda are thus discretionary in practice, and the discretionary use of referenda is highly controversial.

In theory policy referenda are used either to resolve deadlocks with legislatures or to make decisions on issues that were not in contention at the time of the preceding election. In such general terms, it might seem unreasonable to object to the use of referenda. The trouble is that when discretion is involved a referendum may be invoked as a ploy when the result is likely to be favourable. A clear-cut example of this was the poll held in 1973 in Northern Ireland concerning the future of the border with the Republic. Voters were asked whether they wished to remain part of the United Kingdom. There was never any doubt that the result would be a 'yes' majority; the original boundaries of Northern Ireland were drawn so as to ensure this. The poll was clearly invoked in order to provide further support for the argument against change. I doubt very much whether such a poll would have been held at all if the result could have gone either way and if a 'no' majority would have been embarrassing.

This strategic use of referenda depends heavily on the superficial attractiveness of equating the collectively preferred outcome with the majority decision. It thus depends upon the very weakness of direct democracy. A well-known ploy in all forms of political interaction is to bind yourself irrevocably to a particular course of action. Thus bound, you cannot be seduced or frightened away from it, and your bargaining position is strengthened. Referenda can be used to establish such commitments. After all, having had a national referendum that favoured the restoration of hanging, it would be much easier for those who agreed with the result to invoke a mandate that they could not betray.

A final problem with all referenda concerns the precise phrasing of the questions and the number of alternatives on offer. The increasing use of surveys has made us all aware that the answer you get depends crucially upon the way in which you ask the question. Some words are more emotive than others, while even sentence construction can have profound influence. Imagine that the country was asked to decide between two defence policies, one very expensive and powerful, the other less powerful and less expensive. Policy A can be described as 'expensive but powerful' or 'powerful but expensive', The very same words have different meanings. Policy B is either 'cheaper but less powerful' or 'less powerful but cheaper'. If I wanted Policy A, I would pose the choice between:

POLICY A: Expensive but powerful
or POLICY B: Cheaper but less powerful.

Where Decisions are Made

If I wanted Policy B, I would ask people to decide between:

POLICY A: Powerful but expensive
or POLICY B: Less powerful but cheaper.

I am still quite certain that the same electorate would vote differently in each case. (I could also greatly enhance the chances of Policy A by throwing in a number of variations on Policy B in order to split the opposing vote.)

To summarize, the problems with all referenda are the problems of direct democracy in general, compounded by the problems of questionnaire design. All forms of direct democracy can be seductively hard to resist, given the superficial attractiveness of equating democracy with majority rule and the rather technical nature of the powerful objections to this. Discretionary referenda compound the problems of direct democracy still further. The paradoxes of decision-making are at their most dangerous when they can be selectively exploited by those in power.

INDIRECT DECISION-MAKING: 'REPRESENTATIVE DEMOCRACY'

None of us lives in a direct democracy. Most of us participate in decision-making only by proxy. We do this by attempting to influence delegates or representatives who are supposed to act in our interests. We are all, therefore, concerned with the problem of precisely who represents which interests, and how. This problem has four components.

It concerns, first, the relationship between us mere mortals and those who act for us. Specifically, this is a matter of whether we are better served by those to whom we delegate authority or by those who act as our representatives. The second aspect of the problem concerns the basis of delegation or representation. This problem boils down to a decision about which political constituencies should be represented in higher-level decisions. The final two aspects of the problem concern how we select those who act for us. Candidates must first be selected. Representatives or delegates must be then selected from these.

These components are related parts of a single problem, as I have said. Too often people forget this and concentrate upon electoral systems, for example, without recognizing that the role of those who are elected, the constituency that they represent and the manner in which candidates are selected all interact with the electoral system to create a single decision-making system. Yet no electoral system can be 'fair' if the candidates presented for election represent nobody or have no power. Conversely, any electoral system can be made much fairer if constituencies are sensitively defined. Thus while it is necessary for the sake of clarity to talk about things one at a time, you should never forget that each aspect of the problem must be thought about in relation to the others rather than in splendid isolation.

Delegates or representatives?

A delegate has a mandate from those who select her to act for them. To delegate power is to hand it down in specified circumstances. It gives no discretion to the delegate when those circumstances do not apply. As we shall see, a mandate of this sort is both a strength and a weakness. All forms of discretion imply flexibility, and there are occasions when flexibility can be very valuable. Unforeseen circumstances may arise and may then be exploited. On other occasions flexibility can be a liability. When opponents know that you *could* concede if you wanted to, they may be more inclined to try to twist your arm. If they know that a concession is beyond your control, you may have a better chance of getting your way.

According to a very strict interpretation of the role of a delegate, the inflexibility of her mandate can be absolute. Thus if I delegate you to vote for Jones at the general assembly of my trade union, it could be argued that you have the power only to vote for Jones. By implication, if you voted for Smith, your vote would be invalid. You would have ceased to be my delegate by exceeding your mandate and would have no other right to vote. This is precisely the circumstance that led to the downfall in 1982 of Sydney Weighell, General Secretary of the British National Union of Railwaymen.

Mandated to vote one way and voting another, he lost his job, even though what he did, *as he saw it,* was in the interests of his union. In the same way if my delegates go into a pay negotiation with management with a mandate to settle for no less than a 10 per cent rise, their acceptance of 8 per cent, even if they honestly see this as being in my interests, is binding on nobody. They simply do not have the power to make such a concession.

The power of delegates is rarely interpreted in this very strict sense. Most of us accept that, within limits, our delegates may also act as our representatives. Nevertheless, delegates who exceed their mandates must rely on the goodwill of their sponsors. If they forfeit this, they do not have a leg to stand on. If they retain it, they have in fact become representatives.

Your representative, on the other hand, *represents* your interests. In this case the mandate is much less explicit, and a representative may have considerable freedom of action in unforeseen circumstances. Accurate representation of interests may occur for three reasons. Your representative may represent you in the fullest sense, being like you in every important respect. This means that her interests are your interests. Trust or power need not be involved, since, by acting in her own interest, your representative acts in your interest as well. Thus, if you are a black working-class Catholic mother of two, and if you consider these to be the important interests that you wish to pursue, you may place your faith in a representative who also has all of these properties because, as 'someone like you', she will act as you would in similar circumstances. She does not have to imagine what you would do. She does what she wants on the assumption that this is what you would want. In practice this form of representation is rarely pushed to the limit, although (particularly in elections with multi-member constituencies) parties are often at pains to put forward a slate of candidates who between them reflect the interests to which the parties wish to appeal. The candidates may include a woman, a black, a trade unionist and so on because parties expect voters to feel happier supporting 'people like themselves'.

If the private interests of represented and representative differ, as they often will in practice, then a representative must be either trusted or controlled. We have already seen that trust is more likely in small communities than in large ones. Thus a small group may select a representative member and feel able to trust her because of the give and take of small-group interaction. A small group of workers could, for example, choose one of their number to negotiate a pay rise for them in the hope and expectation that this person would not accept a management bribe and agree to a pittance for the rest. They could do this in the knowledge that their representative must return to live and work with them and would not want to do so as an outcast. Even when small groups resort to more or less formal decision-making institutions, therefore, the importance of trust gives a representative a rather special role.

In larger and less trusting groups a representative may be subject to control. Control is quite different from a mandate. It usually involves an opportunity for the represented to sack the representative if her performance is unsatisfactory. Control is usually formalized by providing for the periodic selection or reselection of representatives by some means or another. This, of course, is the function that elections are usually held to fulfil. Since the constituencies in most modern states are too large and too varied to be communities in their own right, formal control rather than informal trust is needed to ensure that representatives really do represent the interests of constituents. In effect, elections provide for the recall of representatives, and the threat of replacement is held to give constituents at least limited control over them. Representatives must please their constituents if they are to continue to act for them in the future.

Such control thus provides only an indirect mandate for representatives, who are not told what to do but must do things that please their constituents if they are to remain in office. They cannot therefore claim that they *must* act in certain ways, though they may well claim that either they ought to do so or, if they do not, they will be unable to act at all in the future. Thus the role of a representative and the process by which representatives are reselected are two matters that are intimately connected. If selection procedures are imperfect, so is constituency control. In the absence of trust, representatives cease to represent.

Sometimes we are better served by delegates than by representatives; sometimes the reverse is the case. The advantage of having a delegate is that control is much more rigid, while a direct mandate clearly specifies the ways in which a delegate may act on our behalf. The disadvantage is that mandates rarely cover all contingencies. As a result, they can sometimes be counter-productive.

A good example is the British Labour Party's perennial debates over how the party leader should be selected. At present the leader is elected by an electoral college, consisting of delegates and representatives from affiliated trade unions, constituency parties, and MPs. There has been much discussion about how union delegates and representatives should behave. Some have proposed that all union representatives should become delegates, mandated by union members to vote in certain ways rather than using their discretion. Now, the Labour Party has been described as the most sophisticated electorate in the world. One consequence of sophisticated voting is that, in order to get your own way, you do not simply vote first for the first person on your list, second for the second and so on. The Labour leadership election proceeds in stages by successively eliminating those with fewest votes until one candidate has an overall majority. All sorts of tactical considerations come into play with such a system. If your chosen candidate looks safe on the first ballot, it may well be in your interest to vote for someone else. This may keep a second choice in the running at the expense of your least preferred candidate. If you are super-sophisticated, it may even seem worth voting for your least preferred candidate, Ms X, in the first ballot. This may provoke a 'Stop X' band wagon and ensure her defeat.

The fact that unions have large block votes means that the vote of a single union may well have predictable consequences. The possibilities are so numerous that they simply cannot all be covered by an explicit mandate. Even leaving aside the most Machiavellian strategies, the mandate would still be so complex that it would be difficult to specify and impossible to agree. It would need to take the form: 'Vote for A on the first ballot unless B looks as if she will be eliminated, in which case vote for B. If C is eliminated, vote for B on the second ballot. If neither is eliminated, vote for A. On the third ballot . . . '

The problem of specifying a sophisticated mandate is hard enough for leadership elections, but it is well-nigh impossible for votes on policy. After all, candidates cannot be amended, diluted or otherwise subtly modified in the conference hall. The range of possible proposals on a single policy issue, however, is enormous. To tie your delegate to a particular strategy in a sophisticated election is to reduce your chances of success. It is far more effective to set a representative a general goal (such as 'Do your best to stop Denis Healey and elect Tony Benn') and to allow her a free hand in achieving this.

There is a powerful tradition in Western political systems that Members of Parliament are representatives rather than delegates. The price we all pay for this is that we cannot complain too loudly if our representative departs from the 'promises' made at election time, provided that such departures are made in good faith and reflect genuine attempts to represent our interests in changed situations. Such qualifications, of course, open up considerable scope for controversy. The subsequent judgements we make on the fate of our representatives will combine judgements of good faith with judgements of tactical competence.

Who do representatives represent?

Indirect decisions are thus made by people who represent the wishes of a group of constituents. We therefore need to know quite precisely which people each representative represents. Obviously, the more homogeneous the views of a group of constituents, the more likely it is that a single view will be a fair representation of the whole. Thus if a constituency really does correspond to a community with a large number of common interests, the role of the representative is relatively straightforward. A group of people with conflicting views cannot conceivably be represented by a single individual. When a constituency cuts across several communities with conflicting interests, a representative may face severe difficulties in deciding which views to represent. Thus the position of a representative is much less controversial when she represents an isolated mining community, for example, than when she represents a rather amorphous big-city suburb. A representative can, of course, present a range of views in a debate on an issue. Called upon to act or to vote, however, one view must prevail. The pattern of constituencies in any indirect democracy, therefore, has a crucial effect on the outcome of the decision-making process, though it is important to note that I am here using the word 'constituency' in a rather broad sense. I refer in general to those who are represented rather than to a particular geographical area.

In practice, we have inherited a geographical method of defining political constituencies. The boundaries of constituencies are drawn on maps. In principle, the reasons for this are far from obvious, since there is no reason to suppose that a geographical method of representation will be better than any other. Geographical interests are not particularly predominant in most Western systems. Starting from scratch, we might well decide that social or economic factors provide a more sensible basis for organizing political representation. Historical and practical factors, however, have determined the system that most of us actually use.

Historically, the British legislature developed from the feudal system. The nation was administered on behalf of the monarch by feudal lords. They were rewarded not by salaries but by grants of land. The right to income from this land, and from all those who used it, offset a consequent obligation to administer it. The very restricted nature of communications and the localized nature of the economy meant that smallish geographical areas were the only feasible bases of administration and representation. With the emergence of an elected Parliament, geographical areas continued to form the building blocks of the political system, a system unchanged in this respect even today.

The representation of electoral interests on the basis of geographical constituencies has one enormous practical advantage. It is unambiguous. Once the boundary lines are drawn, everyone falls into one constituency or another. Furthermore, until recent advances in micro-electronics, communication usually involved some form of physical movement, so that it tended to be much easier to communicate over short distances.

If the representative of a geographical constituency acts 'in the interests of her constituents', however, what happens when those interests conflict? The precise practical answer depends upon the electoral system in use, but the problem would be much simpler if constituencies were defined by criteria that ensured that they more clearly reflected communities of interest. Those who live in the same geographical area do, of course, have interests in common. None who live in Liverpool would like to see the city used as a site for nuclear test explosions. None want the air polluted, and few want the local economy to suffer worse recession than other parts of the country. Nearly all want a low crime rate, a pleasant environment, good roads and so on. In short, many outputs of government are necessarily delivered locally, and this generates a local community of interest.

Many outputs, however, are delivered nationally. The performance of the economy, a central concern of contemporary politics, affects local regions differently. More significant, it also affects different nationwide social groups in different ways. Some (casual labourers, for example) are more likely to become unemployed than others (such as tenured university lecturers or established civil servants). Poor people in large families are hit harder by high food prices than are rich bachelors. The self-employed are affected less than employees by wage policies. The wealthy are worst hit by wealth taxes and so on. It is almost certainly true that decisions affecting national policies are more important and more controversial than those affecting outputs that are delivered locally. Yet a system that selects representatives on the basis of local constituencies reflects the interests of national groups only by accident.

Where Decisions are Made

This is not quite as bad as it might seem. In practice, geographical systems of representation can rely upon local housing segregation. If such segregation did not occur, the system would not work. British politics in the mid-twentieth century has been characterized by the interests of two large social classes, which have selected the members of the two main political parties, the Conservative and Labour parties, to represent their interests. Class interests have, very generally, been represented, but only because housing in Britain is intensely segregated on class lines. This segregation reflects a split between council or private tenants on the one hand and private owner occupiers on the other, with further segregation by wealth in the owner-occupied sector. The housing market has thus produced geographical clusters of people with common social and economic interests. Those interests that are not clustered in this way are not represented. These include, for example, the interests of the young, the old, the sick and indeed any other interest that does not correspond closely to socio-economic housing segregation. This problem is exaggerated in a system that embraces many small single-member constituencies and would be eliminated only by a system of pure proportional representation based on a single national constituency. Indeed, the British Boundary Commissioners, who draw up constituency boundaries, are specifically instructed to ignore all 'political' considerations when they do this. They are directed instead to concentrate upon geographical, numerical and, possibly, 'cultural' criteria.

There is no reason in theory why parliamentary constituencies should not be defined on a completely different basis. They could reflect social and economic interests (such as social class, occupation or wealth), demographic criteria (such as age and sex), ethnic criteria (such as race or religion) and so on. Indeed, many other bodies use such bases for representation. The British Trades Union Congress represents workers by union (and hence by occupation) and by sex. Nobody has ever suggested that all Newcastle workers should have one representative and all Birmingham workers another, despite the fact that all Newcastle workers have some trade union interests in common, particularly those that relate to regional economic policy.

Other bases for constituency representation have also occasionally been tried at the level of national politics, although such 'corporate' arrangements have unfortunately become associated with totalitarian government and, in particular, with the organization of the Fascist state. Ireland, however, developing its new constitution in the heyday of such ideas, did set up a Senate reflecting corporate economic and social interests. Candidates for the Irish Senate contest elections for various 'panels'. There is an Administrative Panel, an Agricultural Panel, a Cultural and Educational Panel, a Labour Panel, an Industrial and Commercial Panel and so on. Members of the Irish Senate represent these, rather than geographical, constituencies.

Those who argue against the direct electoral representation of social and economic interests do so on the grounds that it would reinforce social divisions. This is clearly a theoretical possibility, but I am not convinced that people in Britain are less class-conscious than they otherwise would be because the two main classes are locally represented by a single MP. Deliberate refusal to select representatives from constituencies with common interests *might* force the accommodation of conflicts to begin at an earlier stage in the process, but it might equally increase the alienation and disillusion of those who lost out. The reconciliation of conflicts is usually felt to be the task of the second tier of an indirect democracy. In this case it would equally be argued that the clear and unambiguous representation of conflicting interests in a legislature was a good thing.

As it happens, of course, practical arguments have won the day. The facts that geographical constituencies place everyone unambiguously in one constituency and that housing segregation does produce local clusters of national interest combine to make the current system seem the obvious choice. I do not wish to put the case either way, merely to point out that there is a choice. The type of constituency that most of us use to select representatives has historical roots and some practical advantages. We should not forget, however, that it is no more than one among many imperfect solutions to the problem of deciding whom representatives should represent.

How are representatives selected?

The third element in any system of indirect decision-making concerns the method by which representatives are selected. In terms of national politics, this boils down to the system of electoral laws. The process of selection has two main stages. The first is the selection of candidates. The second is the choice, from among candidates, of representatives.

The selection of candidates is usually given much less consideration than the choice of representatives, despite the fact that, in quantitative terms at least, the choice of candidates from the population narrows down the options much more dramatically than the choice of representatives from candidates. Whatever electoral system is used, the inescapable truth is that every British election has 30 million or so electors, 2,000 or 3,000 candidates, and 600 or so representatives. In a given constituency there may be 100,000 electors, four candidates and one representative. The consequence is that 99,996 people are not chosen as a result of the selection of candidates, while three more are not chosen as a result of the election that follows. I would not go so far as to argue that candidate selection is 33,332 times more important than the subsequent election. I would argue, however, that it is a greatly underrated element in the system of indirect democracy.

This problem is further compounded by the fact that electoral law rarely extends to regulating the selection of candidates. This phase in the process is usually covered by a simple provision that more or less anyone who wishes to do so can stand as a candidate. Yet, if a candidate is not backed by the resources of a major political party, her election is extremely unlikely. Despite this, legal 'interference' in the running of political parties, beyond some stipulations about the lengths to which any candidate may go in order to get elected, is usually considered to be an infringement of political freedom.

The process of candidate selection and the precise electoral system in use are in practice closely related. Electoral systems specifically designed to produce proportional representation of parties must devise some legal definition of a party. On the basis of this specific definition, some interest groups must be ruled not to be parties, so the taboo against 'interference' is breached. Some electoral systems depend upon party 'lists' that state the order in which candidates are to be elected as the party gets more votes. Such lists place considerable power in the hands of the party hierarchy. Putting someone at the top of the list guarantees her election; putting the same person at the bottom guarantees her defeat (although some list systems allow electors to state their own views about this ordering). This aspect of candidate selection is thus an important element in the decision to introduce, or to resist, an electoral system that uses party lists.

Proportional representation tends to encourage more candidates to stand and tends not to result in one-party government. These two quite separate considerations combine to increase the number of viable alternatives on offer and thus to reduce the practical consequences of candidate selection. In contrast, the first-past-the-post system tends to reduce the number of viable alternatives. Candidate selection is thus at its most crucial.

It is difficult to generalize about the candidate selection. This is one of the reasons why political scientists, being in the business of making generalizations, tend to ignore it. A few common features can, however, be noted.

The first and most important is that candidates tend to be selected by those who are active in the party at some level or another. Party activists tend to be a self-appointed bunch of people, and there is good reason to suppose that their views do not correspond with those of the mass electorate. They are usually active because they have some particular views that they wish to promote. They want their candidate to succeed, of course, but they wish her to succeed in a particular way that corresponds with their views. Their need for a popular candidate is thus moderated by the desire for one who thinks like them. This factor becomes more important as the seat in question becomes an increasingly safe bet for the incumbent party, and the election result will therefore be less dependent upon the precise candidate selected. In a highly marginal seat, where a few votes either way might make the difference between winning and losing, party activists may feel more constrained to put up someone capable of attracting widespread support rather than an unpopular candidate who happens to share their own views of the world.

In the second place, candidates are usually chosen as a result of some formal selection process within the party. As we have already seen, any such process is subject to paradox and manipulation and may well produce odd results. Furthermore, there is scope for those activists who become expert at manipulating the system to acquire a powerful influence over the selection process.

We voters are often unaware of the process of candidate selection. We are usually faced with a simple choice between the candidates of rival parties. The extent to which their selection affects our decisions will depend upon whether we are likely to vote habitually for the same party, regardless of its candidates, possibly because we feel that the party is the one that always acts in our best general interests. The greater the level of habitual voting, the more important is candidate selection.

Given a set of candidates, the precise electoral system in use obviously affects the result. There is extensive and heated debate about the 'best' electoral system. Much of this debate concerns the desirability or otherwise of the coalition governments that proportional systems undoubtedly make more likely. I will return to this matter shortly. Leaving aside the matter of coalitions, the debate can be briefly summarized.

One possibility is a first-past-the-post system, which is used in Britain and is based on single-member constituencies. In this system the candidate with more votes than any other – the one who gains a *plurality* but not necessarily a *majority* of the votes – is the winner. The main alternative is usually seen as proportional representation (PR). PR is, in fact, a general term covering a host of different systems. At one extreme the whole country may be treated as a single constituency, and seats may be allocated to political parties in almost perfect proportion to the votes they gain. The single transferable vote system (STV) system used in Ireland, by contrast, uses smallish multi-member constituencies and a ballot in which voters rank candidates in order. STV produces proportional representation of parties only if voters tend to vote in sequence for the candidates of the same party. It does, however, leave candidate selection rather more in the hands of voters. Other systems (for example, that used in Germany) correct at a national level the disproportionate results of a first-past-the-post system, awarding additional members to disadvantaged parties.

General arguments in favour of the first-past-the-post system claim that it is more important to vote for the candidate than for the party, and that single-member constituencies prevent representatives from passing the buck when the problems arise. They also stress the fact that parties do not need to be legally recognized and that party oligarchs do not control candidate selection. In addition, a virtue can be made of the unrepresentative nature of first-past-the-post results if they encourage government responsiveness. This electoral system greatly magnifies changes in electoral opinion. If 7 or 8 per cent of voters change their minds, this usually produces a landslide defeat for the government. Those who favour a first-past-the-post system argue that this exaggerated feedback keeps governments on their toes.

Arguments in favour of PR depend to a large extent upon 'fairness' and, by implication, upon efficiency. In the first place, proportionality is seen as a good in itself, equated with democracy. In the second place, PR systems are more effective at representing national, as opposed to regional or local, interests. It is claimed that this is not only good in itself but also efficient, reducing the possibility of unwanted decisions. In the third place, if first-past-the-post systems are responsive, they achieve this by being volatile. Advocates of PR stress the continuous lurches of policy that result. Some have even argued that many of Britain's recent problems could have been avoided if some policy (almost *any* policy) had been settled upon and implemented for a long time. Plurality systems certainly do encourage continuous policy shifts.

Where Decisions are Made

I do not wish to enter into this debate, which is always heated and rarely useful. I must say, however, that it seems to me that few people these days vote for candidates rather than parties, although they are always grateful for a good candidate rather than a bad one. As a consequence, any arguments that stress the merits of not needing to recognize the existence of political parties are anachronistic.

PUTTING ON THE PRESSURE

Democracy is not majority rule. The arguments against direct democracy hinge upon the fact that in a system of one-stage decision-making by all it is almost impossible to distinguish between the choice-preferred-by-most and the choice-most-preferred-by-all. Indirect decision-making is a process involving two or more stages. At each of these stages it is possible for inputs to be made that may correct the problems of intense minorities, of paradox or of discriminating between collective preferences and the collected preferences of all. One influential version of democratic theory, the 'pluralist' view, lays particular stress upon the political pressure that may be exerted by groups that intervene in the political process. Indirect democracy, it is claimed, allows such groups more avenues of influence.

We have also seen that some form of feedback mechanism must be introduced to guarantee the effective allocation of resources when politics replaces the market. The competitive market provides feedback when dissatisfied consumers fail to buy if they are offered a bad deal. Private companies wanting to maximize profits must therefore take account of consumer preference. Consumers of most public services, on the other hand, are 'locked in'. They may stop consuming only by emigrating. An alternative method for consumers to express dissatisfaction is to complain. Governments can discriminate between intensities of dissatisfaction, however, only if complaining costs resources. If complaining is free, then we will all be complaining most of the time. No one will be able to tell, from our complaints, which are the most urgent problems. This problem is compounded by the fact that once we are complaining anyway it tends to make sense to exaggerate our complaints. Say your bus was ten minutes late and you missed 600 seconds of valuable drinking time. If you decided to moan about this, you might elaborate a little, claiming to have missed a train and therefore the plane that was to take you on the holiday of a lifetime. If effective complaints cost resources, however, you will make them only when you are genuinely aggrieved.

Individuals can rarely complain effectively in isolation. They must organize themselves into groups in order to exert concerted pressure. The logic of allowing pressure groups a role in the decision-making process is now clear. Those groups that are prepared to do most in order to change something can be assumed to feel most strongly about it. If they can exert a greater influence on decision-making than others, there is some chance that those who feel most strongly are more likely to be satisfied than the apathetic, who will not think it worthwhile spending time, energy and money on exerting political pressure. For example, people may form a pressure group in order to resist the location of a new airport near their homes. Another group may promote twenty-four-hour-a-day opening for pubs and bars. If the airport group meets with more success by dint of the time and effort expended on their campaigning, this might be thought to be no bad thing. Their willingness to try harder might be taken as an indicator of their concern. In this case, those who are more concerned will have more influence on what happens.

There are a number of obvious objections to this argument. In the first place, while time and energy might seem to be evenly distributed throughout the population, this becomes less clearly the case the more closely you look at things. There is an uneven distribution in the availability of *spare* time in the population, and some groups are better off than others. At one extreme we may find a relatively poor working-class family with several children; both parents must work, and at least one is a shift worker. At the other end of the scale we may find a recently retired professional couple, whose children have left home and live far away. There is a huge

Where Decisions are Made

chasm of difference between the two households in terms of the time available to each for political activity. While it may well be true that if you really want to do something, you can find the time, that is not the point. If we use the time that people spend on exerting pressure as a measure of the intensity of their feeling, we face the problem that spare time may be so precious to one household that its members are provoked into political action only by the most intense feelings, while time is so freely available to another household that it finds pressure-group activity worthwhile even when it feels much less strongly about an issue.

The same problem exists in the case of the other resources needed for the successful exertion of group pressure. These include energy, skill, experience, self-confidence, knowledge, contacts, professional qualifications and, of course, money. A retired couple may have less energy to spare than a young professional, while a manual labourer may simply be too exhausted to play politics after a day's work. Skill, at least latent political skill, is probably the asset most evenly distributed throughout the population, although it tends to become effective only as a result of experience. The belief that political action is pointless is a great disincentive to action, yet self-confidence can develop quite dramatically as a result of a single successful experience of pressure-group activity. Skill, experience and self-confidence thus interact to prompt those who have acted successfully in the past to do so again. In the same situation others who have not crossed the threshold of action (not necessarily because they are more apathetic) stay at home. Thus you will often find that once one local pressure group has been successful new pressure groups will be easier to form in the same community. Once the proposed airport has been stopped, for example, the threatened closure of the local school may be easier to block as people develop the experience and confidence needed for the successful application of political pressure.

When it comes to getting things done, knowing the right person can be invaluable. At worst, you can find out who to talk to rather than being passed from pillar to post by the front office. At best, you may have a mole to leak inside information to you or a powerful bureaucrat to cut corners on your behalf. If the matter comes to court or to an inquiry, you will need professionals. How much more effective you will be, and how much less money you will need, if your pressure group includes lawyers, architects, surveyors, accountants and all of those others whose sayings carry clout in their chosen fields.

Finally, and there is no getting around this, pressure is much easier to exert if you have money. Groups need organization, and money can save you a lot of time when it comes to organizing things. If you can buy secretarial and research assistance, you won't need hordes of volunteers. If you can pay lawyers or surveyors, you can guarantee to interest them in your cause. It is even possible these days to hire professional pressure-group consultants, who can provide skill, experience, self-confidence, contacts and all the rest. In short, despite the theory, money can replace many of the other requirements for successful pressure-group activity. I have often thought that if I suddenly become a millionaire, it would be great fun to occupy myself by making small bequests to needy pressure groups. This is probably one of the most economical methods of changing the world.

Pressure groups are thus rather imperfect solutions to the problems of allocating resources efficiently. A version of politics that simply handed over a significant role in the decision-making process to some sort of free market in political groups would produce some very odd results. One group might be much less concerned than another, yet would impose its will because it consisted of rich, self-confident professionals with extensive contacts and lots of spare time, while the other group had none of these undoubted assets. If governments are concerned to get accurate feedback on their decision-making, however, they can take account of the uneven distribution of pressure-group resources when assessing intensity of feeling. They might, for example, assume that a group of old-age pensioners who camped all night outside the Houses of Parliament felt more strongly than a group of students who did the same thing. They might assume that the students would see this as something of an adventure, while for pensioners it would be a last resort. Alternatively, a concerned government can attempt to reduce some of the more unequally distributed requirements for successful participation. It can dispense with the need for professionals, provide open access to information and encourage community groups that may develop experience and self-confidence in the organization of collective action.

In short, to allow pressure groups a role in decision-making offers scope for efficient feedback. It provides the information that, correctly interpreted, enables account to be taken of varying intensities of preference. It also allows a powerful minority interest to dominate a majority, even when both feel equally strongly. The value of pressure-group activity must therefore always be evaluated in practice rather than enshrined in general theories.

The other possible advantage of taking account of political pressure is that decision-making becomes, to a certain extent, informal and flexible. We have already seen that all formal decision-making structures are beset by paradox, inconsistency and a tendency to construct a social whole by adding individual parts. Once more, the benefits of informality are potential rather than automatic, and the risks are huge. When discussing the use of secret ballots within trade unions, we saw that public voting may be better than secret ballots at identifying collective preferences. Group activity and discussion may well serve to identify desired alternatives that may not be apparent to isolated individuals. In a similar way, when groups interact in the decision-making process they may identify collective solutions that before were simply not apparent.

Maybe two residents' groups are fighting each other over the siting of a new airport. The choice has hitherto been presented as the need to site the airport next door to either Group A or Group B. The two groups may discover, as a result of putting on political pressure, that the most effective course of action is to attack the need for any new airport at all. Group A may rather like the idea of a new airport in the back garden of the members of Group B. Group B in turn may rather want a new airport a long as it is built somewhere else.

Each group faces a 50 per cent chance of success if both approach the matter in isolation, since the airport will surely be built on one site or the other. When they join forces they have a 60 per cent chance of defeating the whole project. They may well prefer to take the gamble. The net result for each is a 60 per cent chance of no airport (not bad) with a 20 per cent chance of an airport somewhere else (good) and a 20 per cent chance of one in their back garden (awful). This may seem better than a 50 per cent chance of an airport at home or a 50 per cent chance of one away from home. The result of pressure-group activity in this case is that a mutually preferred outcome is indentified, and the combined groups then work towards it.

The crux of this particular argument is that pressure-group activity is more sociable than voting and hence is capable of achieving more sociable outcomes. Once more, this is because the exercise of political pressure is *some* indicator (however imperfect) of intensity of preference. If people are disposed to do so, this valuable information can be put to good use.

In general, the problems of where decisions should be taken and who should take them tend to be problems of government rather than of community. One of the great virtues of a community is its ability to make communal decisions, to identify communal preferences and so on. When decision-making is removed from the community it makes a great difference whither it is removed. The trouble with direct decision-making systems is that they proceed as if communities existed even when they do not. In such cases the mechanical collection of individual preferences does not necessarily produce a collective preference and may produce serious paradoxes. Indirect or representative systems have generally evolved, or have been designed, in response to the unsuitability of direct decision-making by communities. They take account of the fact that most social groupings are large and diverse, breaking each decision down into a series of decisions taken by smaller groups and allowing several stages at which decisions may be digested, and even modified, before they become binding. This is not to say that indirect systems are free from paradox or other faults. Any number of specific decisions may well be regarded as abominations by those forced to suffer them. In nearly all circumstances, however, direct 'democracy' is even less appropriate. It is significant that many of the most bitter and bloody social conflicts have arisen from attempts to impose majority rule in the name of democracy. When people appeal to the 'democratic' will of the majority it is wise to suspect their motives.

8

How Governments Decide

Choosing a government and exerting political pressure are two of the *inputs* of decision-making. However, it would be naive indeed to assume that the same inputs always produce the same result. The actual policies that are implemented are the *outputs* of the system. Inputs are transformed into outputs by a mechanism that is sometimes described as a 'black box'. This description implies that we may observe what goes into and what comes out of this box, but also that the complex and mysterious mechanisms inside defy understanding. This is a neat picture, but, like many neat things, it is unsatisfying. Therefore in this chapter I shall lift the lid off the black box of government decision-making and at least peer at the mechanism inside.

At first sight there appears to be two varieties of box, containing rather different mechanisms. Some governments comprise a single political party in complete control. In this case it might seem that once the single party has gained power it simply does what it wants (although quite what it wants to do is conditioned by many of the things that we have already discussed). The second variety of black box is used when no party has overall control of government, when coalitions of parties are needed for effective decision-making. In this case it is popularly believed that the black box contains a smoke-filled room into which beer and sandwiches are periodically inserted and within which all sorts of deals and compromises are thrashed out. The output of this smoke box is popularly portrayed as a policy package that bears little relation to the policies that attracted voters to parties in the first place.

Now, it is undoubtedly true that single-party governments function in rather different ways from coalitions, but it is as well to bear in mind the various aspects of collective decision-making that I have already discussed. Most crucially, we must remember that coalitions exist *within* parties as well as *between* them. Smoke-filled rooms, sandwiches and compromise are, quite simply, part of the process of government. It is just that different smoke-filled rooms are crucial to different types of system.

ONE-PARTY GOVERNMENT

In Britain and the United States people are accustomed to one-party government. They tend therefore to think of the winning party and the government as more or less the same thing. The distinction between party policy and government policy is blurred or non-existent. There are, of course, occasional rows over the use of the machinery of government to promote party policy positions. This was the case, in 1983, with the proposal to use British government funds to back a campaign to oppose unilateral disarmament.

In general terms, however, the British system of government is rather odd in this respect. Power rests very firmly in the hands of a Prime Minister who is, after all, the Queen's Prime Minister as well as leader of the party. Even if the party could exert authority over its leader, it could not do so over the Prime Minister. Why, then, is the Prime Minister not a dictator? Any attempt to answer this question depends upon some of the most wonderfully elusive aspects of power, legitimacy and authority. The crucial thing we need to work out is what it takes to break a Prime Minister in office. Since Prime Ministers can and have been broken, their power cannot be absolute.

In order to get rid of an unwanted Prime Minister you require a blend of formal authority and practical power. Particularly in Britain, where formal powers are often defined rather vaguely, practical power politics is more important than most formal texts seem to imply. In the USA both politicians and the public have a highly developed sense of the importance of formal powers defined in the Constitution and interpreted by the Supreme Court. Even there President Nixon resigned before he was formally impeached. The possibility of impeachment was an element in all of the power broking that went on, but this possibility would have seemed remote indeed if power had not already begun to slip through his fingers.

Since Britain has no written constitution, the formal powers of Prime Ministers are not entirely clear. In February 1974 Edward Heath apparently lost a general election but did not vacate 10 Downing Street for several days. To have stayed longer might have provoked a 'constitutional crisis', but no one could really say whether or not he was acting *ultra vires*. Between elections the convention is that the Prime Minister resigns if the government is defeated in the House of Commons in a major policy vote and in the following vote of no confidence. When this happens because the incumbent government has lost its majority, the resignation tends to be followed by an election. When it happens because of a major rebellion within the government party, then an election need not be called. A new Prime Minister may be appointed, although an election cannot be ruled out.

In terms of practical politics it is spectacularly destructive for members of a government party to rid themselves of an unwanted leader in this way. The 'split' party risks devastation in the subsequent election, and all sides lose out if things are pressed all the way to their logical limit. Good chess players can usually see that their position is hopeless many moves before the final checkmate. In the same way, most politicians choose to resign key jobs before they are forcibly removed from office. Once the end becomes inevitable, there is no point in acting it out in glorious technicolor, blood and all. Thus both Anthony Eden and Harold Macmillan lost authority in office as a result of either misjudgements or scandals. Each accepted the inevitable with a good grace rather than forcing their party to drag them kicking and screaming through the front door of Number 10.

The constitutional fact that Prime Ministers can be removed is crucial, but it is crucial much more as a threat than as the actual dénouement of a power struggle. But how can a Prime Minister be under so great a threat that she is forced to resign? We are dealing here with political nerve, will, credibility and resilience as well as the deployment of forces within the governing party. Prime Ministers who are new to office tend not to resign. Political will and resilience are high, while the opposing forces have, presumably, just been defeated, so that their morale is low. On the other hand, Prime Ministers who have been in office a long time tend to resign rather easily. Will and resilience are weakened as ambitions have been fulfilled and as a result of the unremitting pressures of office. The need to establish credibility by beating opponents is less cogent at the end of a career than at the beginning. Such things are less important, less worth fighting for.

Will, of course, is a very elusive concept. Generals can tell you that a collapse of will may spread like wildfire. Sportsmen can tell you that in a game such as tennis, in which victory depends upon playing and winning even the very last point, will may collapse for strange and unpredictable reasons. The clear leader can quickly slump to defeat after dropping three set points. Gordon Liddy trained his will by holding his hand in a candle flame and thence achieved spectacular notoriety in the Watergate affair. The clearest political examples are to be found in dictatorships. Tyrants who have previously crushed all opposition suddenly take off to enjoy their Swiss bank accounts as a result of events which, a year or so earlier, would have presented no problem at all.

The main practical manifestation of prime ministerial will is a willingness to engage in brinkmanship. Few political threats are costless. Threatening a Prime Minister that you will bring her down if she does not do what you want is worth attempting only if the threat is heeded. If it is not, actually carrying out the threat is often counter-productive, since most of the best threats damage the threatener as much as the threatened. Actually evicting the PM from office is an apocalyptic achievement, threatening political ruin for all concerned. Knowing this, a tough Prime Minister dares opponents to challenge her.

Prevention, of course, is better than cure. Most Prime Ministers survive more by avoiding opposition than by defeating it. They have long since discovered that the most effective way of doing this is to compromise potential opponents by offering them important (not *too* important) government jobs. Which politician, skilled at justifying anything to anyone, cannot justify to herself the acceptance of such a job? The grounds are easy. Think of all the *good* that can be done from a position of power, even if a little compromise here and there is the order of the day. This explains a phenomenon that sometimes puzzles people, the presence in the Cabinet of some of the PM's traditional enemies. They are not sacked, however gratifying this might be in the short term, because they are more dangerous outside the Cabinet than in it. After all, the British doctrine of collective responsibility means that no Minister may publicly dissent from a Cabinet decision, however much she privately disagrees. Successfully applied, this tactic boils most of the government decision-making problem down to one of conflict within the Cabinet. This conflict reflects the different shades of opinion in the party that have been pre-emptively compromised by being offered office. Power relations within the Cabinet depend an awful lot upon the way that the PM chooses to run things. A number of general observations can be made, however.

In the first place, the doctrine of collective Cabinet responsibility means that privately dissenting Ministers must publicly defend Cabinet decisions which which they disagree, or they must resign. A Minister who threatens to resign is rather like a cat with nine lives threatening to commit suicide. Resigning damages the Cabinet briefly. In the short term it also tends to make the ex-Minister more popular with her fans. A power base *can* be established outside the Cabinet. However, those outside the Cabinet are weakened by the fact that they may threaten only to vote against the government. This either results in government defeat, an awful prospect for all but the most utterly disgruntled, or it will not, and the rebellion will be crushed. In other words, each Cabinet member is dealt one resignation card at the beginning of the game. A Minister can threaten to play it over and over again but can actually play it only once. Once the resignation card is used up, the only threats that remain involve the most desperate measures. The greatly weakened bargaining power of a Cabinet exile undermines the real power of any threat to resign.

In the second place, the PM can sack members of the Cabinet, and can sack them whenever she feels like it. This gives her ultimate power over the Cabinet, although the risks of opposition from the back benches increase if significant opponents leave for whatever reason. Just as a Minister can resign only once, she can be sacked only once. Having been sacked, a dissident moves largely beyond prime ministerial control. The PM is forced to balance the undoubted formal authority that she has to sack opponents against the practical erosion of her power base if she does.

British Prime Ministers are thus forced to temper very extensive formal powers with practical politics. Co-opting and compromising potential opponents by inviting them into a Cabinet bound by a doctrine of collective responsibility, they must then contend with the threat of resignations. Able to evict her enemies from the Cabinet at the stroke of a pen, a PM may prefer to have her enemies where she can see them rather than leaving them to plot away on the back benches. In each case the threat involved is like a threat to use a sledgehammer to crack a nut. Yet, even though threatening to bring down the government may seem rather an extreme way to force the PM to bend a little, this ultimate formal sanction is the bedrock over which practical power ebbs and flows, often in an unpredictable manner.

COALITION GOVERNMENT

The main difference between coalitions and one-party governments is that a general election does not automatically determine the composition of the government. It is all very well to describe the British Labour Party as a coalition. So it is, but when the Labour Party wins an election the whole coalition is swept into office. Each element in the Labour coalition comes as part of a package. With true coalition government the package is put together after, rather than before, the election.

There are two key elements in coalition negotiations. Cabinet seats and policies. Not only do the member parties have to decide who is going to be Prime Minister, Foreign Secretary and so on, but they must also decide which of those various solutions to the nation's problems that they have put before the people will actually be put into effect. The development of an agreed coalition policy package also contains two elements. The first is compromise, and the second is logrolling, the trading of concessions on one policy for agreement upon another. In each case one of the key factors in the ensuing negotiations is the relative bargaining power of the participants.

Bargaining power

In the wheeling and dealing that leads to a coalition government the parties exploit their bargaining power. Once more, formal power is moderated by practical politics. Once more bargaining power is measured in threats. When I am attempting to extract some concession from you, whether it is a Cabinet seat or an agreement on free transport for schoolchildren, I am in a much better position when I can threaten you. And the more I threaten you, the more powerful I am. My threats, of course, must be credible. In terms of practical coalition politics, my threat to keep you out of power is really credible only if there is an alternative coalition that I can join with some hope of success. If I simply threaten to keep you out of office by staying out of office myself, I am threatening to cut off my nose to spite my face. You probably will not take me seriously. Such threats are easy to make, but they are also easy to disbelieve. You will notice that even the most spiteful of people whom you are likely to meet tend still to be in possession of their noses.

Thus in the following example one party has no credible threats that it can make:

	Crimson Party	Pink Party	Pastel Blue Party	Azure Party
Seats	30	30	30	10

The Azure Party contributes essential seats to no majority government. If it joins with the Pastel Blues, the two parties are still in a minority. If the two join with the Pink Party, there is a majority, but the Azures are then redundant. They can hardly expect any joy out of the coalition, since if they ask for anything at all, they will be booted out. There are no credible threats available to the Azure Party, which consequently has no power. It will almost certainly not be in the government coalition, and if it manages to sneak into office, this will be because it asks for nothing and gets nothing.

The Pastel Blue Party, however, is in a stronger position. It is an essential member of the two winning coalitions, being able to form a majority with either the Pink Party or the Crimsons. It can squeeze concessions out of the Pinks by threatening to do a deal with the Crimson Party. It can squeeze concessions out of the Crimsons by threatening to deal with the Pinks. The other two parties are in a similar position. In terms of size alone, therefore, all three have equal bargaining power, while the Azure Party has none.

Coalition bargaining power often bears only a very general relationship to the success of the parties at the preceding election:

	Fat Party	Thin Party	Short Party	Scrawny Party
Seats	40	20	20	20

In this case all parties have some bargaining power. Any one of the three smaller parties can combine with the Fat Party to form a majority, and they may all combine to keep the Fat Party out, but the Fat Party is an essential member of *three* winning coalitions. Put another way, there are four winning coalitions that carry no passengers (Fat/Thin, Fat/Short, Fat/Scrawny and Short/Thin/Scrawny.) Three of these contain the Fat Party, and only one does not. The Fat Party may be only twice as big as the Scrawny Party, but is more than twice as powerful.

The oddities of bargaining power are at their most extreme when a small party finds itself in a quite disproportionately strong position:

	Safe Party	Solid Party	Tiny Party
Seats	48	48	4

The Tiny Party is an essential member of the Tiny/Safe and Tiny/Solid coalitions. It finds itself with the same bargaining power as parties twelve times as big. When it comes to extracting concessions in coalition negotiations, the Tiny Party can expect considerable joy. There might even be a Tiny Prime Minister.

All this, of course, concerns *potential* power. In practice, it rarely seems to be the case that small parties press their theoretical bargaining advantages to the limit. Sometimes, however, they do. In the dying days of the 1974–9 British Labour government, a number of small parties held the balance of power, and all sorts of spectacular demands were made in the run-up to the final vote of confidence. Even more dramatically, Charles Haughey became Irish Prime Minister in 1982 after agreeing to an unprecedented expenditure package for the inner Dublin constituency of a single key independent TD, Tony Gregory. Gregory's vote appeared for a time to be the one thing that stood between Haughey and power, and Gregory's constituents did very well as a result. By and large, however, a number of factors seem to militate against the 'cynical' use of disproportionate power in coalition negotiations.

The first has already been mentioned. It is political nerve or will. Most small parties are very pleased at the prospect of *any* participation in government. Every politician would like to be a Minister with an official car, a large staff and a place in the limelight. Those who are not involved in politics simply for the sake of power often have deep convictions about what needs to be done. The possibility of office offers the promise of actually *doing* something. In either case, to exploit bargaining power means to make threats, and herein lies the rub. Coalition negotiations tend to be conducted by party leaders. Once the leader of a small party has won a seat in the Cabinet, why should she put all that goes with it at risk by making threats on behalf of less significant colleagues? It is credibility, the known willingness to exploit and enact potential threats, that underlies bargaining power. Such willingness may evaporate once a few hitherto undreamed of concessions have been won. It may seem unnecessary to put these on the line in order to extract more, even if the theoretical chances of success are considerable.

Once more, Ireland provides a good example. There have been several coalitions between Fine Gael and Labour, with Labour being quite definitely the smaller party in terms of seats. Formally, however, Labour was an equally important member of each coalition, having just the same power to make or break the government as Fine Gael. Yet Labour has clearly been treated, and even tends to see itself, as the junior coalition partner. It has yet to exploit its bargaining leverage to the full. Significantly, it has usually been the party leadership that has favoured coalition and the rank-and-file that has opposed it in the absence of really major concessions.

The second practical constraint upon theoretical bargaining power concerns the electorate. Voters can take a dim view of a party that exploits a disproportionate bargaining advantage and may punish the culprit at the next election. This cuts both ways, however, since tactical voters may see a small party in a new light if it flexes its muscles, and may realize that their support is not necessarily wasted. On balance, parties seem to assume they are more likely to be punished than rewarded by voters for exploiting their bargaining power to the full, though evidence for this is hard to muster. I suspect that in practice this is a rationalization of the previous point. If small-party politicians are generally unwilling to risk modest gains in the hand in exchange for much greater rewards in the bush, they will be tempted to invoke their 'duty to the electorate' as a justification of their decision.

In the third place, 'disproportionate' bargaining power is affected by party policy. A coalition needs not only to carve up the Cabinet but also to agree upon a programme of policies. One of the most important things that any new coalition must do is to issue an agreed policy package. Such an agreement often takes up a large proportion of the time spent upon negotiations and clearly has a most important symbolic and practical place in the whole process of coalition government.

Agreement is obviously much easier to achieve between those with similar policies than it is between those who are poles apart. This factor has a dramatic effect on practical bargaining power:

	Safe Party	*Soft Party*	*Solid Party*
Seats	48	4	48
	Left ⟵		⟶ Right

Compare this Soft-Centred example with that involving the Tiny Party. The distribution of seats is identical, but I am sure we would all agree that the Soft Centre is much better placed than the Tinies. Even though it is a sad fact of life that Soft Centres are rarely as big as you expect, they may still make an enormous difference. It appears in this case to be almost impossible to keep the Soft Centre out of government. True, there are three winning coalitions that carry no passengers. One of these, however, the Safe/Solid coalition, is very unlikely because when it comes to negotiating a policy compromise both the Safe and the Solid parties will find it easier to do business with the Soft Centre. Indeed, if we consider only policy and forget about the Cabinet, a Safe/Solid alliance looks almost inconceivable. If these two are forced into bed with one another, they will probably agree on policies very much like those wanted by the Soft Centre. They can therefore do much better by dealing with the Soft Centre from the start. In pure policy terms, therefore, the

Soft Centre can afford to be very greedy indeed. The only threat that the other parties can make is to deal with each other. If they do this, however, they will gain less than if they give the Soft Centre almost everything that it wants. Taking Cabinet seats and coalition policy together, and provided that the Soft Centre is not too greedy over Cabinet seats, it can do very well indeed on policy.

The disproportionate power of small parties in coalition bargaining applies, in practical terms, only to parties of the centre. While it may be true that supporters of small centre parties do better than they deserve on the basis of election results, it does not necessarily follow that the electorate as a whole is worse off. By using disproportionate power to drag government policy towards the centre, voters at one end of the spectrum are made better off at the expense of voters at the other end. The net result may or may not increase overall voter satisfaction. It is certainly not true, however, that voters as a whole are inevitably worse off as a result.

Small parties at the extremes of the political spectrum are in quite a different position. The Tiny Party, for example, is unlikely to go into government with the Safe Party, which has to concede fewer items of policy to its Solid rivals. Tinies can try to deal with Solids but cannot expect too much. The Solid Party, after all, has a nice Safe alternative, which is genuinely viable. When it comes down to it, the Tiny Party has little with which to threaten the Solids. If they do join the government, it will be very much as poor relations.

Thus those in Britain who oppose proportional representation on the ground that it would give too much power to small parties have in mind the Liberals and the Social Democrats. Such parties might well become the king makers if coalitions were the order of the day, though, as we have seen, this might not necessarily make voters worse off. It is unlikely that either the Communist Party or the National Front, however, would find much practical scope for exploiting any theoretical bargaining gains by forcing their way into government.

However, and this is a point that is not always appreciated when conditions are considered, the practicalities of bargaining power do not affect the parties of government only. 'Out' parties can have an impact on government policy, even if they never achieve office. For example, the Tiny Party might succeed in dragging policy to the right because it undermines the bargaining position of the Safe Party, which must moderate its demands to take account of a possible Solid/Tiny coalition. The Safe Party, thus weakened, may demand less, and the policy of the Safe/Solid coalition may consequently move to the right. In practical terms, the Communist Party or the National Front might exert more influence if Britain had coalitions and if the centre parties weakened their demands to forestall possible coalitions of the far left or far right.

Quite how much political capital can be made by small parties in this context is not clear. They might cry, 'Vote for us: we won't get into government, but coalition policy won't be as far to the left as it will be if you don't vote for us', but this is a rather esoteric point and one that would probably take quite a lot of selling. Nevertheless, a party can exert influence on government even if it never makes the Cabinet.

Finally, there are some parties that stay out of government because they refuse to compromise even when they could. This is usually because they have deep-rooted beliefs and principles that they are simply not prepared to concede. When such parties are large, they can have a very important effect upon coalition politics. In extreme cases they can cause a complete stalemate. It is hard enough, after all, to build a government majority when all are amenable to bargaining. To control over 50 per cent of the seats when possibly only 70 per cent are even on offer, however, can be a Herculean task. It may require getting all other parties to agree:

	Hardline Party	*Wheeling Party*	*Dealing Party*	*Bargaining Party*
Seats	34	22	22	22

If the Hard-Line Party refuses to make any concessions, the other three must either concede everything or thrash it out among themselves. The unavailability of *any* alternative government opens the door for very unpredictable and chaotic bargaining.

This is the situation that has sometimes faced Italian politicians, when the Communists have refused to go into government. It was even more dramatically in evidence in the French Fourth Republic, when two parties, the Communists and the Gaullists, refused to be moved, a situation that undermined the whole constitution. It is interesting that these rather untypical examples are usually cited by those who oppose coalition government. In such cases there is clearly a case for the claim that coalition systems cause serious problems. In most other cases, given a willingness by the parties to negotiate, a deal does tend to emerge, and coalition governments are among the most stable that can be found.

Logrolling

We have so far considered only one dimension of policy. We have arranged parties from left to right and talked about coalition in terms of policy compromises. This, however, is only half of the story. Governments make policy on many matters. Some of these are related, and some are not. Consider, for example, socio-economic policy and religious-ethnic policy. It is quite possible, as in Belgium, for these matters to be completely independent, so that people may equally support left- or right-wing Flemish parties, or left- or right-wing Walloon parties.

Imagine that two religious groups, the Lions and the Christians, are well represented in Parliament. The Lion Party and the Christian Party feel strongly about their religious beliefs. They have views on the economy too but get less worked up about these. Two other parties, the Hard Left and the Hard Right, feel much more strongly about the economy, although they do have views about Christians and Lions. The Hard Right and the Lions can between them form a majority coalition. But the Hard Right tends vaguely to favour Christians, while Lions tend to favour left-wing economics. They may still do a deal based not upon traditional 'split-the-difference' compromise but upon rolling logs. This involves trading policies rather than making compromises on them.

The Lions may want to eat the Christians so much that they are prepared to abandon their left-wing economics in this cause. The Hard Right wishes to construct an enormous gold memorial to a certain Nobel Prize-winning economic guru, Morris Fanshaw. They are so keen on this project that they are prepared to abandon their Christian beliefs if this means that the memorial will be built. The logrolling begins. A Hard Right/Lion coalition emerges. The ensuing policy package involves eating Christians and lionizing Morris Fanshaw. Neither side has compromised. Instead each has given up something in exchange for something else. They have engaged in logrolling.

Logrolling has a rather complex effect on practical bargaining power, an effect seldom considered by those who write on coalitions. The most important general consequence of logrolling is that parties with more extreme views find themselves at much less of a bargaining disadvantage than would otherwise be the case. As we have just seen, even two very extreme and opposed parties, such as the Hard Right and the Lions, can find ways to deal with each other and to form a government if both are prepared to give something up in order to get what they most want. In political systems in which there are a number of important dimensions of political debate logrolling is likely to erode the disproportionate power of small centre parties. This disproportionate power arises from their being in a better position to make policy compromises. Logrolling replaces policy compromises with policy trading, a process that gives no particular advantage to those at the centre of the ideological spectrum.

People who dislike coalition government usually appeal to the possibility of logrolling as an argument in favour of single-party government. It is naive, however, to assume that logrolling does not go on within single parties and Cabinets. Indeed, the United States, bastion of big-party government, is where the term 'logrolling' originated and where logrolling has been developed into a sophisticated political skill. Ethnic, religious economic and regional groups trade furiously to bid for the presidency. Small 'key' states receive special attention. Any legislator who wants to push a Bill through the House needs to 'buy' support for her pet scheme with promises of support for the pet schemes of others.

Logrolling, as a form of trade, is usually held to increase overall well-being. It is certainly one way of tackling the problem of intensity. People get those things that they feel strongly about by conceding that which they value less. If one group can find another with complementary preferences, both may be made better off by rolling logs and getting what they want rather than by splitting the difference and getting what neither wants.

Logrolling, however, does have disadvantages. The very process of giving each that which each most wants, rather than forcing compromises, can undermine the 'collective' nature of the decisions taken. The typical logrolling deal can bring together a rather odd collection of minorities, each voting for its own private reasons and none acting in the light of a perception of the community as a whole. In addition to this, it is clear that logrolling can quite dramatically increase the provision of selective government benefits. You may vote for my new bridge if I vote for your new hospital, and this will increase the chance that both will be built, while other taxpayers, who get direct benefits from neither, may be forced to foot the bill. The reason for the increase in selective government provision is that the type of group that is often best placed to roll logs is the one that has intense preferences about its own selective benefits, yet is prepared to let other groups have their own selective benefits if that is the price that must be paid.

In short, logrolling is a form of political trade that may increase individual benefits without necessarily increasing benefits to the community as a whole. Whatever else it does, however, it transforms the nature of coalition bargaining, eroding some of the disproportionate power of centre parties and providing a clear role for those with more intensely held views.

WHO DECIDES WHAT IS DECIDED?
SETTING THE POLITICAL AGENDA

Things are not always what they seem. Decision-making is a difficult enough topic without adding extra complications, but I'm afraid that we've so far ignored one vital element in the process. This is the little matter of deciding what is to be decided.

I like coffee, you like tea and we both hate malted milk. We are sitting at home trying to decide what to drink, and I offer you a choice between coffee and malted milk. You've no hesitation in picking my favourite beverage. If the choice is between tea and coffee, we face a head-on confrontation. I can avoid this, to my advantage, if I manipulate the choices open to us.

There are three basic levels at which the political agenda is determined, almost regardless of the decision-making process involved. The most fundamental aspect of this process concerns the origins of the basic objectives that people pursue. Throughout this book I have presented politics as the collective realization of certain goals. These goals do not just emerge out of thin air, although some, such as basic food and shelter from the elements, are fundamental enough to be shared by almost everybody. Most other desires develop as a result of the process of living in society. The desires for television sets or motor cars, for example, seem almost natural these days for those of us who live in the developed West. A quick trip to a desert island or another century, however, would quickly show us that cars and TV sets are simply the things that we want here and now. We have somehow learned to want them.

Thus the main items for inclusion on the political agenda are themselves a result of the process of social interaction. Moreover, such desires can be generated quite artificially. This, after all, is the business that makes the advertising people rich. Their job is to make people want things that they did not want before, would never even have dreamed of, had it not been for that natty little commercial slipped into the

How Governments Decide

middle of an exciting episode of *Dallas*. There can be little doubt that the advertising media sometimes work. Why else would people want to buy pogo sticks or edible underwear? This, of course, is the problem of false consciousness that I discussed earlier. We saw that false consciousness is both clearly plausible and impossible to determine. It is thus evident that the generation of desires, the deepest and most fundamental aspect of agenda-setting, is one of the most difficult to get to grips with.

The second level at which the political agenda is set is that of means rather than ends. Once more, this concerns the things that people want from politics, but it relates more to the best ways of achieving these than to the ends themselves. Such matters tend to be associated with the technical evaluation and implementation of specific policies and hence to the preserve of experts and bureaucrats.

The world is a difficult and complicated place. Few of us understand everything. We rely on others to understand bits of the world for us, regarding these people as experts in their chosen fields. One important aspect of politics is the implementation of policies. One important set of 'experts', therefore, is the group of people who are skilled at implementing policies, the bureaucrats.

As with many of the topics treated in a few pages in this book, understanding the power of experts and bureaucrats presents an enormous problem, although the basic dimensions are relatively straightforward. Consider my young son. He likes to watch what I think is too much television. He often comes downstairs in the morning and wants the television on. He can switch it on himself but is not very good at tuning it. He depends upon me, the expert, to change channels. Now, I can tackle him on the matter of watching too much TV, explaining the difference between false consciousness and real desires, but he would not be impressed. He would see this as a straightforward conflict of wills, a conflict that I am not always willing to engage in early on a Sunday morning. The answer is simple. I tell him that there is nothing on TV at the moment and let him switch the set on. I twiddle the tuning knob furiously and with no success whatsoever. He accepts my expert judgement and switches to the much more educational open-air pastime of tormenting our neighbour's cat. He is in my hands; I know it, and I exploit the fact to my own ends. I do not need to dispute with him over his conscious desires. I avoid the dispute, to my own advantage, by presenting it as a non-issue. There is nothing on TV, so the matter of watching it does not arise.

So it is with experts. They have the power to cross things off the political agenda by ruling them out as unfeasible. They may not use this power, but they have it nonetheless. If an economist tells me that it is not possible to reduce unemployment by increasing government expenditure, I am sure enough of my ground to disbelieve her. If she tells me that it is not possible to do both of these things *and* to reduce inflation at the same time, I am unsure enough to be forced to take *somebody's* word on the matter. If nobody else says anything different, I may well accept that what she says is true. I am hardly in a better position than my 2-year-old son.

Competing experts, of course, may tell different stories. In such circumstances their power will be greatly undermined. There is something in the maxim that it is not always a good idea to bring bad tidings to the king. Being a recognized expert has to do not only with saying the right things but also with saying the things that people want to hear. The recent political success of monetarist economists, for example, may be related to their superior ability. There is little doubt, however, that if the same people had said the same things twenty years ago, they would have been no less right or wrong. They would nonetheless have been less successful as recognized experts.

It is as well, therefore, not to get too bowled over by the power of experts. There is a real sense in which there is a market for expertise, just as there is for anything else. And market trends are fashioned by many things other than the truth. When experts form a monopoly, however, they are in a much stronger position. This goes some way towards explaining the power of a bureaucracy. Administrators are experts at administering. If bureaucrats join forces to tell you that something can't be done, then it is tempting to believe that you can't do it. This aspect of bureaucratic power depends upon the presentation of a monolithic front, something greatly assisted by the widespread dissemination of the belief that administrators are non-partisan functionaries whose job is to do what they are told. In some bureaucracies, such as the British Civil Service, the atmosphere and the hierarchical structure act to discourage dissent from the official line. Specialization of functions means that issues tend to be dealt with by a single organizational pyramid, which acts as a filter and which presents decision-makers with a number of highly processed options.

Thus some of the bureaucrats concerned with transport planning may project a dramatic increase in the demand for air travel. They may consequently 'advise' that a new airport is needed. Predicting that existing airports will sink beneath a sea of chaos, misery and irate air travellers, their advice may be hard to resist. As they are the only people with access to the necessary information, and therefore the only people able to make confident predictions, the power of the bureaucrats in this matter may be almost unchallenged.

Even bureaucrats are human, of course, and nobody likes to have her advice rejected. Even bureaucrats with no particular axe to grind, therefore, can fight their case very vigorously. Their power is greatly enhanced by their monopoly of expertise, and this monopoly is a product of their control over information. This goes a long way towards explaining why bureaucrats often guard their information as if their very lives depended upon it. In a sense, their professional lives *do* depend upon it. Their authority is greatly undermined if all sorts of freelance experts are free to make conflicting predictions on the basis of the same information. This is no doubt why it is harder to get across to 'official' information in systems, such as Britain's, with an established and entrenched bureaucracy. There is probably little that is genuinely sinister about this process. Few of us, if we are honest, could put our hands on our hearts and say that we prefer competition to monopoly when it is we who control the monopoly.

While administrators may act to advance their interests as

administrators, they may also act to advance their interests either as individuals or as members of a social class or other grouping. Accordingly, they may consciously or unconsciously manipulate the alternatives that they present to decision-makers. Perhaps the most obvious example concerns the administration of unemployment, sickness and retirement benefits. By definition, those who do the administering are employed, able-bodied and not yet retired. They will be taxpayers, subsidizing the interests of those whose destiny they control. It is not surprising, therefore, if the unemployed often feel that the bureaucrats whom they deal with see them as the 'enemy'. In many cases this is no doubt true, as consciously or unconsciously, bureaucrats further their own interests as employed able-bodied taxpayers rather than the interests of their clients.

It seems usually to be the case that there is a preponderance of middle-class men in the Civil Service. In Britain there is a significant over-representation of ex-public school pupils and Oxbridge graduates. Whatever the reasons for these distortions, it is clear that the interests of the bureaucrats do not always coincide with those of the people whom they serve. Even the most scrupulous administrator is likely to present advice from a particular perspective. Systematic discrepancies between the interests of administrators and those of the administered will inevitably lead to systematic distortions of the advice they offer. This means that the political agenda will be similarly influenced, since feasibility is at least in part a matter of opinion.

To summarize, the second level of agenda-setting reflects the fact that the making of decisions is much more than the informed selection of a single option from a set of explicit choices. Choices are both informed and made explicit by those with potentially conflicting interests. To be able to decide what is, and what is not, an issue is to have enormous power to affect the eventual outcome. After all, the Mafia leaves you a choice even when it makes an offer you can hardly refuse.

Finally, all decision-making procedures may be manipulated even if means and ends are accepted and options identified. Not only the content of an agenda but also its order can be critical. Items high on the list may be rejected when they would stand a better chance at a later stage, after the options have been narrowed. This is the sort of problem faced on a Sunday drive, when deciding on a pub at which to stop for lunch. You *always* drive past the first one, in the hope of something better. Thirty miles further on you realize that the first was indeed the best, but closing time is fast approaching. There is no time to go back, so you settle for something much worse. If I, as the driver, really wanted to stop at the first pub, I would take another route and contrive to pass it shortly after passing a couple of low dives full of fierce-looking people.

This process is really an extension of one of the paradoxes of decision-making that I discussed in an earlier chapter. We saw then that the order in which decisions are taken can arbitrarily affect the result. But the order in which decisions are taken is usually within someone's control. Anyone who has run a meeting will know the advantages of putting controversial items low on the agenda. Eager to get off to the pub, people who might well have come into the meeting puffed full of self-righteous wind start shifting uneasily in their seats as closing time approaches. They become much more inclined to agree to *anything* rather than face a long-drawn-out row and miss last orders. Thus whenever you are looking for hidden power take a close look at whoever decides the order of agenda. Short of being appointed an absolute dictator, this is one of the powers that I would most like to have in a matter on which I held strong views.

HOW GOVERNMENTS DECIDE

All government decisions are taken by coalitions. These may be explicit, as they are in multi-party Cabinets, or they may be the implicit result of in-fighting within a single government party. A coalition is forged on the basis of the bargaining power and the objectives of its members. Bargaining power depends upon threats, and political objectives can be reasonably assumed to comprise a mixture of ideology and ambition. The key bargaining threat in coalition negotiations is the threat to destroy the government, a threat that can damage both threatener and threatened if it should be enacted. In this sense dissidents within one-party government are probably in a weaker position than those in multi-party Cabinets, in which it may be easier to blame others for destroying the government. Similarly, it is easier for a Prime Minister to sack dissident members of a one-party Cabinet than it is in a multi-party coalition. The allocation of Cabinet posts is a product of often delicate coalition negotiations, and a precipitate sacking may destroy the coalition and hence the government.

When it comes to policies, the inescapable fact is still that one government policy is produced as a result of the myriad preferred policies in the electorate. All coalitions result in policy compromises. While the compromises reached by one-party coalitions are sometimes put directly to the electorate, those reached by multi-party coalitions arrive after the election. When the electorate feels strongly about several important dimensions of policy, however, logrolling between parties at least offers politicians scope for making more people happier than they would be with the policy package of any single party.

The decision to choose a particular option depends upon the alternatives that are on offer. The selection of these alternatives is in itself a crucial aspect of politics. This selection process may be influenced, consciously or unconsciously, by those who have particular interests. Such influence is particularly strong when those involved control a monopoly of information and access. Thus the role of the bureaucracy is crucial, since it often does possess such a monopoly.

Finally, it is worth remembering that what is decided is not necessarily put into practice. Two key institutions are involved in the interpretation and implementation of decisions, the legal system and the Civil Service. Each is properly the subject of a quite separate book. This book is about the politics of making, rather than of implementing, decisions. It should, however, be obvious that the ability that administrators have to influence things when they inform decisions will be at least as potent when it comes to enforcing them. In many societies the senior judiciary is an even more untypical cross-section of the community than the bureaucracy. (This is certainly true in Britain, where the number of working-class lady judges is probably zero.) This does not mean that once governments have finally decided, their decisions are inevitably distorted when they are actually put into practice. It does mean that a potential for distortion inevitably exists.

9

Politics between Governments

Politics between governments is one of the best practical examples of anarchy in action. When discussing why we need governments and when we don't need governments, I presented a choice between regulation by government or by community. We are free to explore the circumstances in which each is more appropriate and to come to our own conclusions. Nearly all of the land surface of the planet, however, is these days divided between sovereign governments. The fact that each is indeed sovereign within its territorial limits means, effectively, that no international government may have jurisdiction over the same area. National jurisdiction may, of course, be ceded to an international organization, but by and large such jurisdiction can be retrieved by withdrawing from that organization. Thus member states of the EEC give up some of their sovereign powers but may retrieve these by pulling out of the European Community. While no individual can exist as a total outcast from society, it is at least conceivable for many states to be self-sufficient enough to exist as international outcasts. In addition, the vast range of often conflicting interests between nations makes it unlikely that every nation on the planet would ever see itself as a member of a single worldwide community and therefore prepared to submit to a single international government. All of these factors have conspired to ensure that we have nothing even vaguely like an international government with anything approaching the powers over its 'subjects' that all national governments undoubtedly possess. There are, of course, many, many international organizations,

Politics between Governments

but these are institutions much more for co-ordinating and regulating anarchy than for replacing it.

Perhaps the best example of this was the behaviour of the United Nations over Unilateral Declaration of Independence made by the Smith regime in Rhodesia. The Smith regime attracted widespread international disapproval by declaring UDI in order to protect white power in Rhodesia, and the UN response was to institute sanctions against it. This represented a typically 'anarchistic' attempt to exile Rhodesia from the international community (which by and large failed because Rhodesia maintained cordial relations with South Africa, a country that remained at least a partial member of this community). The prospect of asserting UN authority in Rhodesia by force of arms was never really a serious possibility, not least because of the unwelcome precedent that it would have set for other situations. The UN and other international organizations are thus designed to co-ordinate international anarchy rather than to impose international government.

The whole field of international relations is a subject in its own right. Since this book is concerned to explore the processes of politics in general rather than the details of international relations in particular, I have chosen to concentrate upon a set of problems that rather nicely illustrate this aspect of anarchy in action. These examples are concerned with the international regulation of a set of matters which are quite clearly beyond the jurisdiction of national governments – the sea bed, inner space and the Moon. Each of these presents serious problems of international collective action since each provides a scarce but valuable collective resource that may be destroyed by chaotic exploitation. Before moving on to discuss each in detail, however, I would like to consider the problems of resource exploitation in general.

'THE TRAGEDY OF THE GLOBAL COMMONS'

A parable that illustrates the problems of exploiting scarce natural resources is 'The Tragedy of the Commons'. A number of herdsmen have access to a piece of common land, and all have the right to graze their sheep on it. This land, like all land, can support only so many sheep; too many sheep and it suffers ecological collapse. The vegetation disappears; the topsoil is washed away; another dust bowl is created. Each herdsman is able, in the absence of any external constraint, to graze as many sheep as he wants on the common. As there are a number of herdsmen, if they all greedily want to graze as many sheep as they can, the land is in grave danger.

Each herdsman reasons as follows: 'If I want to put an extra sheep on the common, then my extra sheep will hardly make the difference between eco-disaster and the continuation of the land as a useful resource. Only if everyone keeps on buying and grazing extra sheep will we all have a problem. If all of my fellow herdsmen do this, however, my extra sheep will be neither here nor there. The commons will collapse whatever I do. If the others restrain themselves, the commons are safe. I can take advantage of this by grazing the extra sheep anyway.' Either way, the logic of self-interest suggests putting an extra sheep on the land. If everyone thinks the same way, then they all do the same thing. Another common turns to dust. There are several potential endings to this story, some more likely than others.

In most capitalist societies, the answer to the dilemma of grazing lands is to abolish the notion of common land and to divide it up into parcels, each the 'property' of one herdsman. This brings about a situation in which each herdsman cuts his own throat, but nobody else's, by over-grazing.

Another ending to 'The Tragedy of the Commons' would be for some strong external agency, such as a government, to intervene and force the herdsman, for their own good, to co-operate in observing some system of quotas that restricts the total herd to the optimum level. No one will like being forced, but each is better off if the government punishes all who step out of line. The land survives, as does the principle of the commons. This type of government solution to a collective-action problem is, of course, one of the main justifications for government in the first place. It is more generally applicable than the privatization of the commons, since some common resources, such as the atmosphere or the air waves, simply cannot be parcelled up and awarded to individuals as their own private property.

A third important solution to 'The Tragedy of the Commons' is the type of conditional co-operation that we described earlier as anarchy. Each herdsman may agree to restrain himself provided that all others do the same. In a large and diverse group more or less formal institutions may be needed to monitor behaviour and to spot defection. Given the unlikelihood of world government, this tends to be the solution adopted for international collective-action problems. International organizations serve to monitor behaviour and to co-ordinate collective action by members against those who stray from the straight and narrow.

Global commons come and go with the march of events and the progress of technology. With the exception of the Antarctic, there are now no significant land-based commons. However, developing technology has opened up new frontiers and consequently new commons. In traditional territorial terms, we can now think of commons existing in the oceans, on the Moon and in inner space. In rather different terms, high levels of energy consumption and pollution have forced us to consider global stocks of non-renewable energy, and the global environment, as common resources. In all of these cases the self-interested action of individual nations can combine to produce general disaster. Fisheries become exhausted, and acid rain destroys crops, while no international government agency is powerful enough to force recalcitrants to co-operate in collective solutions.

The examples that I have selected show that 'The Tragedy of the Global Commons' is a many-sided problem. In particular, it is a problem that concerns two matters that we have already discussed in the context of national politics, the prevention of spillovers and the apportionment of property in the absence of government. The original 'Tragedy' depends upon the coexistence of common land and private sheep. The private sheep have spillover effects on the common land. The consequent collective-action problem may be solved by reducing the spillovers with regulation or co-operation, by privatizing the land and forcing the people to suffer their own spillovers or by collectivizing the sheep and reducing the private incentives for antisocial behaviour.

Of today's global commons, the ocean can at least technically be divided between proprietor nations, since boundaries can be defined and policed. This would probably reduce the spillovers that result from the over-exploitation of ocean resources such as fish and minerals. The practical problem that arises is a result of the absence of an international government that can recognize and enforce such property rights. The politics of the ocean is thus characterized by international conflict over *possession*.

On the Moon, where our most recent commons can be found, the problem is eased by the vast expense of any lunar activity. As far as we know, our tiny incursions have thus caused few spillovers (though perhaps the little green men have all just died of common colds). This may be the reason why the international community has taken an untypically collective attitude towards the Moon. As no government has lunar jurisdiction, there is no lunar private property, and the Moon belongs to us all (at the moment).

The ether presents a different collective-action problem. The air waves cannot feasibly be 'owned', since radio signals respect no national boundary. Radio interference can be caused by a sovereign government acting within its own jurisdiction and cannot be physically policed. The radio spectrum has one special and important property, however. As far as we know, it cannot be permanently destroyed, although it can be rendered useless by overcrowding at any single point in time. Radio interference is an almost perfect example of a negative spillover. Given the impossibility of policing ownership, the tragedy of the broadcasting commons has thus far been regulated by typically anarchistic co-operation.

THE POLITICS OF THE OCEAN

The ocean has three basic components, all of which are in contention. There is the surface of the sea and the problem of who may sail upon it. There is the sea bed and the problem of who owns what lies beneath it. There is the water between the two and the problem of who may catch how much of what swims around in it. Each component of the politics of the ocean has a different history. By far the longest concerns the ocean wave and who may sail thereon.

Territorial limits

Ever since *Homo sapiens* invented the boat there has been a lot of interest in the matter of who should sail boats where. The threat of sea-borne invasion has meant that nations have always had a strategic interest in the waters around their coasts. Ideally, they would all like to control as much of this water as possible, but two factors restrain them.

The first is the practical problem that effective control costs money, while ineffective control is worthless. I could sit in Honolulu and claim the entire Pacific Ocean as my very own. The cost of maintaining a navy large enough to enforce that claim would, however, be enormous. The cost of failing to do so would be that the world would stop taking me seriously.

The second factor restraining nations from claiming huge chunks of sea as their territorial water is reciprocity. International decisions about territorial waters have been relatively anarchistic, while international enforcement is non-existent. Countries with claims to territorial waters tend to have large fleets of both cargo and fighting ships. One nation's territorial water is a restriction of the high seas for every other maritime power. Thus, if a nation wishes to expand its claims to territorial sea, it must reckon with the prospect that others will reciprocate and that the loss of freedom on the high seas will offset the gain in home waters. This may particularly be the case if an expansion in other nations' waters has the effect of closing a corridor of high seas through the middle of a well used strait. While cargo ships have a right of innocent passage through territorial waters, most nations otherwise treat their territorial sea in precisely the same way as they treat land over which they have sovereignty. The loss of straits and passages in this way thus causes considerable inconvenience to naval powers.

A large quantity of the oil pumped out of the Middle East, for example, is exported via the Strait of Hormuz, the only way out of the Persian Gulf. This strait is controlled by three islands, traditionally occupied by Britain. When Britain withdrew in November 1971 they were seized by Iran, which has subsequently used control of the territorial waters, and hence of the Strait, to put pressure on its old enemy Iraq.

Conflict over territorial seas has thus mainly been between developed countries with strong navies (such as Britain and the United States), which want narrow limits and maximum freedom and movement, and less developed countries with weaker navies, which need international agreements to reserve larger areas for their own jurisdiction and have much less interest in a loss of high seas elsewhere. The common resource is freedom of movement in the high seas. The individual national interest is national security and the ability to control movement in coastal waters.

Current claims to territorial waters range between 3 miles and 200 miles from the claimants' coastlines or from 'straight baselines' that close off bays, fjords and the like. These claims represent an interesting blend of theory and reality. One obvious 'natural' limit to the territorial sea is the area that can be controlled from land, since it is of little use to claim something that cannot be controlled. The traditional 3-mile limit became current in the eighteenth century and was based upon the maximum range of a shore-based cannon. Three miles may seem a long way for an eighteenth-century cannonball, but this limit was fixed on the assumption that the most powerful cannon, with the wind behind it, might conceivably be able to fire this far. After some debate over whether claims to territorial waters made on this basis were valid only when actual cannon were in position to do the job if needed, the more hypothetical solution of recognizing 3-mile limits, regardless of the disposition or power of real artillery, became widely accepted.

Three miles is now the minimum claim. It is now more or less beyond international dispute that any water within

3 miles of a nation's coastline (and nearer to that nation's coastline than to any other) should be treated as its territorial sea. The position is far less clear-cut with respect to the 200-mile limits claimed by some Latin American states with weak navies.

We have already seen that the absence of a powerful world government means that international law and agreements can be enforced only by the collective action of nation states. In the absence of international agreement – and none has yet been forthcoming on the limits of the territorial sea – even more pragmatic political considerations prevail. An ambitious claim to territorial waters, recognized by few others, is particularly ambiguous. Even if the claimant is prepared to attempt to defend such a claim, she must come to terms with the fact that tacit acceptance by others of a lesser jurisdiction is much cheaper and much more effective than the continuing need actively to police the claim. Naval losses in 1982 by both Britain and Argentina in the disputed 200-mile exclusion zone around the Falkland Islands illustrate this point only too well. The limits of sovereignty have traditionally been fixed by the boundaries that can be defended with reasonable economy. Nations and empires that have ignored this principle have usually done so at considerable cost.

The sea bed

The sea bed presents a problem more closely related to 'The Tragedy of the Commons'. Pearl fisheries and coral reefs have been traditional subjects of dispute. In 1858 Britain asserted ownership of under-sea mineral deposits mined from Cornwall. Developing technology, and in particular the growing importance of oil combined with off-shore drilling technology, have vastly increased the importance of such issues in the past fifty years or so.

Matters were brought to a head by the United States in 1945, with a claim to all natural resources beneath the sea bed of the continental shelf 'beneath the high seas contiguous to the coasts of the United States'. Very quickly nearly all coastal nations claimed the right to what lay beneath their continental shelves, regardless of whether these were within territorial waters or not.

The recent development of the relevant technology has meant that, with the exception of an oyster bed here or there, no country has had a traditional claim to areas of the sea bed. The possibility that this was a common resource seems scarcely to have been considered. Negotiations have centred much more upon the technical problems of drawing boundaries around what were always acknowledged to be continental shelves 'belonging' in some sense to adjacent coastal states. The sea bed has thus been subject to a classical enclosure movement.

The result has been international agreement upon, though not always compliance with, a convention that defines the limits of the continental shelf 'owned' by adjacent nations. This defines a boundary at a depth of 200 metres, or beyond where the depth of water allows the exploitation of natural resources. So vague a definition depends quite clearly upon the level of technology of the nation concerned, yet even this definition is disputed by some. Many Latin American countries claim the same 200-mile limits, regardless of depth, that they claim for their territorial seas.

Such disputes as have taken place, however, have generally related to boundary lines dividing the continental shelf between two adjacent or facing nations, for which the general limit is ambiguous. Such bilateral disputes have usually been quickly resolved, however. This is probably because the issue of physically defending the claim is less important than the development of some form of internationally recognized agreement. In the absence of such an agreement, commercial exploitation of under-sea resources (particularly by multi-national oil companies) is much less likely.

A very clear example of this process is the North Sea. When it became obvious that there was a lot of oil and gas under the North Sea, agreement about who owned what became imperative. The location of the dividing line between the British and Norwegian sectors was complicated by the existence of the Norwegian Trench. This is a deep depression in the sea bed (descending to a depth of 500 metres) that runs along the Norwegian coast. It limits the breadth of the Norwegian continental shelf to a maximum of 11 nautical miles. The original British claim was that this trench marked the dividing line between the respective shelves and thus that nearly all of the North Sea hydrocarbons were British. Not surprisingly, Norway disagreed, arguing in favour of using the median line between the two coasts. As pressure built up to develop the North Sea, and as it became clear that the technology was available to do this, Britain conceded the Norwegian position. Failure to agree would have cost both sides dearly. Britain and Norway were in direct conflict in the sense that gains of sea bed by one represented losses by the other. Yet both were locked into a position of enforced co-operation. At worst, both would lose heavily if continuing disagreement meant that the oil companies who controlled the technology would refuse to drill in murky waters.

The division of the North Sea is a very good example of the way in which politics between nations can be conducted without an international government. To date the incentives to agree over the disputed boundaries of continental shelves have tended to outweigh other considerations. Perhaps this is because the benefits of increased access to the continental shelf are often speculative rather than immediate. It is in some senses rather remarkable that so little should have been resolved in this area, that competing claims should stand side by side, yet intense overt conflict is relatively rare. Probably it is significant that the necessary technology and hardware is still expensive. This means that under-sea resources themselves are not effectively in short supply at the moment. Economic and technical limits are thus more constraining than geographical boundaries. The deep-sea bed still resembles the Garden of Eden more closely than most other objects of political contention.

Fisheries

Most fishing grounds have traditionally been exploited by many nations, which have often come to feel that they have special claims that have nothing to do with geographical proximity. (Thus British fishermen developed what they considered to be a traditional 'right' to fish in Icelandic waters.) Furthermore, fish stocks are clearly under threat from over-exploitation, a situation greatly exacerbated by efficient modern methods and equipment. Thus conservation is an issue, and fish stocks are sometimes even regarded as a common resource. This last point should not be exaggerated. Conservation is often used as an argument but usually as part of a case to extend exclusive national rights over a particular area. With the exception of international concern over the potential extinction of the whale, the cause of conserving common fishery resources is most frequently espoused when it coincides with a particular national interest. (The happy coincidence of public welfare and private interest makes, of course, for a most attractive political stance.)

Fishery disputes have tended to be acrimonious. In March 1973 a 50-mile exclusive fishing zone was unilaterally declared around Iceland. Seven months later the British Navy fired live rounds at Icelandic patrol boats. Fish feed on plankton, and plankton are mainly found in shallow waters around coastlines. Thus many of the best fisheries are found quite close to the territorial sea of the nations concerned. The result has been that fishery disputes have tended to be related to disputes over territorial seas and quite separate from disputes over continental shelves. Just as countries with powerful navies tend to want to restrict claims to territorial sea, those with large long-distance fishing fleets, such as Britain, Japan and the Soviet Union, need as little restriction on common fisheries as possible. Indeed, the pressures for and against exclusive fishing zones are greater than those relating to territorial waters. Few productive fisheries can be found in those parts of the high seas that are so far beyond coastal waters that some state is not likely to claim them. The undisputed high seas are not much good for fishing. Furthermore, a very small proportion of the world fish catch is traded internationally, while fishing is often an important source of employment. Direct national economic interests are therefore at stake.

Finally, pressure for international agreement on fishing limits is far less urgent than that for agreement over continental shelves. Fishing does not depend upon expensive technology controlled by multinational corporations. It is much more the province of small businessmen with relatively small capital investments. Fishing, therefore, continues in disputed waters. The mutual interest that two nations might have in carving up an under-sea oilfield do not arise over fisheries. One nation's gain in a fishery dispute is very much another's loss, although both may lose if competitive over-fishing actually destroys the resource.

Everything points to an issue with much more underlying scope for contention than any other current aspect of the politics of the oceans. Even if a strong international regulatory agency existed (and it does not), the scope for specific quarrels is enormous. It is probably significant that, with Britain's entry into the EEC, the international allocation of North Sea fishing zones has presented the Community with one of its most intractable problems. This led, in early 1983, to another brief fishing skirmish, this time between Britain and Denmark. For Britain to allow other member states into its fisheries represents a straightforward loss. The fishery issue, taken on its own, affords little scope for compromise. The final resolution of the problem, to the undoubted detriment of British fishermen, depends in practice upon reciprocal concessions over quite different aspects of community policy.

THE POLITICS OF INNER SPACE

Global broadcasting commons

Taking radio broadcasting as a whole, there is one very important common resource. This is the broadcasting frequency spectrum. As we have noted, radio signals do not respect national boundaries, while one radio signal interferes with another broadcast on a similar frequency within a certain range. Only a certain range of frequencies is economically and technically viable for use as a broadcasting medium. The radio broadcasting frequency spectrum is thus not only a common but also a scarce resource. Its overall size increases with the march of technology as higher frequencies become viable. At any point in time, however, it can be thought of as fixed. This resource has also the great advantage of being inexhaustible. A radio signal leaves no permanent pollution, and unlike many natural resources, such as oil or clean air, the spectrum cannot be permanently 'used up'. It can, however, be so heavily used as to be almost useless at any given time.

Since radio broadcasting is so crucial to modern life, with entertainment, public service, scientific and military applications, the real possibility exists of a 'Tragedy of the Broadcasting Commons'. If everyone broadcast at will, the spectrum would be a noisy mess and almost worthless. We would most immediately notice this as CB fanatics boomed out in the middle of *News at Ten*, but we would quickly discover in many other ways just how dependent we are these days upon radio communications.

In addition to the problem of the over-use of this scarce resource, significant technical problems arise from using it efficiently. Different radio frequencies have different characteristics in terms of range, quality, susceptibility to interference, expense of broadcasting and receiving and so on. We are all familiar with the difference between longer-range medium-wave broadcasts, with their cheap receivers and interference problems, and shorter-range VHF radio, needing more expensive tuners, but providing better quality and less noise when they are set up properly. Such variations are greatly multiplied across the whole range of the spectrum, The technical problem concerns identifying the frequencies that are best for specific uses. The research required is both expensive and a common good for all users.

Since the emergence of satellite space stations, a further common resource has become apparent. Satellites orbit the Earth at a rate that is determined by their height above the Earth's surface. The first satellites circle 1,000 kilometres up and were available to an Earth station for a period of twenty minutes three times a day. Satellites are much more useful aids to telecommunication when they orbit the Earth at precisely the same speed at which the Earth is rotating.

Viewed from the ground they then appear to be stationary. This means that an Earth station can always have the same space station in view. There is no need for a whole chain of satellites on the same orbit, passing over the sky one after another, and requiring expensive tracking equipment on the ground. Geostationary satellites orbit the Earth at a height of 36,000 kilometres. One such space station can cover 42 per cent of the Earth's surface, an area 17,000 kilometres in diameter. Thus very few geostationary satellites are needed to provide a global network.

Geostationary satellites are more expensive to launch than others, whose precise position is less crucial. Like all satellites, they have a fixed life because they must carry fuel or compressed gas to power small rockets that occasionally correct distortions in their orbit produced by the Moon and other heavenly bodies. They can only carry so much fuel, and when this runs out they progressively drift out of position. Normal useful life is about seven years. In addition, a single space station actually requires three satellites – one in use, a spare one in orbit and another ready to launch. Nevertheless, satellite broadcasting is actually cheaper than the old-fashioned terrestrial alternative, although receiving aerials and equipment are more expensive.

It has not yet proved possible to design highly directional aerials for use on satellites, and so, like all other broadcasting stations, they interfere with one another. In addition, there is only a limited band of frequencies, a 'window', that can simultaneously penetrate the ionosphere and the atmosphere without being distorted or absorbed. The frequencies within this window must be those capable of carrying a large number of telephone or television channels. This means that relatively few frequency bands are suitable. At the same time, interference between satellite systems reduces the number of geostationary radio stations that can be operated well below the number that could actually be slotted into the 36,000-kilometre orbit. A further practical problem is that by the time that geostationary stations were viable all suitable frequency bands had already been allocated to terrestrial users.

In short, the 36,000-kilometre geostationary orbit is an immensely valuable common resource, the use of which requires international co-ordination or regulation if it is to be at all effective. It is a prime example of one of the new technological commons.

Solutions for terrestrial broadcasting

The possibility of a 'Tragedy of the Terrestrial Broadcasting Commons' was realized early on. The earliest attempt at a solution was made in 1906, by an international conference in Berlin. The outcome was the allocation of certain frequency bands to certain users. (Those below 188 kHz went to coastal stations, those between 188 kHz and 500 kHz to military and naval stations.) In addition, a set of Radio Regulations emerged, governing transmission power, aerials and so on. Specific frequencies were not allocated; they were simply recorded, on a first-come-first-served basis, when someone staked a claim. The second relevant conference, in 1927 in Washington, did make frequency allocations within certain technological limits. At this stage the allocations were recommended rather than required. It was not until the 1947 Atlantic City conference that an International Frequency Registration Board (IFRB) was established. As technology developed, so did the range of the usable spectrum, and subsequent conferences extended international regulation to take account of this.

The IFRB does not allocate frequencies to users – that power remains with sovereign governments. So the system of international regulation is complex. In the first place, certain parts (bands) of the frequency spectrum are *allocated* to types of use, such as sound broadcasting, television, radar and so on. This is done by an international conference. (The terms 'allocated', 'allotted' and 'assigned' have different formal uses in Radio Regulations.) Within a given band specific frequencies (channels) are *allotted* either to countries or to larger geographical areas. This is usually done by a regional conference. Actual use of a given channel is *assigned* to a station by the government under whose jurisdiction the station falls. This usage is governed by international regulations, and the assigning government is responsible to other governments for their observance. The assignment is made by the relevant government, which issues a broadcast licence, and must be notified to the IFRB, which tests it in principle against international regulations, registers it and publishes it in the Master International Frequency Register.

Criteria for use are broadly as follows. Every frequency assignment must conform with the frequency allocations for types of use. If one does not, it can continue only if it does not cause interference with another station, existing or new, operating in accordance with Radio Regulations. If interference occurs, use contrary to allocation must stop. A new frequency assignment must not interfere with a station already assigned under Radio Regulations and entered in the master Register. If interference does occur, the governments concerned must agree upon how to eliminate it and can use the IFRB to arbitrate.

I have gone into the system for organizing terrestrial broadcasting in some detail not only because it is complex but also because it provides a rather sophisticated way of balancing the need for international and national regulation. The system has also been rather effective by comparison with solutions to other global commons problems. It could perhaps have applications elsewhere. What, therefore, are its technical and political consequences?

In the first place, there is always a very strong incentive for two radio stations that interfere with one another to co-operate unless one is trying to jam the other. Neither wants the interference, and both clearly lose out if it continues. It may, therefore, be that co-ordination of the broadcasting spectrum is inherently easier, because of such incentives, than the more conflict-ridden problems of allocating fishing limits or under-sea mineral rights.

In the second place, complex (for the layman) technical issues mean that co-ordinated research may dramatically increase efficiency. If co-operation at this level means that the broadcasting cake is made much larger, all can benefit.

In the third place, the first-come-first-served principle, which operates by putting the onus on new stations not to interfere with existing ones conforming to regulations, can be justified in terms of technical efficiency, if not fairness. This is a thorny problem. A planned and fair allotment might well give frequencies to countries that cannot use them now but want to keep the option of using them when they are able. These frequencies cannot then be currently used by those who could use them immediately and want to do so. However, nobody likes having things taken away from her. Frequencies could be permanently and fairly allocated to all, including those who could not use them, while some temporary arrangement allowed access to others until they were required by their 'owners'. In practical terms, temporary users would come to feel that they had acquired squatters' rights, either refusing to vacate the frequency when asked or seeking a compensating frequency elsewhere. Such a system could clearly work, however, and would doubtless be 'fairer' than the status quo.

Fourthly, the most interesting aspect of the current state of international broadcasting frequency management is its very relaxed attitude towards the rule of law. Radio boffins are engineers. Engineers are pragmatic and clearly prefer the maximization of efficiency to the imposition of inflexible rules. The general principle is that stations must conform with Radio Regulations, but those that do not conform may continue to broadcast until they interfere with those that do.

This is analogous to using traffic lights to define rights of way rather than to force people to stop regardless. A red light would mean 'stop' if there were a car facing a green light at the same junction but 'go' if there were not. The possibility of irreversible traffic accidents, which contrast with the temporary nature of broadcasting collisions, makes this intriguing possibility rather less attractive than it might seem at first sight. In the dead of night, of course, there are some who treat traffic lights like this anyway. (And in the dead of night, some US traffic signals are indeed switched to flashing lights that convey this message, flashing orange in one direction, meaning go with care, flashing red in the other, meaning stop, then go when the road is clear.)

The pragmatic solution to the broadcasting problem depends upon the inexhaustibility of space as a carrier of radio signals. Squatters do no damage if they leave when required. Deep-sea mineral rights could not be allocated on the same basis, since squatters would be using up exhaustible resources while the 'owners' were attempting to gain the ability to exploit them. Noise pollution, however, is a possible application. Instead of imposing absolute noise limits and enforcing these regardless of the effect of the noise, limits could be set but imposed only if there were a legitimate complaint. (In general, the distinction between rules that are enforced regardless and rules that may be enforced only by an injured party is one of the practical differences between criminal and civil law.) Certainly, when common resources are inexhaustible, this principle may well be appropriate, provided that squatters' rights do not develop.

Finally, the two-tier enforcement structure works well because governments have a strong incentive, for reasons we have discussed above, to come to an agreement over some kind of co-ordination of broadcasting frequencies. Governments are required to control stations within their jurisdiction according to international regulations. Their need to participate in international broadcasting decisions and agreements is sufficient to encourage them to do so.

Solutions for space stations

The problem of sharing out the 36,000-kilometre geostationary orbit appears technically to be a problem of allocating frequency bands. There is room for a large number of satellites in the 36,000-kilometre orbit before they begin physically to interfere with one another. The problem of radio interference, given the limited range of suitable frequencies, all of which have already been allocated, emerges much sooner. Fortunately, the physics of radio transmission in these frequency bands permit shared use by satellites and other types of operation, while comprehensive and complex computer searching of the Master File enables suitable frequencies to be selected. (Remember that frequencies not logged in the Master File do not have international 'rights'.)

Thus recent radio conferences have become 'Space conferences', concentrating upon allocating and allotting satellite frequencies. Technical considerations are overwhelming, and computer models abound. Such models are necessary before frequency assignments to specify satellite networks can be made. The government concerned is obliged to make complex calculations to determine whether its system will interfere with others already registered on a first-come-first-served basis. If interference is likely, co-ordination is required. This problem is complicated by the fact that the necessary calculations require technical data relating to other satellite systems. For obvious reasons, this may not be forthcoming. The 1979 Radio Regulations now require all potentially affected administrations to be contacted. Governments controlling existing systems need not respond and involve themselves in coordination, though they may pay a price for this in interference. Once more, pragmatism triumphs over regulation. Once more, the first to come tend to be the best served.

The 'efficiency versus fairness' problem is much greater for space stations than for terrestrial broadcasting, for a number of reasons. The frequency 'window' is restricted, and the need for efficient frequency-sharing agreements means that useful frequencies are in short supply. The economic and technological gap between those who can use space stations now and those who might want to do so in the future is much greater with satellites. To allocate space-station frequencies to all who might want them is probably unfeasible, given current technology.

There is also a real sense in which each nation does not need its own satellite system, since one satellite covers 42 per cent of the Earth's surface. The geostationary orbit, in this respect, looks rather like a natural monopoly. It would be grossly inefficient to have ten competing gas companies all supplying gas to different users on the same street. (Imagine how often the road would be dug up if that were to happen.) It would be grossly inefficient, even if it were technically feasible, to have 150 national geostationary satellite systems.

This factor may generate very serious problems in the

future. It would give considerable power to potential 'electronic colonialists'. Nationally owned and operated satellite networks would be in a powerful position *vis à vis* those who were without space stations but wanted to use them. On top of this, those with existing networks would be impossible to dislodge from this position, and their arguments would be potent. Such networks represent a huge investment and would not be relinquished lightly. Furthermore, it is virtually impossible to alter the frequencies, power, direction and so on of an inaccessible satellite in orbit, while making similar alterations in a terrestrial station is relatively simple by comparison. This would further strengthen the hand of those with functioning satellite systems. There are no easy concessions that they could be asked to make – only the abandonment of an entire system.

If geostationary space stations are a 'natural monopoly' good, the most obvious solution would be government provision, but in this case the government would need to be international. The obvious solution is thus extremely radical. The IFRB has no powers of enforcement, and the neat answer adopted by IFRB for terrestrial broadcasting would not apply.

To summarize, geostationary satellites present technical problems that are simply an extension and complication of frequency spectrum management. However, the rather different nature of the good supplied may present problems that are impossible to resolve in the context of autonomous actions by sovereign governments. A 'Tragedy of the Broadcasting Commons' may result if conventional solutions do not apply and if radical alternatives are opposed by entrenched interests. There can be no doubt that one efficient solution would be a powerful international agency with a monopoly over the provision of geostationary satellite services. In terms of practical politics, this does not seem likely. It will be interesting, if this should happen, to observe the reactions of those pragmatists who make scientific policy.

THE POLITICS OF THE MOON

If space travel ever becomes any cheaper, the Moon will be the next great frontier. As a consequence, there has been considerable international interest in whether it is possible to stake a claim to a patch of the Moon's surface. At one time it even seemed as if all that would be necessary would be to raise a single national flag in order to claim the entire celestial body. Certainly, to judge from what happened after the opening of previous new frontiers, an unseemly scramble seemed likely.

A stop was put to that possibility with the 1967 Space Treaty, signed two years before the first lunar landing. This put the Moon in the same category as outer space, which has never been considered subject to national expropriation, since sovereignty cannot legally be claimed without reference to dry land. An important consequence of there being no national sovereignty on the Moon is that there is no private property, since no government has the authority to grant title to this. The 1967 Treaty was ambiguous over whether this prohibition on expropriation extended to lunar resources or merely to lunar real estate. By analogy with the high seas, which cannot be 'owned' but from which anyone is free to extract resources, it was agreed that the United States probably had the right to keep the first precious samples of Moon rock all to itself. The position, however, was unclear, and samples of Moon rock were made available in theory to any government that wanted them.

An attempt was made to clarify this position with the 1980 Moon Agreement. This specifically prohibits national expropriation of lunar resources and demands an 'equitable' (as opposed to 'equal') sharing of benefits derived from these. Since 'equitable' is a term that requires legal interpretation, and since no one has legal authority over the Moon, the most radical proposal in the Moon Agreement was the establishment of an 'international regime' to govern the Moon as soon as the extraction of lunar reserves becomes feasible. The agreement is vague, however, about what this international regime might look like.

Politics between Governments

In terms of international law, therefore, the Moon and its natural resources are seen as the 'common heritage of mankind'. In terms of practical politics, three factors are clearly important.

In the first place, only two of the world's nations are now, or seem likely to be, in a position to exploit the Moon, and then only at vast expense. The rest of the world obviously has a very strong interest in establishing the Moon as a common resource. It has nothing to lose and possibly a great deal to gain. While an international agreement on the Moon that was adopted in the face of opposition from the two lunar powers would have had little meaning, it would not have been problematic to find sufficient nations to ratify it. The USA and USSR have, in fact, gone along with the Moon Agreement, having extensively used their influence to modify its drafting.

The second and overwhelming practical dimension of lunar politics is the fact that the USA and USSR are also the world's two nuclear super-powers. The two main uses of the Moon are military and scientific. There can be little doubt that the major impetus behind the Space Treaty and the Moon Agreement was international concern that high-technology warfare would be spectacularly escalated by military use of the Moon. Military use is specifically excluded by both agreements, while the prohibition on national expropriation greatly reinforces this. The desire to exclude military use probably explains the concern of both the USA and USSR to see something like these agreements adopted. It seems likely that neither would have welcomed the immense drain on national resources that a lunar arms race would have implied, with little net relative advantage to either side.

Finally, policing the Moon Agreement or the Space Treaty presents considerable practical problems. Not only are the only two nations that are in a position to break the agreement the world's two strongest powers, but they are also the only ones likely to be in a position ever to detect many types of violation. Thus, while the Moon may be legally regarded as our greatest common resource, it is a funny sort of common in practice. Out of 150 or so nations who collectively 'own' it, only two have access to it or know what is going on on it. The remainder are all in favour of retaining it as a common, and the two gate keepers go along with them. No other government has the power or authority to enforce any agreements that might concern it. In short, the Moon is a common because it suits those who could expropriate it not to do so, or at least not to say that they have already done so.

GLOBAL COMMONS, GLOBAL SPILLOVERS

The Moon illustrates quite nicely the fact that there can be no true international commons. Common ownership, like private ownership, requires some form of government jurisdiction and enforcement. Global commons are thus more to do with common interests than with common ownership. International law most closely approaches the notion of common ownership in recognizing something that is beyond ownership such as the high seas, outer space or, by implication, the broadcasting frequency spectrum. Orderly and equitable exploitation of these requires some form of international regime, such as the International Frequency Registration Board in the case of broadcasting. International regimes tend to have few powers of enforcement. They tend, therefore, to work better when the incentives for nations to co-ordinate are many, as is the case with broadcasting, than when there are squabbles over the sharing out of a fixed cake, as is the case with under-sea minerals. I suspect that international regimes will work even less well with regard to something, such as the Moon, that *could* be owned privately but is simply declared legally to be beyond ownership.

Since all countries need to exist in the world, and need to give and take in order to do so, international law is not without force. It is, however, a form of politics without government that resembles individualist anarchy. As long as the benefits of belonging to the international community exceed the benefits of defying international law, order is maintained. Once this situation is reversed, international law is replaced by the confrontation of national powers.

Politics between Governments

National actions that cause large and damaging international spillovers, such as the generation of radio interference, produce collective-action problems that highlight common interests. When common interests are outweighed by the interests of individual nations, national action results instead in squabbles over national jurisdiction over a hitherto 'unowned' resource. The sea bed, therefore, is more commonly regarded as something that is up for grabs than as a common resource.

Overall, however, politics between nations does at least give us a glimpse of life without government. The international community, of course, is a small one, with about 150 members, and it is not particularly harmonious. Nevertheless, it does exist in a state of *relative* order, while the vast majority of international disputes are settled at the negotiating table. It is probably significant that each of the last two world wars have resulted in the emergence of organizations, the League of Nations and the United Nations, that some hoped would become international governments. When each was set up, the world community seemed to be in a state of chaos and in need of a powerful agency to regulate its interaction. It is also significant that neither organization has ever come close to being a world government. The practical problems are probably insuperable; the practical consequences show us that government is not inevitable, at least when communities are small.

10

Conclusion: the Politics of the Future

One of the central threads that has run through this book is the relationship between government and community. This relationship, however, is not static. It changes as communities change. Not only is the nature of politics very different in different cultures; it is also very different in the same culture in different eras. Politics today is nothing like politics a century ago. Politics a century hence will no doubt be quite different from politics today. One of the main forces that drives this process is the development of new technology and the interaction of this with the nature both of communities themselves and of the techniques of government.

Thus new technology influences the economic system and the structure of community interaction. The invention of television has meant that people stay at home for their entertainment rather than going out and meeting others. The invention of computers has meant that governments can plan and control on a much more comprehensive scale than they previously could. Any discussion of politics is no more than a freeze-frame view of some scene in the middle of an endless drama. Nevertheless, by making inferences from how the plot has developed in the past, we may at least speculate upon what is likely to happen in the future and set our view of today in some sort of context. We obviously run a high risk of failure, yet someone who absolutely refused to predict the future would not even get out of bed in the morning for fear that the floor might have disappeared overnight. Since technology is one of the main driving forces behind social

Conclusion: the Politics of the Future

development, our speculations about the future depend heavily upon speculation about the ways in which new technology will influence social relations.

The interaction between technology and politics is one of the least studied and least understood aspects of our existence. Even at the most basic level, it is almost impossible to decide which is the cart and which the horse. Even Marxists, who at least have something to say on the matter, are often unclear about whether new technologies generate changes in society or vice versa. In practice, of course, I have put the question too simply, since cause and effect can clearly flow in both directions. Thus the development of nuclear weapons technology did not just happen and then go on to transform inter-state politics. Inter-state politics generated a need for nuclear weapons technology and underwrote the cost of developing it. Once developed, however, nuclear weapons transformed inter-state politics in ways that were clearly not foreseen when the original demand for them was created. The end result has been a stalemate in which both sides are forced to run very hard, at great cost, in order to stand still. It is a stalemate that leaves all sides just where they were before they started, only facing greater risks of disaster and spending huge proportions of their national wealth on unused and unusable hardware. This was hardly foreseen when the first nuclear weapons research was commissioned, yet we can now see that it was an almost inevitable consequence.

In the same way, microchip technology developed out of the space race, a physical manifestation of rivalry between the USA and the Soviet Union. Who knows whether it would have developed if such rivalry had not existed? Nevertheless, microchip technology will have unforeseen effects on our lives that will stretch far, far beyond great-power confrontations. The same can be said of almost any new scientific discovery. Scientists are no doubt making important discoveries all of the time, and many of these no doubt just happen without any political stimulus. However, those discoveries that are defined as important, and are thus developed into usable technologies, are very often selected as a result of the political and social preoccupations of the day. Rennaissance scientists, after all, had a hard time with their new theories of the solar system because their discoveries ran directly counter to the interests of the ecclesiastical politicians in positions of power. No one who matters these days sees much mileage in proclaiming the Earth to be the centre of the Universe, so we tend to regard the Solar System as politically uncontroversial.

Whatever else can be said about the relationship between politics and technology, it is clear that new technologies can transform politics in unexpected ways. The last industrial revolution marked the beginning of modern class politics. Some are now arguing that recent developments in microelectronics, affecting both information processing and communication, are producing a revolution in information technology that will be as fundamental in its effects as the industrial revolution. In this chapter, therefore, I want to take a brief look at the possible effects of the information technology revolution upon the politics of the future. Doubtless many other new technologies may also emerge to transform our lives fundamentally. Some, such as genetic engineering, are already visible on the horizon. Others we can only guess at. I have not chosen to concentrate upon information technology because it is the only radical development that awaits us. I have chosen it because, of the various possibilities on the agenda, the information technology revolution is under way, with a dynamic that already seems inexorable.

As I have already mentioned, technological development affects both the techniques of government and the structure of communities. Information technology is already beginning to have an effect on the practice of politics, though this has progressed further in the USA than anywhere else. I have discussed the possibility of a resurgence of interest in 'direct democracy' via cable TV. The problem here is that direct democracy is unsatisfactory for all sorts of technical reasons, yet it has an understandable populist appeal. Cable TV combined with computerized audience research, however, provides something that can be considered to be almost a

Conclusion: the Politics of the Future

completely new communications medium. It will become possible for different sectors of an audience to be fed different information, using this new system of 'narrowcasting'. This basic technique is already in operation in the USA, where it is used by politicians in their increasingly refined and selective computerized direct mail campaigns. In Britain computer bureaux have recently been offering this service to advertisers, and advertising magazines have been introduced that are delivered free to a carefully defined and selected target audience. If narrowcasting does develop as a result of the introduction of cable TV, it could have considerable effects on the practice of politics.

At the moment 'broadcast' media offer the same message to all, usually at a national level but at the very least on a broad regional basis. In Britain newspapers are national. They are available to, if not read by, all. This is a powerful constraint upon what politicians can say. Ideally, of course, politicians would like to say completely different things to different people, in order to increase their chances of election. National and broadcast media, however, prevent them from getting away with being all things to all people. Having presented one set of promises, their performance can easily be judged. Most important of all, they are allowed only one set of excuses for failure. If multi-channel cable TV becomes a dominant medium, a real opportunity will present itself for politicians to make a whole range of quite incompatible promises. Each set of promises can be tailored to suit a carefully defined audience and could be followed up by a similarly tailored set of excuses. The overall accountability of politicians, not to mention the coherence of their policies, could be seriously undermined.

This would affect the whole basis of representative decision-making, of which the control of representatives by those represented is a key element. Such control is exerted by holding representatives accountable for their actions and must inevitably be undermined if different accounts can be given to different people. Most cable TV systems are organized on a city-by-city basis, for example. This clearly offers the chance for regional variations in promises and excuses. Thus viewers in some of Britain's depressed industrial cities could be offered promises of action to reverse decline, while those in the relatively affluent metropolis could be offered the promise of a dash for growth, regardless of the fate of the regions. Multi-channel cable TV also offers specialist services, however. There might be a black channel, a women's channel, a youth channel, an arts channel and so on. Ambitious politicians could take different stands on each in an attempt to be different things to different people.

The potential dangers of narrowcasting are only recently becoming apparent. More widespread and traditional fears about the effects of information technology concern centralized data banks and the possible implications of these for social control and the invasion of privacy. On the one hand, information is power, and centralized information may mean centralized power. On the other hand, centralized information may be much more easily leaked, intentionally or unintentionally, to those who have no right to it. Legislation is being introduced in many countries to enforce standards of data protection, but such legislation can never be wholly effective for a number of reasons.

Information as a commodity has some interesting and unusual properties. Once created, it can be reproduced very cheaply and quickly, while still being immensely valuable. (This is a property of software in general, a matter to which I will shortly return.) This means that the theft of information, and in particular the theft of electronically stored information, can be difficult to detect. The information, after all, may still be there after it has been 'stolen'. In the second place, information, once stolen, can never be 'given back'. Once someone has learned your innermost secrets, only a frontal lobotomy or major shock treatment can render these 'unlearned'. There is a real sense in which no subsequent legal action can restore the status quo that existed before the theft or misuse of data. If the data is valuable, even quite severe penalties may not deter a potential thief.

There are, therefore, considerable dangers to personal privacy resulting from the establishment of centralized data banks. It is difficult to see, however, how these can be

Conclusion: the Politics of the Future

controlled. My suspicion is that general attitudes about the information that is or is not private will change. After all, such matters are not necessarily cut and dried. While many who work in private businesses regard their incomes, for example, as a matter of considerable secrecy, most people who work in the state sector are paid salaries that are a matter of public record. Each group probably regards the situation as perfectly normal. Those who have something to hide, of course, will probably not find it too difficult to get around the problem by adopting several identities. This point relates less to the problem of privacy, however, than to the problem of social control.

The fear of social control is not always very well founded. People are sometimes rather bowled over by what they imagine computers can do, forgetting two simple facts. In the first place, computers do only what they are told. Any system for the effective social control of a population of 60 million would almost certainly be too complex to specify, even if a whole team of terribly clever people put their minds to it. In the second place, computing power, while vast, is not infinite. Even if an effective social control system could be specified, I doubt that any foreseeable computer installation would be capable of operating it to control a large population.

I do not wish to be too sanguine about this, however. Limited control is clearly made much more likely by computer-based techniques, and the use of computers for data storage offers the temptation to analyse and monitor what is going on. One obvious example concerns the recent proposal for machine-readable passports. The numbers going into and out of a country, of course, is much smaller and more tractable than the number living there. Machine-readable passports would offer the possibility of monitoring population movements in and out, of identifying those who move in and out many times a year and, possibly, of looking into the affairs of these people a little further. Those whom governments wished to exclude would be excluded much more reliably. Governments attempt to do these things at the moment, of course. Computers may help them to be more effective. Thus the issue is rather like the problem of TV democracy. Government monitoring of population movement goes on at the moment but has yet to become an issue because it is relatively ineffective. When it becomes more effective, it may become an issue. Whatever happens, attempts at control are much more likely to be directed at certain target groups, such as suspected criminals, frequent international travellers and the like, than at the population as a whole. This does not make such control any less of an issue, though it does make nightmares about a computer-controlled totalitarian society just a little far-fetched.

Much more plausible is computer-based planning that relates not to individuals but to areas, regions or sectors of the economy. This is almost certain to develop in both the public and the private sector. Insurance companies, for example, will be able to match insurance premiums to the risks they accept in a much more detailed fashion. At the moment motor insurance premiums are calculated on the basis of a few, relatively crude, criteria. Much more sophisticated analyses of risk could be attempted if all of the relevant information on insurance claims were collected and centralized in a coherent manner. (One of the interesting side-effects of computerization is the need to develop systems for the collection of information, since computers can only analyse data that are presented systematically.) Similar diagnostic or risk assessment systems could easily be developed for tax authorities, money lenders, town planners, traffic engineers and so on. As centralized data bases grow, so will the *potential* effectiveness of these techniques. This may not please those who dislike central planning as such, since it will certainly make central planning easier. Other than this, there is nothing inherently sinister in such a development, which may certainly make attempts to maximize social efficiency more effective.

One side-effect of the sophisticated analysis techniques that will become available may well have significant political consequences, however. When discussing taxation I drew attention to the different problems presented by optional and compulsory services, in particular to the fact that it is possible to tax only the users of optional services, while compulsory

Conclusion: the Politics of the Future

services must be funded more generally. The distinction between optional and compulsory services, however, is itself a product of technology. Consider the road system. All roads are, in theory, optional. However, it is at present feasible to treat only trunk routes in this way by monitoring use and, possibly, by charging user tolls. The costs of monitoring every highway and byway cannot cover the benefits, and the general road system is in practice treated as a compulsory good, at least for all road users. If it were possible to log the movements of each car, however, it might well be feasible to charge each car owner a road tax that was directly proportional to her usage of the road system. She could even be charged rather more for using expensive roads, rather less for cheap ones and so on.

In general, much more comprehensive monitoring of the usage of social services would not only make central planning easier but would also make more selective taxation a possibility. This, of course, would continue to be an ideological matter. The decision about how broadly the benefits of a road system were to be distributed, for example, would remain a political one. Nevertheless, the range of feasible options might be extended and new ideological solutions put on the agenda.

In general terms, however, one of the most fundamental new policy problems that will emerge from the revolution in information technology will concern the vastly increased importance of a new type of commodity, software. Software is information and knowhow, whether it is contained in data bases, in computer programs, in video programmes of one sort or another, in research findings or whatever. It has always presented a problem in capitalist societies that depend upon the protection of private property rights and the consequent emergence of a market in which private property is traded. Hardware is relatively easy to control. I can sell you my car without too much fuss because I can possess it. It is a tangible sort of thing. You can see that I have it. You know when you have got it, and I can prevent you from getting it if I want to, either physically or by using the full force of the capitalist legal system. If you do not physically possess this piece of lasting hardware, you can't get much good out of it. Information is different and has always been so. That is why we have copyright and patent laws that serve to make particular pieces of information someone's property. If you photocopy this book and sell it on street corners, you are breaking the law because you are infringing my copyright. You are, in effect, stealing my information from me rather than buying it on my terms.

Copyright and patent laws have always been rather difficult to enforce because information is intangible. While I can catch you red-handed in possession of my car, I will find it much harder to catch you red-handed in the possession of my secrets. If I invented a wonderful new fizzy drink and protect the formula with patents, just how close can a competitor come to my brainchild before I can justifiably accuse her of copying it? When I compose a new symphony of sparkling originality, quite how must you change it before you can claim to have come up with something different? Most businesses that rely upon successful innovation accept these days that patents can only give them a head-start over the competition. They realize that they would be foolish to rely on these for ever. A brand new chemical compound may, of course, be easy enough to specify. But a new concept in the design of electronic circuits, for example, is both transparently clear for all to see as soon as it hits the market and, quite possibly, difficult to pin down precisely. This is just as well. Otherwise whoever invented the wheel would by now be the richest person in the universe.

Any commodity, of course, is a mixture of hardware and knowhow. It is the balance of these that makes something easier or harder to sell in an unregulated market. As the information technology revolution progresses, however, it is clear that software is becoming more and more the main element of value. In any new computer installation, for example, the cost of the programs and the operating systems that put the hardware to work often now exceeds the cost of the processors themselves. (And this conceals the fact that a large part of what you pay for when you buy computer hardware goes to defray research and development costs. If

Conclusion: the Politics of the Future

these software expenses are excluded, computers can be sold much more cheaply, as recent victims of computer 'piracy' are finding out to their cost.) As the software element increases in importance, the need for some form of 'artificial' government action to define and enforce property rights increases. Even the freest of free markets in information needs a heavy dose of government intervention to protect the proprietorial rights of sellers. If information technology moves to the centre-stage of economic development, the role of government may thereby be changed, and the willingness of even the most buccaneering entrepreneurs to rely upon government protection will thereby be increased.

In practical terms, therefore, information technology is unlikely to have an enormous impact. It may increase the force of populist demands for mass participation in day-to-day decisions. It may reduce the need for consistency imposed upon politicians by the current national mass media. It may change, or at least sharpen, popular perceptions of what is a person's private business and what is not. It may aid central planning and offer alternative methods of charging for public services. It may push the new commodity of software into a central position in economic development, thereby changing the role of government as protector of property rights. All of these factors are important, but none is as important as the potential transformation of the structure of communities that may also result.

The last industrial revolution was called a revolution because it transformed society. It resulted in the emergence of a new class system, the nature of which was at least partially determined by the technology involved. Among many aspects of this transformation two were 'deskilling' and 'social concentration'.

Traditional skilled crafts were replaced by more routine occupations as a result of the mechanization of production. This had at least two important consequences. In the first place, a skill, especially a skill in short supply, provides some economic power. Since skills must be passed on, those who have skills also have some control over their supply. By restricting access to these, they have some control over their economic bargaining power. Unskilled jobs are undifferentiated in the sense that anyone can do them. This weakens bargaining power unless something is done about it. The need to do something about it has doubtless contributed some underlying impetus to the rise of the modern trade union movement. Meanwhile, the relatively undifferentiated nature of the new jobs that were created undoubtedly contributed something to the development of a broader view of common interest based not on trades and occupations but on social classes. In the second place, deskilling tended to mean that each individual made a smaller and less tangible contribution to any given product. The new workers thereby became more alienated than the traditional artisans, less able to derive any intrinsic satisfaction from the job that they found themselves doing.

In addition to destroying old skills, the industrial revolution resulted in the factory system. It was the factory system that enabled the economies of scale made possible by new technology to be realized in practice. This had the effect of concentrating workers in larger and larger economic units. It speeded up the process by which people realized that they had much broader common interests with fellow workers. Even today it is well known that workers in large factories tend to be more 'radical' than those who work on their own or with one or two others.

The next industrial revolution may have similar consequences, mainly to do with the growing economic importance of software. By and large, people who make hardware need to be in contact with it, to mould it, to manipulate it and to assemble it. Since software is intangible, it does not require such physical contact. And since the revolution in information technology will also be a revolution in communication, the need for people to be concentrated in one place will also disappear.

Those who produce software can work just as well from home, as the old artisans did. But, unlike the old artisans, they can live a long way from the market, if that is what they desire. Their product does not need to be transported physically but can be beamed around the world in seconds.

Conclusion: the Politics of the Future

Producers of software have always been free from the constraint of having to live where the work is. Producers of traditional software, such as writers and artists, have indeed exploited their ability to live in cottages in the West of Ireland, on Greek Islands, in Paris, Florence or whatever else seemed a nice place to be. The proportion of the population producing the new software will grow in the coming years, and this may have considerable social consequences.

The process of concentration will obviously be reversed. Modern cities, a product of this concentration, will fulfil a very different role. The need to be close to markets will be reduced, and the steady process by which metropolitan centres have grown in importance and population may well be halted. This is already evident in the United States, where new industries have tended to settle in the 'sunbelt'. Since they can be located anywhere, why not locate them in places where the winters are warm and the housing cheap? Britain, of course, has no sunbelt, but there is already evidence of a growing tendency to consider the pleasantness of the local environment when making location decisions. This reflects the declining importance of transportation costs as the importance of software increases. This, of course, can only accelerate the decline of traditional cities as the economically active become more geographically mobile. They will become able as well as willing to move away from deteriorating environments, leaving the economically inactive and unemployed behind and thus speeding the rate of decline.

This process of dispersal, if it takes place, may also reduce the solidarity of social classes. No longer concentrated in a single work place, common interests will become harder to perceive. With more and more people working from home, even the nature of the family may change. The breadwinner will no longer need to disappear for most of the day, winning bread. This is a factor that will no doubt be good for some marriages and bad for others but will certainly make a difference.

The process of deskilling will once more be important, though it is likely to have a more traumatic influence on the white-collar sector. Blue-collar workers will obviously be affected by computer-controlled automated production, but this will, in a sense, be no more than another stage in a continuous process of change. Many white-collar jobs will be deskilled for the first time as computer-based management systems become more effective. High-level management decisions will still be needed, but important lower-level management tasks, such as stock or credit control, invoicing, distribution management and so on, can already be handled automatically. The development of an increasingly alienated white-collar sector is clearly possible as former managers become minders of the new machines.

The overall effect of such developments is likely to change the nature of community. Although futurology is a hazardous profession, the signs that we can see at the moment seem to suggest that such changes will tend to increase, rather than decrease, the role of government. Information technology may make governments not only potentially more effective; it may also make them more necessary.

The reasons for this are related to the defining characteristics of a community. Communities require both stability and interaction if the enlightened give and take that can replace government is to emerge. Information technology will almost certainly reduce *face-to-face* interaction, though it will open up new forms of electronic communication. Such communication will be easy, even at long range and across national boundaries. The geographical concentration of interests will thus become much less important. This will pave the way for new types of community both to identify themselves and to become conscious of common interests.

Traditionally, the 'fit' between community and government has been considered in terms of geography. Those who have argued in favour of anarchy have done so on the basis of communities regulating some more or less well-defined territory. Indeed, the very concept of a widely dispersed world community of, for example, unemployed physicists is a rather hard one to grasp. If the new communities that emerge as a result of the revolution in information technology are communities without territories, more widely dispersed and defined by much more specialized sets of common

Conclusion: the Politics of the Future

interests, the problem that will result is how such communities can be governed unambiguously. I suspect – and it is only a suspicion – that the weakening of geographical communities will lead to a strengthening of the power of governments, although my main reservation concerns the extent to which sophisticated electronic interaction can lead to strong personal relationships. These days we tend to believe that it cannot. These, however, are very early days, and we have not yet begun to develop a feel for what is likely to happen. What is almost certain is that the developing technology will alter the basis of community. We can be sure, therefore, that it will change the nature of government.

Notes on Further Reading

This is usually the section of a book such as this in which reams of boring material are listed because the author is scared of missing something out. You should have realized by now that I don't scare easily and should not be surprised, therefore, to find my recommendations rather brief. It is worth, however, pointing readers in the direction of a few other books, so that those books can in turn point the way a little further down the route. I've related these notes to my chapter headings and chosen recent books where possible.

1 INTRODUCTION

If you really want to find out about politics, there is absolutely no substitute for reading *and interpreting* the newspapers. If you read newspapers looking for politics, you will find politics everywhere. But don't simply stuff your head full of raw information. Interpret what you read, so that you can identify the general themes that a particular story throws light upon. People are often rather snooty about newspapers, dividing them into the quality rags and gutter press. Avoid such distinctions. All newspapers must present a biased and distorted view of the world, although some do present this in greater detail than others. If at all possible, read two newspapers with radically different viewpoints. Stereo vision adds perspective, and systematic reading should enable you to get used to the kinks of any particular source. Read at least one popular newspaper, since one of the things that it is essential to know about any country is the type of political information that most people are getting. British newspapers are comparatively poor in their foreign news coverage. One or two weeklies, such as the *Economist,* do provide systematic foreign coverage as well as filling you in on the type of political information that the business community regards as important.

On the nature of social investigation, I find *What is History?* by E. H. Carr very persuasive. Though intended primarily to re-educate historians, it does provide a lot for other social scientists to think about. On the nature of social science, *Social Science as Sorcery* by Stanislav Andreski is hard to beat. This is basically a debunking job, but for reasons that I discussed in the Introduction, a certain amount of debunking is certainly in order.

2 AND 3 WHY WE NEED GOVERNMENTS AND WHEN WE DON'T NEED GOVERNMENTS

One recent book, *Community, Anarchy and Liberty* by Michael Taylor, provides an excellent discussion of some of the arguments for anarchy. Taylor bases his argument, as I do, upon the notion of community and takes his examples from primitive stateless societies. Taylor's worst failing is to ignore the problems of operating anarchist societies in the modern state-ridden world, but the book is nonetheless an enjoyable introduction to the problem.

Try reading *The Highway Code,* any book on etiquette (the most recent of which is *The Official Sloane Ranger Handbook* by Anne Barr and Peter York) or any book on the criminal underworld to get an idea of the importance of social norms and conventions in regulating communities. (A useful exercise is to classify all of the laws and advice in *The Highway Code* into that which does not require government action, and that which does.)

The question of why we need governments is, of course, the subject matter of some of the 'greats' of political philosophy, including Thomas Hobbes's *Leviathan*, Jean Jacques Rousseau's *The Social Contract* and John Locke's *Two Treatises of Government*. Political philosophers tend to be very possessive about these and insist that you read the originals. Mere mortals read reviews of them, written, as often as not, by political philosophers.

4 WHO IS GOVERNED?

Taylor's *Community, Anarchy and Liberty* has some general comments on what a community consists of. On the specific interests that draw people together much has, of course, been written. One very good analysis of the interaction of language, religion and culture in Ireland is Terence Brown's *Ireland. A Social and Cultural History 1922–79*. This book has much to offer even those who do not have a direct interest in Ireland but who are interested in the relationship between the things that define communities and in national politics.

5 WHAT GOVERNMENTS DO

This is a long chapter and a huge area of study. Much of this, including the problems of collective action, of producing public services and of redistributing well-being, is the subject matter of welfare economics. Most introductions to welfare economics, such as A. J. Culyer's *The Political Economy of Social Policy*, have quite a lot to say about these matters, though many, including Culyer, tend to be much too dismissive of the role of government. A widely read text on the problems of consumer feedback in government production is Albert Hirschman's *Exit, Voice and Loyalty*. This looks at the options open to those who are 'locked into' services such as education, transport or health care that are provided by government. There are, of course, many books on individual policy areas and nationalized industries. There is little to choose between many of these, although a good example is Patrick Dunleavy's *The Politics of Mass Housing in*

Britain. Dunleavy analyses a particular government policy decision that is now widely reviled, the decision to provide the bulk of British public housing in multi-storey tower blocks. His concern is to show how such a policy could have emerged in the face of all of the contemporary evidence that it was ill-advised.

6 MAKING COLLECTIVE DECISIONS

This is one of the very few areas of politics in which complex technical literature does provide a real payoff. Much nonsense is talked about social choice mechanisms, and especially about electoral systems, by those who do not really understand the issues. The worthwhile literature on this subject is not too easily accessible by the lay person. Ian McClean, in chapter 4 of *Dealing in Votes,* gives a readable introduction to the subject. A very solid, though rather technical, review of the whole field can be found in William Riker's *Liberalism Against Populism*. This is not an easy book for the beginner, but it is one worth persevering with for those who really want to find out the many ways in which these things are more complicated than they seem at first sight. Chapters 10 and 11 of Andrew Coleman's *Game Theory and Experimental Games* provide a treatment that lies in its complexity somewhere between Riker and McClean.

7 WHERE DECISIONS ARE MADE

Few serious writers these days advocate direct democracy, so there is little to be found on this. The theory of representative democracy has been developed at great length. The main themes are sketched in by Robert Dahl in *A Preface to Democratic Theory*. This is not, these days, a terribly popular book in the trade, but it does state the pluralist view quite clearly, and it does deal with direct democracy. I've always been a sucker for simplicity, and Dahl presents his case in very simple terms. McClean's *Dealing in Votes* treats pressure groups and provides a useful introduction to the vast literature on this matter. Riker's *Liberalism Against Populism* is also intended as a contribution to the direct versus indirect democracy debate. It does not, however, really come off in this respect and is much more useful as the review of social choice theory for which I have already recommended it. Taylor and Johnston's *Geography of Elections* takes a long look at the precise effects of constituency boundaries, while David Robertson's *A Theory of Party Competition* adapts the welter of American work on choosing governments for a British context. Robertson also looks at some of the effects of party activists and financiers.

8 HOW GOVERNMENTS DECIDE

This is one area in which fiction, 'faction' and biography tend to serve us much better than academic political science. *The Crossman Diaries* is by now a classic in the field, detailing much of the day-to-day infighting that characterizes the nitty-gritty of government decision-making. *The Corridors of Power* by C. P. Snow is a novel that draws heavily on Snow's personal experience to illuminate the interaction between the Civil Service and government. It is less frequently recommended these days than it used to be but no less useful. Virtually every participant in the American Watergate scandal has by now written an autobiography. Nearly all of these are self-serving attempts to vindicate the author, but nearly all throw some light upon the real, as opposed to the formal, power of a US president.

9 POLITICS BETWEEN GOVERNMENTS

In this chapter I deliberately selected rather unusual examples. As a consequence, there is relatively little available to read on them. An exception is the politics of the sea, to which J. V. R. Prescott provides a lucid introduction in *The Political Geography of the Oceans*. Very little has been written on the politics of the Moon, of telecommunications or of space stations, however, save for a few specialist articles.

10 CONCLUSIONS: THE POLITICS OF THE FUTURE

This chapter is based largely on my own private speculations. There is, of course, a literature on the future, and it is mainly rather gloomy. Books such as Alvin Toffler's *Future Shock* and E. F. Schumacher's *Small is Beautiful* tend to concentrate upon the dire consequences of leaving current policies unchanged. Writings on the future, however, are even more a matter of taste than writings on anything else. Perhaps this is why novels tend to dominate the literature. George Orwell's *1984* and Aldous Huxley's *Brave New World* will be well known to all. I tend, however, to subscribe to the view that science fiction is more about the present than the future and would be more inclined to look at histories (for example, of the industrial revolution) to glean some insights into what future technological developments hold in store for us.

References

Andreski, Stanislav, *Social Sciences as Sorcery*, Harmondsworth, Penguin Books, 1974
Arrow, Kenneth, *Social Choice and Individual Values*, New York, Wiley, 1951
Barr, Anne, and York, Peter, *The Official Sloane Ranger Handbook*, London, Ebury Press, 1982
Brown, Terence, *Ireland: A Social and Cultural History 1922–79*, Glasgow, Fontana, 1981
Carr, E. H., *What is History?*, Harmondsworth, Penguin Books, 1964
Coleman, Andrew, *Game Theory and Experimental Games*, Oxford, Pergamon Press, 1982
Crossman, Richard, *The Crossman Diaries: Selections from the Diaries of a Cabinet Minister 1964–70*, London, Hamish Hamilton, 1979
Culyer, A. J. *The Political Economy of Social Policy*, Oxford, Martin Robertson, 1983
Dahl, Robert, *A Preface to Democratic Theory*, Chicago, University of Chicago Press, 1956
Dunleavy, Patrick, *The Politics of Mass Housing in Britain*, Oxford, Clarendon Press, 1981
Hirschman, Albert, *Exit, Voice and Loyalty*, Cambridge, Mass., Harvard University Press, 1970
Hobbes, Thomas, *Leviathan*: available in many editions, e.g. Glasgow, Fontana, 1962
Huxley, Aldous, *Brave New World*, Panther Books, London, 1978
Locke, John, *Two Treatises of Government*: available in many editions, e.g. Cambridge, Cambridge University Press, 1960
McClean, Ian, *Dealing in Votes*, Oxford, Martin Robertson, 1982

References

Orwell, George, *1984*, Harmondsworth, Penguin Books, 1980

Prescott, J.V.R., *The Political Geography of the Oceans,* Newton Abbot, David & Charles, 1975

Riker, William, *Liberalism Against Populism,* San Francisco, W. H. Freeman, 1982

Robertson, David, *A Theory of Party Competition,* London, Wiley, 1976

Rousseau, J. J., *The Social Contract:* available in many editions, e.g. New York, Hafner, 1947

Schumacher, E.F., *Small is Beautiful,* London, Abacus, 1974

Snow, C.P., *The Corridors of Power,* New York, Scribner, 1979

Taylor, Michael, *Community, Anarchy and Liberty,* Cambridge, Cambridge University Press, 1982

Taylor, Peter, and Johnston, R. J., *Geography of Elections,* Harmondsworth, Penguin Books, 1979

Toffler, Alvin, *Future Shock,* New York, Bantam, 1980

Index

(General references to 'government' and 'community' occur throughout the book and so have not been listed below.)

action, collective, 25, 29–36, 44–6, 54–5, 88ff., 134–43
   international, 217–39
administrators, *see* bureaucrats
advertising, 41, 78, 123, 208–9
air, clean, 103, 137–8
airlines, 112, 129–30; *see also* transport
airports, 132, 136, 186, 189, 211
altruists, 20–4, 38
anarcho-capitalists, 27, 47, 62, 134; *see also* libertarians
anarchy, 18–24, 44–66, 216, 252
   international, 216–39
Andreski, Stanislav, 255
architecture, community, 69
Argentina, 223
armies, 90, 115
Arrow, Kenneth, 154–6
art, 35–6, 100, 104

ballet, 131
ballots
   postal, 147–50
   public, 146–50
   secret, 146–50
Bangladesh, 87
bargaining power, 198–205, 250
banks, queuing in, 54–5
Barr, Anne, 62, 255

Belgium, 87, 205
Bell Telephone System, 119–23
Biafra, 87
boundaries, of states and communities, 82–7, 223–7
Boundary Commissions, 179
boycotts, 63–4
brinkmanship, 195–6
Britain, 222–3, 226, 251
   Civil Service, 211–12
   Communist Party, 203–4
   fishing industry, 226–7
   Labour Party, 157, 175–6, 198
   Liberal Party, 203
   National Front, 203–4
   Prime Minister of, *see* Prime Minister
   Social Democrats, 203
British Airways, 129
British Broadcasting Corporation, 101–3
British government, *see* government
British Post Office, 122–3
British Rail, 112–13, 115–16
British Telecom, 119–23
broadcasting, 101–3, 141
broadcasting, politics of, 220, 227–35
Brown, Terence, 256
budgets, government, 96–7
buildings, historic, 125
bureaucrats, 42, 209–13

Cabinet, 2, 194–207

Index

collective responsibility in, 196–7
Cabinet Ministers, 2, 196–7
  resignation of, 196–7
candidates, selection of, 181–5; *see also* democracy, indirect
capitalism, 78–82, 218–9, 247
Carr, E. H., 255
Carroll, Lewis, *see* Dodgson, Charles
cars, private, 110, 130, 247
cartels, 128–30
chivalry, 60–1
choice
  public, *see* decision-making
  social, *see* decision-making
cities, 124–5, 132–3, 251
  decline of, 124–5, 251
citizens' band radio, 228
class, social, 65–6, 77–82
Clay Cross, 10
clubs, 51–2
coalitions, 153, 197–215
  distribution of portfolios in, 198–205
  effect of opposition parties on, 203–5
  logrolling in, *see* logrolling
  policies of, 198–207
  small parties in, 198–207
  stability of, 205
  within parties, 193, 198, 213
Coleman, Andrew, 257
'Commons, The Tragedy of the', 217–39
communication, 178, 242–4, 250–3
communitarians, 47–50, 63, 134
competition, 129–30
  as a good, 129–30
computers, 243–53
Concorde, 132
conservation
  of architecture, 105
  of countryside, 105
consociational democracy, 87
constituencies, 176–81
  demographic, 179–81
  economic and social, 177–81
  geographical, 177–81
  see also democracy, indirect
constitutions, 10, 194

changes of, 167–71
consumer feedback, *see* feedback
consumption, vicarious, 104–5
contracts, 26–9, 43–4, 51–2, 121–3
control, social, 245–6
conventions, 56–8
copyright laws, 248
coral reefs, 223
cosmetic surgery, 98–9
covetousness, *see* jealousy
crazes, *see* panics
credibility, 195; *see also* threats
Crossman, Richard, 258
culture, 74–7
Culyer, A. J., 256

Dahl, Robert, 257
decision-making, collective, 92–7, 144–215
  agenda setting in, 208–13
  conditional, 145–50
  direct, *see* democracy, direct
  hierarchies of, 151–91
  indirect, *see* democracy, indirect
  in trade unions, 145–50
  irrelevant alternatives in, 154–6
  paradoxes of, 152–6, 169
  rules for, 154–8, 167–8
  transitivity of, 154–6
  unanimity in, 154–6
defence, national, 99, 106, 116, 132
delegates, 161–2, 171–6; *see also* democracy indirect
  mandate of, 172–3
Democracy
  direct, 157–91, 242
  indirect, 157–91
devaluation, 93
doctors, 116–17
Dodgson, Charles, 156
dogs, 31–2, 99, 139
doors, 60–2
driving, 9, 55–9
drug-taking, 140
Dublin, 200
Dunleavy, Patrick, 256–7

economic interests, 77–82
economics, 15–16
  monetarist, 210
Eden, Anthony, 194

263

Index

education, 64, 108–19
education vouchers, 118–19
efficiency, 39–42, 111
   of government 114–19, 127–8
   of private sector, 114–19, 127–8
electoral law, *see* electoral systems
electoral systems, 181–5
   additional-member, 184
   first-past-the-post, 155, 182–5
   proportional, 182–5
   responsiveness of, 184
   single transferable vote, 184
embargoes, *see* boycotts
etiquette, 59–62
European Economic Community (EEC), 10, 163, 216, 227
European Garden Festival, 153
exchange rates, *see* markets, currency
exhaust gases, 30–1, 137–9
exile, 63–4
experts, 209–13
expropriation, 134–7
external effects, *see* spillovers
externalities, *see* spillovers

factories, 80–1, 250
Falkland Islands, 223
false consciousness, 78–9, 209
family, 69
feedback, consumer, 101, 106, 117, 125–8, 166, 185–91
fishing limits, 225–7
France, 88, 157, 205
   Communist Party in, 205
   Gaullist party, 205
free riders, 32–6, 44–6, 97
free trade, 12

geostationary orbit, *see* satellite orbits
goods
   aesthetic, 104–8
   and services, private, 99, 119–30
   hybrid, 98, 108–19
   numéraires, 38–9, 126–7, 151–2, 166, 186–91
   optional, *see* spillovers, optional
   public, *see* services, public
   staple, 109
Government
   British, 9–10, 193
   British Labour, 1974–9, 200
   coalition, *see* coalitions
   innovation, 90–7
   international, 216–39
   planning, 90–7
   regulation, 112, 121–5, 134–43, 218–19
   single-party, 182, 192–7
   subsidies, 112, 139
greed, 42–3
Gregory, Tony, 200

hangovers, 35
Haughey, Charles, 200
headlights, 58–9
health, public, and hygiene, 33–6
health care, 108–118, 131–2
Heath, Edward, 194
Hirschman, Albert, 256
historic buildings, *see* buildings
history, 15–16, 75–7, 240
Hobbes, Thomas, 256
hog cycle, 41–2
homosexuality, 140
honesty, 28–9
Hormuz, Strait of, 222
housing market, 70–1
human nature, 5, 19–20, 48
human rights, 50
Huxley, Aldous, 259

Iceland, 226–7
ideology, 142, 147, 198–207, 247
incentives, 40
industrial revolution, 40, 80–1, 111, 242, 249
industries, nationalized, 119, 128
inequality, *see* redistribution
inflation, 133–4
information, 163, 243–9; *see also* software
information technology, 40, 163–4, 167, 242–53
innovation, 35–6, 100, 123–4, 129–30
insurance companies, 246
interest rates, 93, 128
interests, common, 67–87, 250
interests, economic, *see* economic interests

Index

International Frequency Registration Board, 230–5
intimidation, 146
Iran, 222
Iraq, 222
Ireland, 84–7, 256
  Fine Gael Party, 201
  Labour Party, 201
  Northern, 10, 72–7, 81, 85–7, 170
  plantation movement in, 135
  Republic of, 73–7, 167, 180, 200–1
  Senate, 180
Irish language, 65
Israel, 84, 87
Italy, 167, 205
  Communist Party in, 205

Japan, 226
jealousy, 42–4
Johnson, R. J., 258
Jordan, 87

laissez-faire, 11–12, 27
Laker, Freddie, 129–30
language, 70–4
law, international, 236–9
League of Nations, 239
Legitimacy, 8–11
libertarians, 47, 50–2, 134
litter, 34–5, 141–2
Liverpool, 152–3
Locke, John, 256
logrolling, 165, 205–13

Macmillan, Harold, 194
majority, qualified, 11, 167–8
  simple, 167–8
mandates, 172–6
market, 110–43, 151–2
  currency, 128
  leaders, 128–30
Marxism, 78–82, 241
McClean, Ian, 257
minefields, 32, 97
monetarism, *see* economics, monetarist
monopolies, 41, 119–23
  natural, 119–23, 234–5
Moon, 219–20, 236–9
moral regulation, 140–1
multinational corporations, 80–1, 127–8, 136–7, 224, 227

'narrowcasting', *see* television, cable
nationality, 74–7
needs, 4–5
Nepal, 6
newspapers, 243
Nigeria, 84
noise, 233
norms, 53–62, 72–3, 92–3, 140–1
Norway, 224–5
nuclear weapons, 116, 241
numéraires, see goods

oil, 124, 223–5
opera, 104–7, 131–2
option value, 104–6
organizations, international, 216–39
Orwell, George, 259

panics, 70–129
parties, political, 181–5; for specific parties, see country headings
  activists in, 182–3
  splits in, 194–7
patents, 124, 248
pay policy, 92–3
philosophy, 15–16
physical sciences, 13–14, 241–2
police, 9, 49–50
political science, 12–16
pollution, 31–6, 137–40
pornography, 140
postal service, 122–3
preference, intensity of, 151–2, 166–9, 185–91, 207
Prescott, J. V. R., 258
pressure groups, 166, 185–91
  professionals in, 188
Prime Minister, 193–7
privacy, 244–5
property, private, 50–2, 135, 218–20, 247–9
proportional representation, *see* electoral systems
psychology, 15–16

queues, 52–5

race, 70–4
radio, *see* broadcasting
railways, *see* transport, 111–13
reactors, pressurized water, 20–2
redistribution, 26, 39–42, 109, 130–40

Index

referenda, 163–71
religion, 70–4, 168
representatives, 171–85; *see also* democracy, indirect
   control of, 173–6
   trust of, 173–6
responsiveness, *see* feedback
revolution, 141
   industrial, *see* industrial revolution
   nationalist, 135
   socialist, 135
Rhodesia, 217
rights, 50, 233
Riker, William, 257–8
Robertson, David, 258
Rousseau, J. J., 256

satellite orbits, 228–30, 233–5
science, *see* physical sciences
schools, 65–6, 75–6
   comprehensive, 65–6
   desegregation of, 118
   grammar, 65–6
   private, 65–6
   secondary modern,, 65–6
Schumacher, E. F., 259
sea
   bed, 223–7
   territorial, 221–3
segregation
   by class, 79–82, 179
   by race, 118
Serpell Report, 115
services, public, 99–143
sewerage, 107
skills, 249–50
slum communities, 49–50
Snow, C. P., 258
Socialization, 64–6, 75–7
social workers, 49–50
sociology, 14–16
software, 243–53
South Africa, 217
Soviet Union, 126, 226, 237, 241
space stations, *see* satellite orbits
speed limits, 93–4
spillovers, 12, 29–36, 44, 51–2, 98–143, 219–20
   compulsory, 102, 106–8, 246–7
   optional, 100–6, 246–7
   production, 119, 123–8
   pure, 98–108
state, corporate, 180
strikes, 145–50
subsidies, 112, 139
Switzerland, 167, 169

taxation, 90, 100–8, 130–4, 246–7
Taylor, Michael, 255–6
Taylor, Peter, 258
technology, 240–53
telephone service, 119–23
television, broadcast, 100–5, 132, 243
   cable, 102–3, 122–3, 163–6, 242–4
   commercial, 102, 121–2
   detector vans, 103
threats, 195–6; *see also* bargaining power
Toffler, Alvin, 259
tolerance, repressive, 78
tower blocks, 34–5, 49–50, 68, 257
Trades Union Congress, 161–2, 179
trade unions
   democracy in, 145–50, 161–2, 172–3, 175–6
   reform of, 145–50
traffic, *see* driving
transport, 108–18, 247
   private, 108–18
   public, 108–18
trust, 26–9

United Nations (UN), 217–239
United States (USA), 167, 169, 193–5, 206–7, 222–3, 236–7, 241

vandalism, 34–5
vanity, 42–4
video recorders, 5, 92, 102
vote-trading, *see* logrolling
voting, *see* decision-making, collective; electoral systems

wars, 82
welfare
   benefits, 131, 212
   social, 36–42, 50–2, 101ff
will, collective, 145–50, 164–5

yardsticks, *see* goods, *numéraires*
York, Peter, 62, 255